PILOT'S GUIDE
TO RECREATIONAL
DESTINATIONS

• EASTERN UNITED STATES •

POLDI MIKULA

BEYOND THE CLOUDS

Published by:
BEYOND THE CLOUDS

Cover Design: David Hirner
© 1999 by Poldi Mikula

"The images used herein were obtained from IMSI's Master Clips ®
and Master Photos ™ Premium Image Collection, 1895 Francisco Blvd. East, San Rafael, CA 94901, USA".

Printed in the United States of America.

Library of Congress Cataloging-in-Publication Data
Mikula, Poldi.
      Pilot's guide to recreational destinations.
Eastern United States / Poldi Mikula. — 1st ed.
        p. cm.
        Includes index.
        LCCN: 99-90433
        ISBN: 0-9671785-0-9

      1. East (U.S.)—Guidebooks. 2. Air travel—
East (U.S.)—Guidebooks. 3. Air pilots—Travel—
East (U.S.)—Guidebooks. I. Title.

F106.M55 1999   917.404'44
               QBI99-762

TABLE OF CONTENTS

iii

CT
DE
FL
GA
IN
KY
ME
MD
MA
MI
NH
NJ
NY
NC
OH
PA
RI
SC
TN
VT
VA
WV
INDEX

CT

DE

FL

GA

IN

KY

ME

MD

MA

MI

NH

NJ

NY

NC

OH

PA

RI

SC

TN

VT

VA

WV

INDEX

MASSACHUSETTS

MICHIGAN

NEW HAMPSHIRE

NEW JERSEY

NEW YORK

CT
DE
FL
GA
IN
KY
ME
MD
MA
MI
NH
NJ
NY
NC
OH
PA
RI
SC
TN
VT
VA
WV

INDEX

CT
DE
FL
GA
IN
KY
ME
MD
MA
MI
NH
NJ
NY
NC
OH
PA
RI
SC
TN
VT
VA
WV

INDEX

CT
DE
FL
GA
I N
KY
ME
MD
MA
MI
NH
NJ
NY
NC
OH
PA
R I
SC
TN
VT
VA
WV

INDEX

CT
DE
FL
GA
IN
KY
ME
MD
MA
MI
NH
NJ
NY
NC
OH
PA
RI
SC
TN
VT
VA
WV

INDEX

GENERAL INFORMATION

Airports were chosen for close proximity to interesting sights and activities. Airport information is given only to help with preliminary decisions about destinations. All information necessary for safe flight must be verified with current directories, charts, and other relevant sources.

☞ *Airport Information:*
An " ★ " indicates the general location of the airport on the state map. Airport attendance hours are listed, but the availability of fuel during those hours needs to be confirmed. Airport diagrams are included only for airports with published instrument approaches and are not to scale. They are for general orientation only and not to be used for navigational purposes.

☞ *Transportation:*
Car rental telephone numbers are local numbers. Central reservation phone numbers are: Alamo 800/GO ALAMO; Avis 800/831-2847; Budget 800/527-0700; Discount 800/622-6201; Dollar 800/800-4000; Enterprise 800/325-8007; Hertz 800/654-3131; National 800/CAR-RENT; Thrifty 800/FOR CARS; U-Save 800/272-8728. Additional taxi and car rental companies serving the airport may not be listed. Some airports offer courtesy cars pending availability. Check with the appropriate FBO.

☞ *Lodging/Restaurants:*
Some lodgings and restaurants operate seasonally only. Call ahead to make reservations.

☞ *Attractions:*
Proximity to an airport was an important factor in choosing an attraction. Please note that the distance to the airport is approximate only. Resort activities available only to registered guests are shown with an "r" following the page number in the index.

ABBREVIATIONS

acft — aircraft
asph — asphalt
ctr — center
conc — concrete
dep — departure
indef — indefinitely
msl — mean seal level
rwy — runway

app — approach
B & B — bed & breakfast
clnc — clearance
del — delivery
hvy — heavy
lgt — light
nm — nautical mile
tfc — traffic

"r" after page number in the index indicates activity at resort generally requiring overnight stay.

Asterisk [*] after Z (Zulu) hours is a reminder to adjust for Daylight Saving Time, one hour earlier.

CONNECTICUT

Groton (GON)
New London Airport
Airport is located 3 miles southeast of town.

☞ *Airport Information:*
Location: New York sectional N41.19.80 W72.02.71
Airspace: Class D 1200-0300Z*
Attended: May-Oct 1200-0400Z*
Nov-Apr 1000-0200Z*
Elevation: 10 feet
Fuel: 100LL, Jet A
TPA: 1010 feet msl lgt acft
1510 feet msl hvy acft
Runway: 05-23: 5000 x 150 asph
Runway: 15-33: 4000 x 150 asph
FBO: Columbia Air Services
860/449-1400

☞ *Communication:*
CTAF: 125.6
Unicom: 122.95
App/Dep: Providence 125.75 (1100-0500Z*)
Boston Center 124.85 (0500-1100Z*)
Clnc Del: 118.55 (0300-0500Z* and 1100-1200Z*)
Ground: 121.65
Tower: 125.6 (1200-0300Z*)
ATIS: 127.0 (1200-0300Z*)

☞ *Transportation:*
Taxi: 860/443-6489; 860/444-2255
Car Rental: Avis 860/445-8585

☞ *Lodging:*
New London/Groton: The **Lighthouse Inn** 860/443-8411 is a 1902 mansion with private beach and a view of Long Island Sound. **Best**

Western 860/445-8000; **Morgan Inn & Suite** 860/448-3000;
Radisson Hotel 860/443-7000
Mystic: **Hilton** 860/572-0731; **Inn at Mystic** 860/536-9604. The
Steamboat Inn 860/536-8300 is a small luxury inn directly on the
waterfront with fireplaces and whirlpool baths.
Noank: An elegant turn-of-the-century mansion with six rooms and
antique furnishings — **The Palmer Inn** 860/572-9000.

☞ *Restaurants:*
Mystic: The **Inn at Mystic** 860/536-9604 features a four-star
restaurant overlooking the harbor. In the heart of downtown you will
find the **Whaler's Inn and Motor Court** 860/536-1506 with a choice
of three restaurants.
Noank: If you want the best lobster, crabs, and clams on the half
shell visit **Abbott's Lobster in the Rough** 860/536-7719. Bring your
own alcohol for this seaside lobster shack. Mouthwatering lobster
rolls and water views are worth the wait in this busy place.

COASTLINE SAILING SCHOOL
(approximately 5 miles from airport)
Eldridge Yard, Marsh Road, Noank, CT 06349; Tel: 860/536-2689

This school offers a wide variety of courses on the Long Island
Sound, some of the best sailing waters in the country. It's primarily a
big-boat school with mostly 30-foot Ericsons. The first two hours of
the basic "Sailing Weekender" are spent on the boat tied to the dock,
learning safety procedures and terminology. But then it's off to sailing
in Fisher's Island Sound. A 4:1 student/instructor ratio gives you
good attention for maximum learning. Cruising courses are available
on various cruising yachts and last 2 to 5 days. Or choose a 6-day
sailing vacation to Martha's Vineyard, which in good weather can be
one of the best sailing trips in the country.

CONNECTICUT ARBORETUM
(bird-watching approximately 4 miles from airport)
Connecticut College, Williams Street, New London, CT 06320;
Tel: 860/439-5020
Open daily.
Admission and tours are free.

The arboretum is west of the Connecticut College campus and
covers 425 acres with a variety of natural ecosystems, hiking trails,
and ponds. Watch a wide variety of birds, including rare, uncommon
or endangered ones—178 species have been counted. Join free

tours from May to October on Saturday and Sunday at 2 p.m.

FOXWOODS RESORT CASINO
(approximately 10 miles from airport)
Route 2, Ledyard, CT 06339; Tel: 800/PLAY BIG

Foxwood calls itself the largest casino in the world. Four thousand slot machines, hundreds of game tables, keno, bingo, poker, and race book will lure you to spend your money. Two hotels, a shopping complex, and a total of sixteen restaurants for everything from a quick bite to an elegant meal entice you to stay. Foxwoods is home to one of the most technologically advanced virtual reality theaters, Cinetropolis. Evening entertainment is provided in the 1,500-seat Fox Theater. Foxwoods is located on the Mashantucket Pequot Tribal Reservation and is run by Native Americans who have been licensed to engage in gaming on their land.

MYSTIC MARINELIFE AQUARIUM
(approximately 6 miles from airport)
55 Coogan Blvd., Mystic, CT 06355; Tel: 860/572-5955
Admission is $13 for adults, $8 for children 3 to 12 years old.
Open daily, except Thanksgiving, Christmas, New Year and last full week in January.

Aquarium houses more than 3,500 types of sealife, including Beluga whales and Atlantic bottlenose dolphins. The 2.5-acre outdoor exhibit has four species of seals and sea lions. Dolphin and whale demonstrations are held daily at the Marine Theater.

MYSTIC SEAPORT
(A maritime museum along the Mystic River approximately 7 miles from airport)
75 Greenmanville Avenue, Mystic, CT 06355; Tel: 888-9SEAPORT;
Internet: www.mysticseaport.org
Open daily, except Christmas.
Admission is $16 for adults, $8 for children 6 to 12 years old.

Mystic Seaport is a 19th-century village portraying America's maritime heritage in an entertaining way for the whole family. Tall ships, homes, industries, and a working shipyard bring you close to the past. It is considered the nation's leading maritime museum. Spend a day in the 19th century as you explore a 156-year-old whaling ship and discover trade shops and hands-on activities for all ages.

Mystic Seaport's Gallery presents the story of America and the sea with ship models, paintings, sailor's art and artifacts as well as figureheads and interpretive exhibits. The most extensive small craft exhibit in the country honors the great boat designers and builders of the past century.

Special events such as the Lobsterfest in May and the Sea Music Festival in June add to the fun. October is the time for the Chowderfest. Taste soup served from the bubbling cauldrons set over wood fires. Contact the above number for exact dates of the festivals. At the Museum Store you will find an array of related books, contemporary marine art, and museum reproductions for that one-of-a-kind present.

The Seaman's Inne restaurant offers traditional New England culinary fare with lighter fare to be found at the Schaefer's Spouter Tavern.

PLAYIN' HOOKY
Thamesport Marina, New London, CT 06320; Tel: 800/322-2754

Captain Robert DeMagistris will take you saltwater fishing on the *"Playin Hooky."* Popular catches are bluefish, striped bass, flounder, and cod. Fish for shark and tuna in deep water. The months of June through October are best.

USS NAUTILUS/SUBMARINE FORCE LIBRARY AND MUSEUM
(approximately 3 miles from airport)
Crystal Lake Road, Groton, CT 06349; Tel: 800/343-0079
Open daily, except Tuesdays.
Free admission.

Take a self-guided tour of the world's first nuclear-powered submarine. Museum displays submarine memorabilia, artifacts, and working periscopes.

VOYAGER CRUISES
(approximately 7 miles from airport)
73 Steamboat Wharf, Mystic, CT 06355; Tel: 860/536-0416
Open daily from May to November.

Cruise to Fisher's Island on the *Argia*, a replica of a 19th-century gaff-rigged schooner with 20th-century appointments. Capacity is 49 persons.

WHILE YOU'RE THERE: **Mystic Whaler Cruises**
800/697-8420 has 1-to-5-day windjammer cruises leaving from
Mystic. The *Mystic Whaler* is a re-creation of a New England
schooner and you are encouraged to lend a hand in sailing the 110-
foot vessel. Capacity is 65 persons for day trips and 36 persons for
overnight trips. *Hel-Cat II* 860/535-2066 is the name of the party
fishing boat operated by captain Brad Glas out of Groton. Private
charter fishing boats out of New London are *West Wind III* 860/526-
9453, and the *Wanderer* 860/739-2801.

Meriden (MMK)
Markham Mun. Airport

Airport is located 3 miles southwest of town.

☞ *Airport Information:*

Location: New York sectional N41.30.52 W72.49.77
Attended: 1300Z* to dusk
Elevation: 130 feet
Fuel: 100LL
TPA: 1103 feet msl
Runway: 18-36: 3100 x 75 asph
FBO: Meriden Aviation
203/238-4400

☞ *Communication:*

CTAF: 122.8
Unicom: 122.8
App/Dep: Bradley 127.8
Clnc Del: 120.65

☞ *Transportation:*

Taxi: 203/235-4434

☞ *Lodging:*

Meriden: **Hampton Inn** 203/235-5154; **Ramada Plaza Hotel &
Conference Center** 203/238-2380; **Residence Inn by Marriott**
203/634-7770

LYMAN MEADOW GOLF & ORCHARD
(approximately 7 miles from airport)
Route 157, Middlefield, CT 06455; Tel: 860/349-8055

This 18-hole course features ponds, rolling hills, and brooks that are characteristic of the countryside. The course was designed by Robert Trent Jones. It is part of a family-owned farm with 27,000 fruit trees adjacent to the course, called Lyman Orchards. In-season farm market offers fresh fruits and vegetables and, if you are still up to it after your round of golf, you can pick your own fruit! For info on farm market call 860/349-1793; pick your own fruit 860/349-1566.

Plainville
Robertson Field (4B8)

Airport is located 2 miles north of town.

☞ *Airport Information:*
Location: New York sectional N41.41.42 W72.51.89
Attended: Oct-Apr 1130-0100Z*; May-Sep 1230-0100Z*
Elevation: 200 feet
Fuel: 100LL, Jet A
TPA: 1000 feet msl for lgt acft; 1500 feet msl hvy acft
Runway: 02-20: 3612 x 75 asph
FBO: Interstate Aviation 860/747-5519

☞ *Communication:*
CTAF: 122.8
Unicom: 122.8
Clnc Del: Bradley 134.5

☞ *Transportation:*
Taxi: 860/582-2885
Car Rental: Interstate Aviation 860/747-5519

☞ *Lodging:*
Farmington: Nestled in a park-like setting is the **Farmington Marriott** 860/678-1000 with indoor or outdoor pool, health club, and two tennis courts. Antique furnishings adorn **The Farmington Inn** 860/677-2821 with 72 guest rooms and suites. Complimentary continental breakfast.

☞ *Restaurants:*
Farmington: **Chuck's Steak House** 860/677-7677; **The Farmington Inn** 860/677-2821 serves four-star northern Italian cuisine.

KAT BALLOONS
(approximately 4 miles from airport)
40 Meadow Lane, Farmington, CT 06032; Tel: 860/678-7921

Give hot-air ballooning a try! Meet at 6 a.m. or late in the afternoon for a 20-to-30-minute setup for launching the balloon, then let the breeze take you across Farmington River Valley. Kat Balloon's crew will be waiting for your wicker basket to set down wherever the gentle currents have taken you. A champagne-buffet reception will be waiting for you back at the Balloonport. Pilots are commercially licensed. Instruction is available. Summer months are best for this activity. Reservations are highly recommended.

Windsor Locks
Bradley Int'l Airport (BDL)

Airport is located 3 miles west of town.

☞ *Airport Information:*
Location: New York sectional N41.56.33 W72.40.99
Airspace: Class C
Attended: Continuously
Elevation: 174 feet
Fuel: 100LL, Jet A
TPA: 1174 feet msl lgt acft
1874 feet msl hvy acft
Runway: 06-24: 9502 x 200 asph
15-33: 6846 x 150 asph
01-19: 5145 x 100 asph
FBO: AMR Combs 860/627-3300

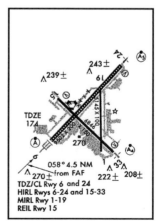

☞ *Communication:*
Unicom: 122.95
App: Bradley 125.8 within 20 miles
Dep: Bradley 127.8 south; 125.35 north and west

Dep: 123.95 northeast
Clnc Del: 121.75
Ground: 121.9
Tower: 120.3
ATIS: 118.5

☞ *Transportation:*
Taxi: 860/559-5902 or 860/550-3456
Car Rental: Dollar 860/627-9048; Hertz 860/627-3850

☞ *Lodging:*
Airport: **Days Inn** 860/623-9417; **Double Tree** 860/627-5171;
Ramada Inn 860/623-9494; **Sheraton Inn** 860/627-5311;
Windsor Lock: **Bradley Int'l Inn** 860/623-2533; **Fairfield Inn by
Marriott** 860/627-9333

NEW ENGLAND AIR MUSEUM
(located at airport)
Bradley Int'l Airport, Windsor Locks, CT 06096; Tel: 860/623-3305
Open daily, except Thanksgiving and Christmas.
Admission is $6.75 for adults, $3.50 for children 6 to 12 years old.

A total of 75 aircraft are on display, including classic private and
commercial planes, bombers, fighters, helicopters, and gliders from
1909 through World War II to present. Children can use the jet
fighter cockpit simulator. Aviation films are shown and guides are
available to answer your questions.

DELAWARE

Wilmington
New Castle Co. Airport (ILG)

Airport is located 4 miles south of town.

☞ *Airport Information:*

Location: Washington sectional N39.40.72 W75.36.39
Airspace: Class D service 1200-0400Z*; other times class E
Attended: Continuously
Elevation: 80 feet
Fuel: 100LL, Jet A
TPA: 1080 feet msl lgt acft
1580 feet msl hvy acft
Runway: 09-27: 7165 x 150 asph
01-19: 7002 x 200 asph
14-32: 4596 x 150 asph
FBO: Dawn Aero 302/328-9695
Atlantic Aviation
302/322-7000

☞ *Communication:*
CTAF: 126.0
Unicom: 122.95
App/Dep: Philadelphia 118.35
Tower: Wilmington 126.0 (1200-0400Z*)
Clnc Del: call 800/354-9884
Ground: 121.7
ASOS: 123.95 (1200-0400Z*)

☞ *Transportation:*
Taxi: 302/656-8151; 302/658-4321
Car Rental: Avis 302/322-2092; National 302/328-5636

☞ *Lodging:*
Wilmington: For living areas with 18th-century furnishings, lodge at
the **Hotel du Pont** 302/594-3100 or 800/441-9019 located
downtown. The **Ramada Inn** 302/658-8511 is 1 mile from the airport.

9

☞ *Restaurants:*
Wilmington: Delicious Italian fare is served at **Raffaele's**
302/658-3988.

WINTERTHUR
(museum and garden approximately 8 miles from airport)
Route 52, Winterthur, DE 19735; Tel: 800/448-3883 or 302/888-
4600; Internet: www.udel.edu/winterthur
Open daily, except on major holidays.
Admission varies.

Four generations of Du Ponts cared for this country estate that today
combines art, history, and natural beauty. Henry Francis Du Pont, a
collector and horticulturist, created an unrivaled collection of early
decorative arts from 1640 to 1860 displayed in a 175-room hillside
mansion. Having studied horticulture at Harvard, he had the gardens
laid out with precision and attention to bloom sequence, texture, size,
and all the other details that make a jewel of a garden. See the
garden aboard a tram or join guided walks. Special events are held
throughout the year.

NOTES:

Boca Raton Airport (BCT)

Airport is located 2 miles northwest of town.

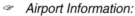 *Airport Information:*

Location: Miami sectional N26.22.71 W80.06.46
Attended: Continuously
Elevation: 14 feet
Fuel: 100LL, Jet A
TPA: 1010 feet msl lgt acft
1510 feet msl hvy acft
Runway: 05-23: 6267 x 150 asph
FBO: Boca Aviation
561/368-1110

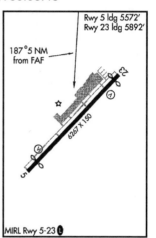

Rwy 5 ldg 5572'
Rwy 23 ldg 5892'

187°5 NM from FAF

6267 X 150

MIRL Rwy 5-23

Communication:
CTAF: 122.8
Unicom: 122.8
App: Palm Beach 125.2
Dep: Palm Beach 127.35

Transportation:
Taxi: Contact FBO 561/368-1110
Car Rental: Budget 561/368-1110

Lodging:
Boca Raton: Boca Raton Resort & Club 561/395-3000 or
800/327-0101 — see entry below; **Best Western University Inn**
561/395-5225; **Radisson Suite Hotel** 561/483-3600

Restaurants:
Boca Raton: French food connoisseurs are at the right place at
Chez Marcel 407/362-9911, for classic French food.

BOCA RATON RESORT & CLUB

(approximately 8 miles from airport)
501 E. Camino Real, Boca Raton, FL 33432;

Tel: 561/395-3000 or 800/327-01016

Mediterranean Revival architecture is prevalent in this area and this resort is not different. Addison Mizner, inspired by buildings he had seen in the Mediterranean, shaped the architecture in this area, including the Boca Raton Resort & Club. Think of pink color, marble columns, sparkling fountains, and pampering in many ways. Golf enthusiasts can take advantage of Dave Pelz's Short Game School. This school teaches the short game only. The philosophy is that to cut strokes off your scores, you have to work on your short game. The 18-hole Resort Course was originally designed in the 1920s and re-designed by Joe Lee in 1988. Tennis is provided for by 22 Har-Tru courts. The resort's location on the Gold Coast makes it a natural for all water sports, such as windsurfing, snorkeling, fishing for big game, and lots more.

WHILE YOU'RE THERE: Go on an exciting tour of the Everglades in an airboat with **Loxahatchee Everglades Tours** 561/482-0313. Nightly turtle-watching tours are offered by the **Gumbo Limbo Nature Center** 561/338-1473 between May and July. Advance reservations are necessary.

Clewiston
Airglades Airport (2IS)

Airport is located 5 miles west of town.

☞ *Airport Information:*

Location: Miami sectional N26.44.52 W81.02.99
Attended: Continuously
Elevation: 20 feet
Fuel: 100LL
TPA: 800 feet msl
Runway: 13-31: 5950 x 75 asph
FBO: Air Adventures 800/533-6151 or 941/983-6151

☞ *Communication:*

CTAF: 123.0
Unicom: 123.0
App/Dep: Tampa 125.3

☞ *Transportation:*
Taxi: 941/983-7945
Car Rental: Henry County Motors 941/983-8188

☞ *Lodging:*
Clewiston: **Clewiston Inn** 941/983-8151

☞ *Restaurants:*
Clewiston: **The Galley** 941/983-3151 is located at Roland Martin's Lakeside Marina, mentioned below. **Sonny's Real Pit BBQ** 941/983-4171.

AIR ADVENTURES
(skydiving at airport)
P.O. Box 787, Clewiston, FL 33440; Tel: 800/533-6151 or 941/983-6151

Aviators are used to lofty surroundings, but nothing compares to free-falling from an airplane at an altitude of about 12,000 feet! Exhilarating to say the least! Give it a try in a tandem skydive. You will be attached securely and safely to a "jumpmaster" to reduce stress and keep anxiety to a minimum. After that you can contemplate the Accelerated Freefall Program. That will teach you basic skydiving skills with eight levels of progression. Tandem jumps start at $165.

ROLAND MARTIN'S LAKESIDE MARINA
(fishing approximately 6 miles from the airport)
920 E. Del Monte Ave., Clewiston, FL 33440; Tel: 941/983-3151 or 800/473-6766

Lake Okeechobee is one of the largest freshwater lakes in the United States and teeming with speckled perch (crappie). You might also catch bluegill, catfish, and bass. Crappies bite year-round, but generally the season is from November to April. The marina provides boat rentals and guides.

Cocoa
Merritt Island Airport (COI)

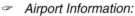

Airport is located 2 miles southeast of town.

☞ *Airport Information:*

Location: Jacksonville sectional N28.20.50 W80.41.13
Attended: 1300-0100Z*
Elevation: 7 feet
Fuel: 100LL, Jet A
TPA: 1000 feet msl
Runway: 11-29: 3601 x 75 asph
FBO: Merritt Island Air Service
407/453-2222

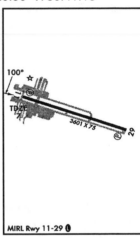

MIRL Rwy 11-29 ●

☞ *Communication:*

CTAF: 123.05
Unicom: 123.05
App/Dep: Patrick 132.65
(1200-0400Z*)
Non radar service 1200-
1400Z* Sat-Sun
Miami Center 124.1
(0400-1200Z)

☞ *Transportation:*

Taxi: 407/784-8294
Car Rental: Enterprise 407/453-8710

☞ *Lodging:*

Cocoa Beach: **Holiday Inn Resort** 407/783-2271 occupies 25 acres of prime Atlantic front property. The **Days Inn Oceanfront** 407/783-7621 has a large pool. Families will appreciate the spacious accommodation at **Wakulla Motel** 407/783-2230.

☞ *Restaurants:*

Cocoa Beach: Having their own fishing fleet guarantees the freshest of seafood at **Bernard's Surf** 407/783-2401. **The Mango Tree** 407/799-0513 is a place for a very special evening. **Spinnaker's** 407/783-7549 is a casual spot on the Cocoa Beach Pier serving sandwiches, burgers, ribs, steak, and chicken dinners.

COCOA BEACH SURFING SCHOOL

(approximately 7 miles from airport)
490 Tina Place, Merritt Island, FL 32952; Tel: 407/868-1980;
Internet: www.ronjons.com (look up the information on the surfing
school under "surf sites")

Gradually sloping sand beaches in Cocoa Beach are ideal for
learning to surf. It is called the surfing capital of Florida for a good
reason. Take a lesson, attend a week-long camp, or just rent a
board and hit the waves.

WHILE YOU'RE THERE: If fishing is on your mind contact **Fish
& Sea Charters** 407/784-0094. They will arrange fishing excursions
for you.

Deland Mun.-Taylor Field (DED)

Airport is located 3 miles northeast of town.

☞ *Airport Information:*
Location: Jacksonville sectional N29.04.01 W81.17.05
Attended: Continuously
Elevation: 80 feet
Fuel: 100LL, Jet A
TPA: 900 feet msl lgt acft
                1100 feet msl hvy acft
Runway: 12-30: 6000 x 100 asph
                05-23: 4379 x 75 asph
FBO: Deland Aviation
                904/736-7333

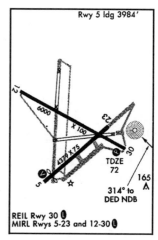

Rwy 5 ldg 3984'

TDZE 72

314° to DED NDB

REIL Rwy 30 ◗
MIRL Rwys 5-23 and 12-30 ◗

☞ *Communication:*
CTAF: 122.8
Unicom: 122.8
App/Dep: Daytona 125.35

☞ *Transportation:*
Taxi: 904/734-6199; 904/734-3417
Car Rental: Contact FBO 904/736-7333; Enterprise 904/738-4013

386 -

☞ *Lodging:*
Deland: **Holiday Inn** 904/738-5200

SKYDIVE DELAND
(located on field)
1600 Flightline Blvd. Deland, FL 32724; Tel: 904/738-3539

Learn to skydive at the school where Tom Cruise did his first jumps for filming *Days of Thunder* in Daytona Beach. With only 30 minutes of training you are able to go on a skydive with a professional tandem instructor. He or she takes care of all the details while you enjoy the thrill of free-fall and a peaceful ride under the parachute. Incidentally, this method was first conceived and developed here and is now used worldwide. Quite a sky-diving community, Deland Municipal also is the location of leading manufacturers of skydiving equipment and hosted the 1993 National Skydiving Championships. Various levels of training are available, with tandem jumps starting at $150. For $75 you can have your jump recorded on a video and roll of film!

Everglades Airpark (X01)
Airport is located 1 mile southwest of town.

☞ *Airport Information:*
Location: Miami sectional N25.50.92 W81.23.40
Attended: 1300-2200Z*
Elevation: 5 feet
Fuel: 100LL
TPA: 800 feet msl
Runway: 15-33: 2400 x 50 asph
FBO: 941/695-2778

☞ *Communication:*
CTAF: 122.9

☞ *Lodging:*
Everglades City: The **Ivey House** 941/695-3299 calls itself a B & B and Backcountry Expertise. The small and homey place has naturalist guides on staff to take you on nearby adventures.

EVERGLADES NATIONAL PARK BOAT TOURS
(approximately 1 mile from airport)
P.O.Box 119, Everglades City, FL 34139; Tel: 800/445-7724
Daily tours.

A thrilling discovery awaits you in the green mangrove maze of Florida's Ten Thousand Islands. Frequent sightings include ospreys, egrets, ibis, rare roseate spoonbills, frigate birds, pelicans and bald eagles. Endangered manatees are often seen in these warm, shallow waters. Canoes may also be rented for a closer look at the Everglades. Tours depart from Park Docks on Chokoloskee Causeway on Rte. 29. November through April is the best time to visit this area.

Fernandina Beach
Mun. Airport (55J)

Airport is located 3 miles south of town.

☞ *Airport Information:*
Location: Jacksonville sectional N30.36.67 W81.27.76
Attended: 1300Z* to dusk
Elevation: 15 feet
Fuel: 100LL, Jet A
TPA: 800 feet msl lgt acft
1000 feet msl hvy acft
Runway: 04-22: 5350 x 100 asph
13-31: 5150 x 150 asph
08-26: 5000 x 150 asph
18-36: 5000 x 150 asph
FBO: Island Aviation Services
904/261-7890

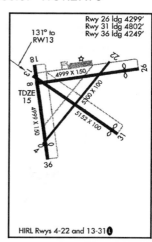

☞ *Communication:*
CTAF: 122.7
Unicom: 122.7
App/Dep: Jacksonville 127.0

☞ *Transportation:*
Taxi: 904/261-7278
Car Rental: Enterprise: 904/261-7890

☞ *Lodging:*

Amelia Island: **Amelia Island Plantation** 904/261-6161 or 800/874-6878—see entry below. The **Florida House Inn** 904/261-3300 or 800/258-3301 has 11 rooms and a downtown location. The pier alongside the **Beach Motel Inn** 904/261-4236 will please anglers at this property.

AMELIA ISLAND PLANTATION
(resort approximately 4 miles from airport)
P.O. Box 3000, Amelia Island, FL 32035; Tel: 904/261-6161 or 800/874-6878

Miles of pristine beach are only part of the splendor at this resort. One of the highlights of the plantation are the 54 holes of challenging championship golf. Designers Pete Dye and Tom Fazio blended dense vegetation, marshland, rolling contours and the ocean in creating some spectacular holes of golf. An award by *Golf* and *Money* magazines are among the many received. Non-resort golfers are able to reserve tee-times only one day in advance. The tennis courts are home to the annual Bausch & Lomb Championships. Pristine coastal wilderness — 1,330 acres of it — invites walking, biking, and jogging on the beach or under century-old oaks. Revitalize at the resort's fitness center, lap pool, or sauna or by having a massage.

WHILE YOU'RE THERE: Fernandina Beach 800/2-AMELIA or 904/226-3542 has restored 30 blocks of Old Town where houses and buildings date to the 1850s and a gracious Victorian charm pervades.

Fort Myers
Page Field (FMY)
Airport is located 3 miles south of town.

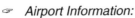

☞ *Airport Information:*

Location: Miami sectional N26.35.20 W81.51.80
Airspace: Class D service 1200-0300Z*
Attended: 1200-0300Z*
Elevation: 18 feet
Fuel: 100LL, Jet A

TPA:	800 feet msl lgt acft	
	1500 feet msl hvy acft	
Runway:	05-23: 6401 x 150 asph	
	13-31: 4997 x 150 asph	
FBO:	Ft. Myers Airways	
	941/936-2559	

```
                                    Rwy 5 ldg 5947'
                                    Rwy 13 ldg 4297'
                                    Rwy 23 ldg 6001'
                                    Rwy 31 ldg 4667'
            ʌ 98±
                                         ʌ 86±
                    100
                                         ʌ¹²⁹
                            ☆ 72
                                         ʌ 74±
                    TDZE
                    16
                 \ 051° 5.8 NM
              ʌ    from FAF
               93
MIRL Rwys 5-23 and 13-31
```

☞ *Communication:*

CTAF:	119.0
Unicom:	122.95
App/Dep:	Fort Myers 126.8
	(1100-0500Z*)
	Miami Center 134.75
	(0500-1100Z*)
Tower:	119.0 (1200-0300Z*)
Ground:	121.7
Clnc Del:	121.7
ATIS:	135.2

☞ *Transportation:*

Taxi:	941/936-5466; 941/433-2255
Car Rental:	Enterprise 941/418-1550
	Page Field Aviation Ctr 941/936-1443

☞ *Lodging:*

Fort Myers: **Days Inn Airport** 941/936-1311; **Budget Inn** 941/ 275-3500; **Radisson Inn** 941/936-4300

☞ *Restaurants:*

Fort Myers: The **Prawnbroker Restaurant and Fishmarket** 941/489-2226 has excellent seafood. It's sometimes crowded and not open for lunch, though.

EASTWOOD GOLF COURSE
(approximately 3 miles from airport)
4600 Bruce Herd Lane, Ft. Myers, FL 33905; Tel: 941/275-4848

This is a *Golf Digest* ranked 18-hole public course that is owned and operated by the city of Ft. Myers. Scenic in design with a woodsy setting, it was laid out by Robert von Hagge-Bruce Devlin and is well liked by players. The nature center in the vicinity attracts plenty of wildlife that adds to the experience.

GATEWAY GOLF CLUB
(approximately 20 minutes from airport)
11360 Championship Drive, Ft. Myers, FL 33913;
Tel: 941/561-1010

This is a challenging but fun course that keeps your interest. Tom Fazio designed the 18-hole Scottish-links layout in between marshlands and lakes. Large mounded traps add interest to the scenery and your game.

OFFSHORE SAILING SCHOOL
(approximately 3 miles from airport)
16731 McGregor Boulevard, Ft. Myers, FL 33908;
Tel: 941/454-1700; Internet: www.offshore-sailing.com

Former Olympian and 12-meter sailor Steve Colgate started this sailing school in 1964 and turned it into one of the largest and best known schools. He writes the course texts, designs the curricula, and oversees the hiring of all instructors. Eighty thousand graduates show that his method seems to work. A large variety of courses and schedules are designed for a rewarding experience.

Key West Int'l Airport(EYW)
Airport is located 2 miles east of town.

☞ *Airport Information:*
Location: Miami sectional N24.33.37 W81.45.57
Airspace: Class D service 1200-0200Z*; other times class G
Elevation: 4 feet
Fuel: 100, Jet A
TPA: 800 feet msl lgt acft;1500 feet msl hvy acft
Runway: 09-27: 4800 x 100 asph
FBO: Island City Flying Service 305/296-5422

☞ *Communication:*
CTAF: 118.2
Unicom: 122.95
App/Dep: Navy Key West 124.45 (1200-0500Z*)
            Miami Center 132.2 (0500-1200Z*)
Tower: 118.2 (1200-0200Z*)
Ground: 121.9

Clnc Del: 121.9
ASOS: 121.125

☞ *Transportation:*
Taxi: 305/296-6666
305/292-0000
Car Rental: Budget 305/294-8868
Avis 305/296-8744
Hertz 305/294-1039

TDZE 46

4800 X 100   4

80   72

298° 4.8 NM
from FAF

REIL Rwy 9 and 27
MIRL Rwy 9-27

☞ *Lodging:*
Key West: **The Reach** 305/296-5000
has a good beach location. Attractions
can be accessed easily from the **Pier
House** 305/296-4600 or 800/327-8340.
The **Curry Mansion Inn** 305/294-5349 is
a restored Victorian mansion with 16 rooms. Watersport rentals are
available on the private beach of the **Holiday Inn Beachside**
305/294-2571. **Best Western Key Ambassador Resort Inn**
305/296-3500

☞ *Restaurants:*
Key West: Fine dining with a casual atmosphere can be had at the
award-winning **Pier House** 305/296-4600. Cuban food at its best is
served at **El Siboney** 305/296-4184.The local specialty, conch
fritters, can be sampled at the **Half Shell Raw Bar** 305/294-7496
among the locals.

CONCH TRAIN TOUR
(approximately 2 miles from the airport)
301 Front Street, Key West, FL 33040; Tel: 305/294-5161
Daily tours.

Relive more than 400 years of history aboard a 90-minute narrated
tour filled with anecdotes, humorous stories, and well-researched
historical facts.

ERNEST HEMINGWAY HOUSE
(museum approximately 2 miles from the airport)
907 Whitehead Street, Key West, FL 33040; Tel: 305/294-1136
Open daily.
Admission $7.50.

Visit and tour the home and gardens of the late author and Nobel

Prize winner. Experience the tranquil environment that motivated Hemingway during his most productive years. *For Whom the Bell Tolls* and *The Old Man and the Sea* came to life here.

FURY CATAMARANS
(snorkeling tours approximately 2 miles from the airport)
201 Front Street, Building 21, Suite 109, Key West, FL 33040; Tel: 305/294-8899
Daily tours.

The Keys are a snorkeler's paradise, with miles of living coral reefs. View rainbow-hued tropical fish through your goggles. Gear and instruction are provided. Three-hour tours are conducted twice a day.

MEL FISHER'S MARITIME HERITAGE SOCIETY MUSEUM
(approximately 2 miles from airport)
200 Greene Street, Key West, FL 33040; Tel: 305/294-2633
Open daily.
Admission is $6.50 for adults and $2 for children.

When a hurricane overcame the galleons *Santa Margarita* and *Nuestra Señora de Atocha*, silver and gold bullion, jewelry, and a fortune in emeralds were lost in the sea. After a long search, 350 years later, these vessels were recovered and are now on view here with some of their loot.

WHILE YOU'RE THERE: Take a look at the underwater world without getting wet on the **Fireball Glass-bottom Sightseeing Boat** 305/296-6293. **Mosquito Coast** 305/294-7178 has guided back-country wildlife tours in kayaks and stops for snorkeling excursions on the way. Rent snorkeling equipment, jet skis, Hobie Cats and windsurfers from **Sunset Watersports** 305/296-2554. Key West's narrow streets of Old Town are best explored on foot. Pick up Sharon Well's Walking and Biking Guide free in local restaurants. Bikes and mopeds are for rent at **The Bike Shop** 305/294-1073.

Lakeland
Linder Reg. Airport (LAL)

Airport is located 4 miles southwest of town.

☞ *Airport Information:*

Location:	Miami sectional N27.59.34 W82.01.11
Airspace:	Class D service 1100-0300Z*
Attended:	1100-0300Z*
Elevation:	142 feet
Fuel:	100LL, Jet A
TPA:	1150 feet msl lgt acft
	1650 feet msl hvy acft
Runway:	09-27: 8500 x 150 asph
	05-23: 5000 x 150 asph
FBO:	Hawthorne Lakeland
	941/644-0433

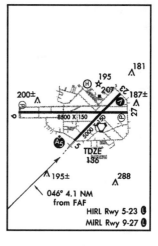

☞ *Communication:*

CTAF:	124.5
Unicom:	122.95
App/Dep:	Tampa 120.65, 119.9
Tower:	124.5
Ground:	121.4
ATIS:	118.025

☞ *Transportation:*

Taxi: 941/648-1849; 941/646-0478
Car Rental: Enterprise 941/647-0866

☞ *Lodging:*
Lakeland: **Sheraton** 941/647-3000; **Holiday Inn** 941/646-5731

INTERNATIONAL SPORT AVIATION MUSEUM
(located on field) Tel: 941/644-0741; Internet: www.airmuseum.org
Open daily.
Admission is $4 for adults, $2 for children.

Originally called the Sun 'N Fun Air Museum, this museum keeps
expanding at an amazing pace. It now contains the extensive
Howard Hughes aviation collection, a wall exhibit paying tribute to
Fred Weick, a pioneer in aeronautical engineering whose designs
include the famous Ercoupe, and a $5 million expansion that will

nearly double the facility's size. This museum is worth a visit not only during the famous annual "Sun 'N Fun" Fly-In in April but anytime during the year.

Live Oak (24J)
Suwannee Co. Airport

Airport is located 2 miles west of town.

☞ *Airport Information:*
Location: Jacksonville sectional N30.18.06 W83.01.39
Attended: Mon-Sat 1300-2300Z*
Elevation: 104 feet
Fuel: 100LL
TPA: 1100 feet msl
Runway: 07-25: 4000 x 75 asph
FBO: Blue Sky Air Service 904/362-4200

☞ *Communication:*
CTAF: 122.8
Unicom: 122.8

☞ *Transportation:*
Taxi: 904/364-1902
Car Rental: Enterprise 904/362-1022

☞ *Lodging:*
Live Oak: **Best Western Inn** 904/362-6000

SUWANNEE CANOE OUTPOST
(bicycle and canoe outfitter approximately 10 miles from airport)
2461 95th Drive, Live Oak, FL 32060; Tel: 800/428-4147

The Spirit of the Suwannee Park, where the Canoe Outpost is located, is a 580-acre wooded facility with 2 miles of frontage along the Suwannee River. Offered are downstream canoe trips on three remote rivers, including Florida's only three whitewater rivers. The outfitter will transport you up river, and provide the canoes and maps; you paddle downstream with the current. Tier prices are charged depending how far upriver you choose to travel. Other choices to see abundant wildlife are by hiking or biking miles of trails.

Miami
(TMB)

Kendall-Tamiami Airport

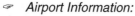

Airport is located 13 miles southwest of town.

☞ *Airport Information:*

Location: Miami sectional N25.38.87 W80.25.97
Airspace: Class D service1200-0200Z*
Attended: Continuously
Elevation: 8 feet
Fuel: 100LL, Jet A
TPA: 1000 feet msl lgt acft
1500 feet msl hvy acft
Runway: 09L-27R: 5001 x 150 asph
09R-27L: 4999 x 150 asph
13-31: 4001 x 150 asph
FBO: Husta Intl. Aviation
305/232-6990
International Flight Center
305/238-8122

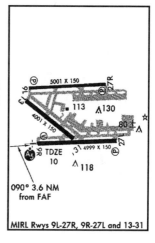

MIRL Rwys 9L-27R, 9R-27L and 13-31

☞ *Communication:*

CTAF: 118.9
Unicom: 122.95
App/Dep: Miami 125.5
Tower: 118.9, 124.9 (1200-0200Z*)
Ground: 121.7
Clnc Del: 133.0
ATIS: 124.0

☞ *Transportation:*

Taxi: 800/527-0700; 305/388-8294
Car Rental: Enterprise 305/233-0310

☞ *Lodging:*

Miami: **Ramada Hotel** 305/595-6000; **Wellesley Inn** 305/270-0359

MIAMI METRO ZOO

(approximately 6 miles from airport)
12400 S.W. and 152nd Street, Miami, FL 33177; Tel: 305/251-0400
Open daily.
Admission is $8 for adults and $4 for children 3 to 12 years old.

A 290-acre state-of-the-art cageless park where you will find a wide variety of animals in natural environments. Favorite animals include white tigers, komodo dragons, koalas, and gorillas. An air-conditioned monorail ride and wildlife shows are included in the admission price.

WEEKS AIR MUSEUM
(located at field)
Tel: 305/233-5197; Internet: www.weeksairmuseum.com
Open daily.
Admission is $6.95 for adults, $4.95 for children.

Opened in 1987, this museum is dedicated to the preservation and restoration of aircraft through the end of the World War II era. On display are about 20 aircraft along with a wide variety of engines and propellers. Most aircraft are maintained in flying condition.

Naples Mun. Airport (APF)
Airport is located 2 miles northeast of town.

☞ *Airport Information:*

Location: Miami sectional N26.09.15 W81.46.53
Airspace: Class D service 1100-0300Z*; other times class E
Attended: 1100-0300Z*
Elevation: 9 feet
Fuel: 100LL, Jet A
TPA: 1009 feet msl single engine acft; 1500 feet msl multi engine acft
Runway: 05-23: 5000 x 150 asph
14-32: 5000 x 100 asph
FBO: Naples Airport Authority 941/643-0404

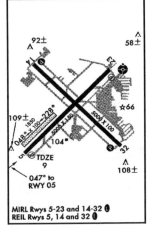

☞ *Communication:*

CTAF: 128.5
Unicom: 123.0
App/Dep: Fort Myers 119.75 (1100-0500Z*)
Miami Center 134.75 (0500-1100Z*)
Tower: 128.5 (1100-0300Z*)

Clnc Del:	121.6
Clnc Del:	118.0 when tower is closed
Ground:	121.6
AWOS:	135.425 when tower is closed
ATIS:	134.225 (1100-0300Z*)

☞ *Transportation:*
Taxi: 941/455-9157; 941/262-1312
Car Rental: Avis 941/643-0900; Dollar 941/793-2226
Hertz 941/643-1515

☞ *Lodging:*
Naples: Watercraft rentals and recreation are available at the **Charter Club Resort** 941/261-5559 or 800/494-5559. Located in Old Naples, the **Lemon Tree Inn** 941/262-1414 is designed with the architectural influence of Old Florida and rich with charm and ambiance. **Naples Registry Resort** 941/597-3232 or 800/247-9810—see entry following.

JUNGLE LARRY'S CARIBBEAN GARDENS
(approximately 6 miles from airport)
1590 Goodlette-Frank Road, Naples, FL 33940, Tel: 941/262-5409
Open daily.
Admission is $13.95 for adults and $8.95 for children 4 to 15 years old.

Fifty-two acres of botanical and zoological preserve, founded in 1919. Cruise between the primate islands to see monkeys in natural habitats and watch animal antics with educational shows.

NAPLES REGISTRY RESORT
(resort approximately 7 miles from airport)
475 Seagate Drive, Naples, FL 34103; Tel: 941/597-3232 or 800/247-9810

Tropical beauty complements an elegant resort on Pelican Bay. Whatever your pleasure, the Registry plays your game. Eighty-one holes of championship golf await on nearby courses designed by legends such as Tom Fazio, Arthur Hill, and Robert Trent Jones, Jr. Play tennis on one of the 15 courts or indulge in health-club treatments. A wildlife preserve known as the "Registry's Backyard" is adjacent. Stroll through an ancient mangrove forest or take the open-air tram. Rent a canoe or kayak for some leisure on the lagoon. Water sports are available on the beach.

WHILE YOU'RE THERE: Discover the history of glass at the **Naples Glass Museum** 941/403-9744. Watch glass blowers at work or view many items on display—from historic tools to exclusive art. Contact **Naples City Dock** 941/434-4693 for information on watersports, boat schedules, and rentals.

Orlando (ISM)
Kissimmee Mun. Airport
Airport is located 16 miles southwest of town.

☞ *Airport Information:*
Location:	Jacksonville sectional N28.17.39 W81.26.23
Attended:	1300-0100Z*
Elevation:	83 feet
Fuel:	100LL, Jet A
TPA:	1000 feet msl
Runway:	15-33: 6000 x 100 asph
	06-24: 5001 x 150 asph
FBO:	Kissimmee Aviation 407/847-9095
	Marathon Flight School 407/846-6128

☞ *Communication:*
CTAF:	124.45
Unicom:	122.95
App/Dep:	Orlando 119.4
Ground:	121.7
Tower:	124.45 (1200-0200Z*)
Clnc Del:	121.7
Clnc Del:	119.95 (0100-1300Z*)
AWOS:	128.775

☞ *Transportation:*
Taxi: 407/847-4867; 407/846-2222; 407/422-5466
Car Rental: Enterprise 407/932-3388

☞ *Lodging:*
Kissimmee: **Days Inn** 407/846-4714; **Doubletree Guest Suites Orlando Maingate** 407/397-0555; **Holiday Inn Hotel Main Gate East** 407/396-4488. A large variety of accommodations can be found

within **Walt Disney World Resort** 407/824-4321.

FLYING TIGERS WARBIRD MUSEUM

(located on field)
Tel: 407/847-7477, Internet: www.warbirdmuseum.com
Open daily, except major holidays.
Admission is $8 for adults and $6 for children.

Primarily a restoration facility of WWII aircraft, it also has a display of about 25 flying vintage military aircraft. Guided tours are conducted lasting about 45 minutes.

HUNTER'S CREEK GOLF COURSE

(approximately 6 miles from airport)
14401 Sports Club Way, Orlando, FL 32837; Tel: 407/240-4653

Hunter's Creek is an 18-hole public course and ranked by *Golf Digest*. Testing your game with long targets, it also has plenty of water hazards.

SEA WORLD

(approximately 10 miles from airport)
7007 Sea Harbor Drive, Orlando, FL 32821; Tel: 407/351-3600
Open daily.
Admission is $39.95 for adults, $32.80 for children 3 to 9 years old.
Check into combination tickets.

It takes a whole day to see this top-notch interactive marine adventure park. One of the big draws is the exciting marine mammal show featuring the killer whale Shamu. Atlantis is a water-coaster thrill ride through a mysterious lost city. Experience a simulated helicopter flight through an Arctic blizzard at the Wild Arctic complex and many other adventures and exhibitions.

UNIVERSAL STUDIOS

(film studio approximately 10 miles from airport)
1000 Universal Studios Plaza, Orlando, FL 32819; 407/363-8000
Open daily.
Admission is $42 for adults and $34 for children 3 to 9 years old.

The largest working motion picture and television studio outside of Hollywood. It's also a theme park where guests are able to "Ride the Movies" like *Terminator 2 3-D*, *Back to the Future*, and *Jaws*. A place to experience technology at its most entertaining.

WALT DISNEY WORLD
(theme parks approximately 8 miles from airport)
Box 10040, Lake Buena Vista, FL 32830; Tel: 407/824-4321
Open daily.
Admission for 1-day, 1-park ticket is $42 for adults and $34 for
children 3 to 9 years old. Combination tickets available.

Disney's magic keeps on working on the young and young at heart.
Whether it's the spires of Cinderella's castle at **Magic Kingdom** or
the educational and cultural attractions at **Epcot** — it's an
exhilarating experience. Interested in how animators create those
wonderful characters and produce those movies? **Disney–MGM
Studios** has tours for that and lots of rides and shows relating to the
motion picture industry. Two major water theme parks take off the
heat of the day.
Golfers will have the pleasure of choosing from 6 different courses to
play their favorite game. Three of them are designed by Joe Lee,
while Pete Dye and Tom Fazio worked on others. A total of 117
holes of highly rated golf are sure to add to your Disney pleasure.

Panama City
Bay Co. Int'l Airport (PFN)

Airport is located 3 miles northwest of town.

☞ *Airport Information:*

Location:	New Orleans sectional N30.12.73 W85.40.97
Airspace:	Class D service 1200-0400Z*; other times class G
Attended:	Continuously
Elevation:	21 feet
Fuel:	100LL, Jet A
TPA:	800 feet msl lgt acft
	1000 feet msl hvy acft
Runway:	14-32: 6308 x 150 asph
	05-23: 4884 x 150 asph
FBO:	Sowell Aviation
	850/785-4325

☞ *Communication:*

CTAF: 120.5

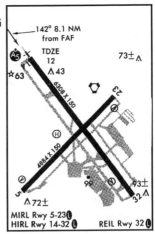

Unicom:	122.95
App/Dep:	Tyndall 119.1 (below 5000')
App/Dep:	119.75 (above 5000') 1300-0500Z*
	Jax Center 119.1 (0500-1300Z*)
Tower:	120.5 (1200-0400Z*)
Ground:	121.65
ATIS:	119.975 (1200-0400Z*)

☞ *Transportation:*
Taxi: 850/763-4691; 904/293-8299
Car Rental: Avis 850/769-1411; Hertz 850/763-2262

☞ *Lodging:*
***Panama City Beach:* Quality Inn** 800/874-7101. The **Mark II Beach Resort** 800/234-8843 and **Emerald Beach Motel** 800/633-3131 have beachfront locations. **Marriott's Bay Point Resort** 850/234-3307—see entry below.

☞ *Restaurants:*
Panama City Beach: A dockside location and award-winning restaurant, **Captain Anderson's** 850/234-2225 serves what the owners call "The World's Finest Seafood Platter." Watch the sunset in the Gulf while dining at **Fiddler's Green** 850/234-3307 at Marriott's Bay Point Resort.

MARRIOTT'S BAY POINT RESORT
(approximately 7 miles from airport)
4200 Marriott Dr., Panama City Beach, FL 32408; Tel: 850/234-3307

Watersports, tennis, golf—a place for an active vacation in a beautiful setting on 1,100 acres. Challenge yourself with a game of golf on the rather demanding Lagoon Legend course which requires long carries over marshes. Looks easier than it is! After playing the Lagoon Legend, playing their Club Meadows seems relaxing and easy. Twelve courts will lure the tennis enthusiast to play some ball. More diversions can be had with sailing, deep sea fishing, scuba diving, windsurfing, and a variety of other water sports. A white sandy beach and emerald green Gulf waters invite for swimming or soaking up the sun. How about a harbor ride on a modern Mississippi paddle-wheeler? And all that with Southern hospitality!

WHILE YOU'RE THERE: The **Miracle Strip Amusement Park** 850/234-5810 is a family-oriented park with more than 30 rides. Experience unique water rides at the **Shipwreck Island Water Park**

850/234-0368. Deep-sea fishing trips, sightseeing trips and dinner-dance cruises are held from Memorial Day through Labor Day at **Captain Anderson's Marina** 850/234-3435. At 1,642 feet, **City Pier** 850/233-5080 is the longest in the Gulf and great for fishing. **Pete's Scuba Center** 850/230-8006 schedules diving excursions to excellent dive sites in the area. Bottlenose dolphins, sea lions, and parrots are the stars at **Gulf World** 850/234-5271.

Pensacola
Ferguson Airport (82J)

Airport is located 7 miles southwest of town.

☞ *Airport Information:*
Location: New Orleans sectional N30.23.93 W87.20.92
Attended: Daylight hours
Elevation: 27 feet
Fuel: 100LL
TPA: 527 feet
Runway: 18L-36R: 3200 x 40 asph
18R-36L: 3200 x 150 turf
FBO: Ferguson Flying Service 850/453-4301

☞ *Communication:*
CTAF: 122.8
Unicom: 122.8

☞ *Transportation:*
Taxi: 850/455-8506

☞ *Lodging:*
Pensacola: **Days Inn** 904/438-4922; **Hampton Inn** 904/932-6800

NATIONAL MUSEUM OF NAVAL AVIATION
(approximately 5 miles from airport)
P.O. Box 33104, NAS Pensacola, FL 32508; Tel: 904/452-3604;
Internet: www.naval-air.org
Open daily, except major holidays.
Admission is free.

Not just the home of the famous "Blue Angels," the National Museum of Naval Aviation is also one of the largest air and space museums in the world. An indoor and outdoor display hold over 100 authentic aircraft from the early days of flight to space travel. A full-scale replica of an aircraft carrier flight deck has aircraft parked on deck. Four original Blue Angel A-4 Skyhawks of the famous demonstration team are displayed in a "diving diamond formation." Visit this museum to see the finest collection of Navy, Coast Guard, and Marine Corps aircraft.

St. Augustine Airport (SGJ)

Airport is located 4 miles north of town.

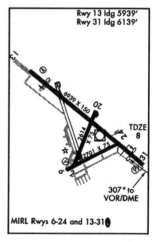

Rwy 13 ldg 5939'
Rwy 31 ldg 6139'

TDZE 8

307° to VOR/DME

MIRL Rwys 6-24 and 13-31

☞ *Airport Information:*

Location: Jacksonville N29.57.52 W81.20.33
Attended: 1100-0200Z*
Elevation: 11 feet
Fuel: 100LL, Jet A
TPA: 800 feet msl lgt acft
1500 feet msl hvy acft
Runway: 13-31: 6939 x 150 asph
06-24: 2701 x 75 asph
02-20: 2614 x 75 asph
FBO: Aero Sport 904/824-1995

☞ *Communication:*

CTAF: 122.8
Unicom: 122.8
App/Dep: Jacksonville 120.75
AWOS: 119.625

☞ *Transportation:*

Taxi: 904/824-6888; 904/824-8161
Car Rental: Avis 904/824-1995; Enterprise 904/829-1662

☞ *Lodging:*

St. Augustine: The **Radisson Ponce de Leon Golf Resort** 904/824-2821 is a beautiful 350-acre property bordering the marshlands of the intracoastal waterway. The **Casa de la Paz** 904/829-2915 or 800/929-2915 is a bayfront B & B.
St. Augustine Beach: The **Beach Club** 904/471-2626 or 800/333-7335 offers fully equipped condos. The **Holiday Inn** 904/471-2555

has an oceanside pool. Adjacent to Anastasia State Park and St. Johns County Fishing Pier is the **Howard Johnson Resort Hotel** 904/471-2575.

☞ *Restaurants:*
St. Augustine Beach: If you like the Caribbean, you will like the **Conch House** 904/829-8646 or 800/940-6256. Seafood and a variety of conch dishes are their specialty. **Jack's Bar-B-Q** 904/471-2055 is more of a shack kind of place with sumptuous barbecued pork, chicken, and beef.
St. Augustine: The **Mill Top Tavern's** 904/829-2329 raw bar is a favorite with locals.

COASTAL KAYAK CO.
(kayak trips approximately 4 miles from airport)
4255 Highway A1A South, St. Augustine, FL 32084; Tel: 904/471-4144; Internet: www.coastalkayaks.com

Guided kayak tours through local St. Augustine waterways, including tours of pristine coastal habitats and historic areas of the nations oldest city. Paddle the Mantanzas Inlet area to observe dolphins, manatees, and numerous sea and shore birds. Trips are suitable for seasoned as well as inexperienced paddlers. Kayak rentals available.

SPANISH QUARTER VILLAGE
(living history museum approximately 4 miles from airport)
P.O. Box 210, St. Augustine, FL 32085; Tel: 904/825-6830
Open daily.
Admission is $6 for adults and $3.75 for children.

Among restored and reconstructed homes and gardens, guides dressed in Colonial clothing re-create the daily lifestyle of the 1740's.

ST. AUGUSTINE SIGHTSEEING TRAINS
(approximately 4 miles from airport)
170 San Marco Ave. St. Augustine; FL 32084; Tel: 800/226-6545
Tickets are $12 for adults and $5 for children 6 to 12 years old.

St. Augustine—America's Oldest City—is a time capsule capturing nearly 500 years of history. It was founded in 1565—42 years before the English colonized Jamestown and 55 years before the pilgrims landed at Plymouth Rock. The city exudes a playful charm created by a contradiction of Old and New World influences. Admire evidence of the Spanish period in the Old Town. Step on and off at attractions, historical sights, restaurants, and shopping.

WHILE YOU'RE THERE: Alligator and reptile shows are at the **St. Augustine Alligator Farm** 904/824-3337, a reptile and wildlife preserve established in the 1890s. **Sea Love Charters** 904/824-3328 runs deep-sea fishing charter, party, and tarpon boats.

Sarasota (SRQ)
Bradenton Int'l Airport

Airport is located 3 miles north of town.

☞ *Airport Information:*

Location:	Miami sectional N27.23.72 W82.33.25
Airspace:	Class C service 1100-0500Z*, check NOTAMS
Attended:	Continuously
Elevation:	28 feet
Fuel:	100LL, Jet A
TPA:	1000 feet msl
Runway:	14-32: 7003 x 150 asph
Runway:	04-22: 5004 x 150 asph
FBO:	Jones Aviation
	941/355-8100
	Dolphin Aviation
	941/355-2902

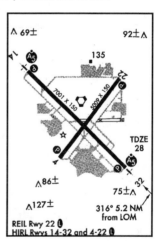

☞ *Communication:*

CTAF:	120.1
Unicom:	122.95
App/Dep:	Tampa 119.65; 124.94 (4000' and below)
	Sarasota 120.1 (provides secondary approach control within 5 miles of airport)
Tower:	120.1 (1100-0500Z*)
Ground:	121.9
Clnc Del:	118.25
ATIS:	134.15
AWOS:	119.225

☞ *Transportation:*
Taxi: 941/349-3952; 941/355-5155
Car Rental: Avis 941/359-5240; Hertz 941/355-8848

☞ *Lodging:*
<u>Sarasota:</u> **Best Western Midtown** 941/955-9841; **Days Inn Airport** 941/355-9721

RINGLING MUSEUM
(approximately 1 mile from airport)
5401 Bay Shore Road, Sarasota, FL 34243; Tel: 941/359-5700
Open daily.
Admission is $9 for adults; children 12 and under are free.

The Ringling Museum is the legacy of circus magnate John Ringling, one of the greatest business tycoons of his day. The complex includes his Venetian-style mansion, a large collection of European Baroque paintings displayed at a spacious 22-gallery museum, and gardens.

THE BOLLETTIERI SPORTS ACADEMY
(tennis academy approximately 3 miles from airport)
5500 34th Street West, Bradenton, FL 34210; Tel: 941/755-1000 or 800/USA-NICK

This is the headquarters of the tennis school that Andre Agassi, Boris Becker, Jim Courier, Mary Pierce, and Monica Seles chose for their top-level training. Even if you don't fit in that league, Bollettieri's Sports Academy's unique teaching methods are applicable to advanced as well as recreational players. The facilities are superb. Programs last from a day to a week.

WHILE YOU'RE THERE: Hold a stingray in the touch tank or look at manatees, sharks, and other marine mammals at the **Mote Marine Aquarium** 800/691-MOTE.

Sebring Reg. Airport (SEF)

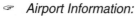

FL

Airport is located 6 miles southeast of town.

☞ *Airport Information:*

Location: Miami sectional N27.27.39 W81.20.54
Attended: Mon-Fri 1300-2300Z*
Sat-Sun 1300-2200Z*
Elevation: 63 feet
Fuel: 100LL, Jet A
TPA: 800 feet msl lgt acft
1500 feet msl hvy acft
Runway: 18-36: 5190 x 150 asph
14-32: 5190 x 300 conc
FBO: Sebring Flight Center
941/655-6455

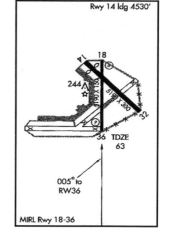

☞ *Communication:*

CTAF: 122.7
Unicom: 122.7
App/Dep: Miami Center 127.2

☞ *Transportation:*

Taxi: 941/382-6119; 941/385-0173
Car Rental: Budget 941/385-0144; Enterprise 941/385-6969

SKIP BARBER RACING SCHOOL

(driving and racing school on Sebring field)
P.O. Box 1629, 29 Brook Street, Lakeville, CT 06039; Tel: 800/221-1131

Famous the world over, Sebring's airport runways and permanent road course are utilized by Skip Barber Racing in three different circuit layouts. Choose from half-day to two-day schools to enhance your skills or get your teenager up to speed safely. Learn advance car control skills such as threshold braking, skid recovery, and accident-avoidance maneuvers.

Tampa Int'l Airport (TPA)

Airport is located 6 miles west of town.

☞ *Airport Information:*

Location: Miami sectional N27.58.53 W82.32.00
Airspace: Class B; see VFR Terminal Area Chart
Attended: Continuously
Elevation: 27 feet
Fuel: 100LL, Jet A
TPA: 800 feet msl lgt acft, 1500 feet msl multi-engine, jet acft
Runway: 18R-36L: 1100 x 150 conc
18L-36R: 8300 x 150 asph, conc
09-27: 6998 x 150 asph, conc
FBO: Raytheon Aircraft Service 813/878-4500

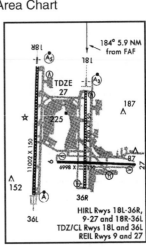

☞ *Communication:*

Unicom: 122.95
App/Dep: 118.15 (001-150º); 119.65 (151-219º);118.8 (220-360º)
Tower: 119.5; 119.05
Ground: 121.7; 121.35
Clnc Del: 133.6
ATIS: Arrival 126.45; Departure 128.475

☞ *Transportation:*

Taxi: 813/253-0121; 813/253-2424
Car Rental: Hertz 813/874-3232

☞ *Lodging:*

Tampa: The **Days Inn Busch Gardens/Magnate** 813/933-6471 and **Holiday Inn Busch Gardens** 813/971-4710 are conveniently located for Busch Gardens visitors. The **Hyatt Regency Tampa** 813/225-1234 has a downtown location. **Tampa Airport Marriott** 813/879-5151

☞ *Restaurants:*

Tampa: Hearty steak and organic veggie lovers will find their fill at **Bern's Steak House** 813/251-2421. Flamenco accompanies

Spanish and Cuban fare at **Columbia** 813/248-4961.

BUSCH GARDENS
(theme park approximately 10 miles from airport)
3000 E. Busch Blvd., Tampa, FL 33674; Tel: 813/987-5082
Open daily
Admission is $40.95 for adults and $34.95 for 3-to-9-year-olds.

African-themed family entertainment park on 330 acres. Take a monorail to view African wildlife roaming the park's plains and waterways. Thrill seekers can get their adrenaline going on incredible rollercoasters or a state-of-the-art flight simulator. There are also bird gardens, bazaars, and Broadway-style musical revues for your entertainment.

FLORIDA AQUARIUM
(approximately 7 miles from airport)
701 Channelside Drive, Tampa, FL 33602; Tel: 813/273-4000
Open daily, except on major holidays.
Admission is $11.95 for anybody 13 years and older.

Discover the underwater world inside the glass-domed Florida Aquarium. Come face-to-face with an impressive variety of fish, birds, plants, and animals, including turtles and alligators. Habitat displays range from beaches to coral reefs and swamps.

MUSEUM OF SCIENCE AND INDUSTRY (MOSI)
(approximately 10 miles from airport)
4801 E. Fowler Avenue, Tampa, FL 33617; Tel: 813/987-6100
Open daily.
Admission is $12 for adults and $8 for children. One IMAX movie included in price.

Hands-on, interactive activities are the trademark of this science center, the largest in the Southeastern United States. The Challenger Learning Center takes you to gravity-defying heights. Investigate space, the solar system, environment, and other subjects.

WHILE YOU'RE THERE: Test the water at **Adventure Island** 813/987-5600, a water park opposite Busch Gardens featuring a wave pool, inner tube runs, and speed slides. July through December are the months for dog racing at the **Tampa Greyhound Track** 813/932-4313.

Tampa (X39)

North Aero Park Airport

Airport is located 17 miles northeast of town.

☞ *Airport Information:*

Location: Miami sectional N28.13.25 W82.22.58
Attended: 1230-2330Z*
Elevation: 68 feet
Fuel: 100LL, Jet A
TPA: 1000 feet msl
Runway: 14-32: 3541 x 50 asph
FBO: Tampa North Aero Services 813/973-3703

☞ *Communication:*
CTAF: 123.05
Unicom: 123.05

☞ *Transportation:*
Taxi: 813/872-8292
Car Rental: Enterprise 813/880-0600

☞ *Lodging:*
Wesley Chapel: **Saddlebrook Resort** 813/973-1111—see below

SADDLEBROOK RESORT
(approximately 3 miles from airport)
5700 Saddlebrook Way, Wesley Chapel, FL 33543; Tel: 813/973-1111

Whether it's golf, tennis, or spa treatments you like to relax with, it's all possible at this first-class resort. Arnold Palmer designed both of Saddlebrook's championship 18-hole courses. Both are formidable because of the difficulty of rolling terrain. Saddlebrook is also world headquarters of the Arnold Palmer Golf Academy, where you can improve your fundamentals of the game. If tennis is your choice sport, you'll find everything you need. The resort is highly rated by both *Tennis* and *Racquet* magazines and features 45 courts. The Hopman Tennis Program has instruction and clinics. After sports, a European-style luxury spa offers massage therapy, hydrotherapy, herbal and seaweed body wraps, moor mud treatments, and aromatherapy. Anglers can find solitude at bass fishing in privately stocked resort lakes.

Titusville 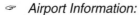 (TIX)

Space Coast Reg Airport

Airport is located 5 miles south of town.

☞ *Airport Information:*

Location: Jacksonville sectional N28.30.83 W80.47.97
Airspace: Class D service Mon-Fri 1200-0200Z*
Sat-Sun 1300-2300Z*
Attended: 1300-0100Z*
Elevation: 35 feet
Fuel: 100LL, Jet A
TPA: 1000 feet msl lgt acft
1500 feet msl hvy acft
Runway: 18-36: 6001 x 100 asph
09-27: 5001 x 100 asph
FBO: Discovery Aviation Center
407/267-6043
Gateway Aviation
407/267-1345

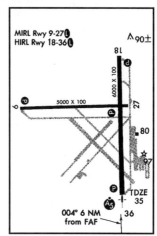

☞ *Communication:*

CTAF: 118.9
Unicom: 122.95
App/Dep: Patrick 134.95 (1200-0400Z*)
Non radar service (1200-1400Z* Sat-Sun)
Miami Center 124.1 (0400-1200Z*)
Tower: Executive 118.9 (1200-0200Z* Mon-Fri)
(1300-2300Z* Sat-Sun)
Ground: 121.85

☞ *Transportation:*

Taxi: 407/267-7061
Car Rental: Budget 407/268-5414

☞ *Lodging:*

Titusville: **Best Western Space Shuttle Inn** 407/269-9100; **Days Inn** 407/269-4480

KENNEDY SPACE CENTER

(approximately 7 miles from airport)
DNPS, Kennedy Space Center, FL 32899; Tel: 407/452-2121;
Internet: www.kscvisitor.com

Open daily, ecxept Christmas Day.
Complex is free.
Ticket for shuttle tour and one IMAX film is $19 for adults and $15 for children 3 to 11 years old.

Visit the complex where NASA prepares and launches the Space Shuttle. Tour the launch areas by bus, walk among authentic vintage spacecraft, view an IMAX big-screen film, and attend live briefings on launch preparations. The Apollo/Saturn V Center brings the space program to the moon to life through dramatic multimedia shows and hands-on displays and real Apollo flight hardware. Visits are most rewarding during an actual launch. Updated launch information is available by calling 407/867-4636. Complimentary car passes are available 3 months in advance to a viewing site six miles from the launch area.

MERRITT ISLAND NATIONAL WILDLIFE REFUGE
(approximately 10 miles from airport)
Box 6504, Titusville, FL 32780; Tel: 407/861-0667
Visitor center open daily from November to March.
Closed Sundays from April to October and on federal holidays.
Admission is free.

Blessed with a favorable coastal location, tropical-like climate, and a vast and diverse range of habitats, Merritt Island remains unsurpassed as a refuge for wildlife. Freshwater impoundments, saltwater estuaries, brackish marshes, and woods provide habitat for more than 330 species of birds, 31 mammals, 117 fishes, and 65 amphibians and reptiles. Depending on the season you may see concentrations of waterfowl, raptors, manatees, alligators, and loggerhead sea turtles. A self-guided auto tour route of 6 miles lets you see wading birds, shorebirds, and waterfowl. Foot trails wind through forests and marsh. Best time to visit is during the spring, fall, and winter. Hunting is permitted in accordance with the refuge hunt leaflet. The visitor center has information on fishing, boating, and canoeing as well as excellent brochures. There are no overnight or eating establishments on the island.

WHILE YOU'RE THERE: The **U.S. Astronaut Hall of Fame**
407/269-6100 honors American space heroes. Interactive exhibits allow guests to experience the thrill of the astronaut adventure for themselves. A 1,000-foot fishing pier is the centerpiece of **Jetty Park** 407/783-7111, an ideal location to kick back and land snapper, snook, and redfish.

Winter Haven
Gilbert Airport (GIF)

Airport is located 3 miles northwest of town.

☞ *Airport Information:*
Location: Jacksonville sectional N28.03.78 W81.45.20
Attended: 1200Z* to dusk
Fuel: 100LL, Jet A
TPA: 1000 feet msl
Runway: 04-22: 5006 x 100 asph
11-29: 3999 x 100 asph
FBO: Winter Haven Air Services
941/293-2501

☞ *Communication:*
CTAF: 122.7
Unicom: 122.7
App/Dep: Tampa 120.65, 119.9
ASOS: 133.675

☞ *Transportation:*
Taxi: 941/324-9166
Car Rental: Enterprise 941/293-2501

☞ *Lodging:*
Winter Haven: Holiday Inn 941/294-4451; **Howard Johnson**
941/294-7321

FANTASY OF FLIGHT
(aviation attraction approximately 10 miles from airport)
I 4, Exit 21, Polk City, FL 33868; Tel: 941/984-3500; Internet: www.
fantasyofflight.com
Open daily, except Christmas and Thanksgiving.
Admission is $21.95 for adults, $10.95 for children 5-12 years old.

This attraction provides aviation-themed flight experiences and
exhibits. Discover the excitement of experiencing the sights, sounds,
and motion of aerial combat in a Corsair flight simulator. Take a
tethered balloon flight to 500 feet in their newest attraction, "The
Great Balloon Experience." History buffs will enjoy the "History of
Flight Tours" or the 35 aircraft on display.

GEORGIA

Atlanta
Fulton Co. Brown Field(FTY)

Airport is located 6 miles west of town.

☞ *Airport Information:*

Location: Atlanta sectional N33.46.75 W84.31.28
Airspace: Class D service 0800-0759Z*; other times class E
Attended: Continuously
Elevation: 841 feet
Fuel: 100LL, Jet A
TPA: 1600 feet msl lgt acft
2000 feet msl hvy acft
Runway: 08-26: 5796 x 100 asph
14-32: 4158 x 100 asph
09-27: 2801 x 60 asph
FBO: Brown Jet Center
404/699-2277
Hill Aircraft 404/691-3330
Raytheon Aircraft Service
404/699-9260

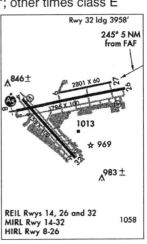

☞ *Communication:*
CTAF: 118.5
Unicom: 122.95
App/Dep: Atlanta 121.0
Tower: County 118.5; 120.7 (0800-0759Z*)
Ground: 121.7
Clnc Del: 123.7
ATIS: 120.175 (0800-0759Z*)

☞ *Transportation:*
Taxi: Contact FBO
Car Rental: Enterprise 404/691-3330

☞ *Lodging:*
Atlanta: The **Houston Mill House** 404/727-7878 is a lovely English

44

fieldstone home that has been turned into a B & B. **Comfort Inn** 404/696-2274; **Days Inn Downtown** 404/659-1285; **Masters Economy Inn Six Flags** 404/696-4690; **Ramada Inn Downtown** 404/659-2660

☞ *Restaurants:*
Atlanta: All-American food and rock n' roll memorabilia decor are found at the **Hard Rock Cafe** 404/688-7625. Enjoy regional cuisine in a historic, restored plantation home amidst trees at **Anthony's** 404/262-7379. Satisfy your craving for Mediterranean food at **Fairlie Poplar Cafe & Grill** 404/827-0040.

CNN CENTER
(broadcasting studio tour approximately 8 miles from airport)
1 CNN Center, Marietta Street at Techwood Drive, Atlanta, GA 30303; Tel: 404/827-2300
Open daily.
Tours are $7 for adults and $4.50 for children under 12 years old.

Get a feel for international news broadcasts by joining a guided studio tour at the CNN Center. Glass-enclosed overhead walkways allow you to get close to the high-tech, fast-paced business of producers and anchorpersons. Visitors are invited to reserve a seat in the studio audience for CNN's program "Talk Back Live."

SIX FLAGS OVER GEORGIA
(amusement park 1 mile from airport)
7561 Six Flags Road, Austell, GA 30168; Tel: 770/739-3400
Open March to October. Spring and fall open on weekends only.
Admission is $32.99 for adults and $16.50 for children under 48" tall.

Batman–The Ride is the newest addition to the Six Flags theme park. It's a suspended, outside-looping ride—a real thrill for rollercoaster fans. Dozen of rides, including rollercoasters and water rides as well as concerts and musical revues, are ready for your entertainment.

Augusta
Daniel Field <small>(DNL)</small>

Airport is located 1 mile west of town.

☞ *Airport Information:*

Location:	Atlanta sectional N33.28.00 W82.02.36
Attended:	1200Z* to dusk
Elevation:	423 feet
Fuel:	100LL, Jet A1
TPA:	1200 feet msl
Runway:	05-23: 3900 x 100 asph
	11-29: 3732 x 150 asph
FBO:	Augusta Aviation
	706/733-8970

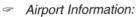

```
                          Rwy 23 ldg 3612'
                          Rwy 11 ldg 3406'
                          Rwy 29 ldg 3417'
                            161° 5.7 NM
                            from FAF



          3732 x 150



MIRL Rwys 11-29 and 5-23 ◐
REIL Rwys 11 and 29 ◐
```

☞ *Communication:*

CTAF:	123.05
Unicom:	123.05
App/Dep:	Augusta 126.8 (1145-0400Z*)
	Atlanta Center 128.1
	(0400-1145Z*)
Clnc Del:	128.1
ASOS:	135.275

☞ *Transportation:*

Taxi: 706/722-3501
Car Rental: Enterprise 706/737-3222

☞ *Lodging:*

Augusta: **Holiday Inn** 706/737-2300; **Super 8 Motel** 706/738-5018;
Radisson Riverfront Augusta 706/722-8900

☞ *Restaurants:*

Augusta: Try **The King George Restaurant & Riverwalk Brewery**
706/724-4755 for traditional English specialties and hand-crafted
brews. Japanese food is served at **Mikoto's** 706/855-0009. For
American cuisine visit **Sixth at Watkins** 706/722-8877. **Villa Europa**
706/798-6211 serves German, Italian, and American fare.

FORT DISCOVERY – NATIONAL SCIENCE CENTER
(approximately 2 miles from airport)
One Seventh Street, Augusta, GA 30901; Tel: 800/325-5445 or

706/821-0200; Internet: www.nscdiscovery.org
Open daily.
Admission is $6 for adults and $5 for children.

Located on the Riverwalk, a six-block, treelined garden esplanade along the Savannah River levee, is Fort Discovery. It is a science and technology playground dedicated to reach America's youth with 250 interactive exhibits, demonstrations and a hi-tech theater. Check out the simulated moonwalk, indoor lightning storm, and pendulum swing.

JONES CREEK GOLF CLUB
(approximately 6 miles from airport)
4101 Hammonds Ferry, Evans, GA 30809; Tel: 706/860-4228

Rees Jones has been at work in this heavily wooded area to design a course that has been ranked as the top public course in Georgia by *Georgia Golf News*. Opened in 1986, it features creeks, ponds, and over sixty sand bunkers. Test your skills on this 18-hole course, especially No. 13!!

WHILE YOU'RE THERE: Boats may be rented at the **Augusta Riverwalk Marina & Boat Rentals** 706/722-1388.

Brunswick
Mc Kinnon Airport (SSI)

Airport is located 5 miles east of town.

☞ *Airport Information:*

Location: Jacksonville sectional N31.09.10 W81.23.48
Airspace: Class E service 1100-0258Z*; other times Class G
Attended: 1200-0100Z*
Elevation: 20 feet
Fuel: 100LL, Jet A
TPA: 1020 feet msl non-turbine acft
1520 feet msl turbine acft
Runway: 04-22: 5421 x 150 asph
16-34: 3313 x 75 asph
FBO: Golden Isles Aviation 912/638-8617

☞ *Communication:*
CTAF: 123.05
Unicom: 123.05
App/Dep: Jax Center 126.75

☞ *Transportation:*
Taxi: 912/638-3790
Car Rental: Avis 912/638-2232
Hertz 912/638-2522

☞ *Lodging:*
Sea Island: **The Cloister** 912/638-3611 or 800/732-4752—see entry below.
St. Simon's Island: The **King and Prince Beach and Golf Resort** 912/638-3631 or 800/342-0212 is an elegantly quiet beach resort with the usual activities, such as golf, tennis, swimming, riding, and biking. The **St. Simon's Inn** 912/638-1101 is near the village, a block from the beach. **Days Inn** 912/634-0660

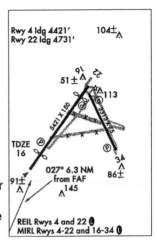

```
Rwy 4 ldg 4421'          104±
Rwy 22 ldg 4731'              A

                      91  22
                  51±  A
                           A 113
               5421 X 150
  TDZE                        P
  16                        3
                            A
              027° 6.3 NM    86±
  91±         from FAF
   A            A 145
                A

REIL Rwys 4 and 22
MIRL Rwys 4-22 and 16-34
```

THE CLOISTER

(full service resort and golf approximately 2 miles from airport)
100 First Street, Sea Island, GA 31561; Tel: 912/638-3611 or 800/732-4752

Sea Island is best known for The Cloister Hotel, opened in 1928. This classic resort has earned five stars from Mobil for 20 consecutive years. The Spanish Mediterranean style speaks of its historic charm while providing first-class amenities that are aimed to please you. Fifty-four holes of golf on immaculate courses are apt to keep you golfers busy. When you add in 18 tennis courts, 2 pools, spa facilities, horseback riding, windsurfing, fishing, sailing, skeet shooting and biking, you wonder how you can do it all. Former president George and Barbara Bush chose it for their honeymoon and returned several years ago to celebrate their wedding anniversary.

WHILE YOU'RE THERE: Try your luck fishing for barracuda, snapper, amberjack, and other fish in the Atlantic Ocean or Intracoastal Waterway. Fishing outings are organized at **Golden Isles Yachts** 912/638-5678. Rent bikes from **Barry's Beach Service** 912/638-8053 or **Benjy's Bike Shop** 912/638-6766 to pedal St. Simon's paved bike paths. **Southeast Adventures** 912/638-6732 has bird and dolphin watching tours.

Dahlonega
Lumkin Co.Wimpys
Airport (9A0)

Airport is located 3 miles northwest of town.

☞ *Airport Information:*
Location: Atlanta sectional N34.34.76 W84.01.24
Attended: Unattended
Elevation: 1311 feet
Fuel: Not available
TPA: 2300 feet msl
Runway: 15-33: 3035 x 50 asph
FBO: Not available

☞ *Communication:*
CTAF: 122.9

☞ *Transportation:*
Car Rental: Hardy Ford 706/864-6504

☞ *Lodging:*
Dahlonega: **Econo Lodge** 706/864-6191; **Super 8 Motel** 706/864-4343.

☞ *Restaurants:*
Dahlonega: Sample Southern fried chicken and honey cured ham at **Smith House** 706/864-3566.

APPALACHIAN OUTFITTERS
(river trips approximately 2 miles from airport)
Office: 24 North Park Street, Outpost: Highway 60 South, Dahlonega, GA 30533; Tel: 706/864-7117 or 800/426-7117
Season is approximately from April through September.

Explore the beauty of the North Georgia mountains by way of its spectacular rivers. The Chestatee River, once home of the Cherokee, is ideal for canoeing, kayaking, tubing, or fishing. Guide service, rentals with shuttle service, and canoe clinics are offered.

CONSOLIDATED GOLD MINES
(approximately 5 miles from airport)
185 Consolidated Road, Dahlonega, GA 30533; Tel: 706/864-8473
Open daily.
Admission $10 for adults, $5 for children.

Dahlonega, a Cherokee word meaning "precious yellow metal," is the
site of America's first major gold rush in 1828. Consolidated Gold
Mines was once the largest mining operation in the East. Visitors can
take a tour that leads 450 feet into the tunnel system made by
miners before the turn of the century, where you can see gold veins
and geological formations. Or how about trying your luck at panning?

WHILE YOU'RE THERE: Experience the beauty of north
Georgia woodlands by mountain bike. Rent a bike or take a guided
trail tour with **Mountain Adventures Cyclery** 706/864-8525.

Folkston
Davis Field (3J6)

Airport is located 3 miles southwest of town.

☞ *Airport Information:*
Location: Jacksonville sectional N30.47.85 W82.01.66
Attended: Unattended
Elevation: 68 feet
Fuel: Not available
TPA: 1068 feet msl
Runway: 18-36: 2500 x 50 asph
FBO: Not available

☞ *Communication:*
CTAF: 122.9
Unicom: 122.9

☞ *Lodging:*
Folkston: **Days Inn** 912/496-2514; **The Inn at Folkston** 912/496-
6256 or 888/509-MAIN

☞ *Restaurants:*
Folkston: Southern food in a down-to-earth restaurant can be had at

Okefenokee's Restaurant 912/496-3263.

OKEFENOKEE NATIONAL WILDLIFE REFUGE
Suwannee Canal Recreation Concession
(approximately 7 miles from airport)
Route 2, Box 3325, Folkston, GA 31537; Tel: 912/496-7156 or 800/
SWAMP-96

Okefenokee Swamp is a vast cypress swamp covering some 600 square miles of wilderness the Indians called "land of the trembling earth." Shallows and backwater shelter close to 20,000 alligators. Wildlife includes 30 species of snakes as well as pumas, bears, deer, otter, and hundreds of species of birds. If you choose to visit in spring you will find the gators at their most active, flowers in bloom, and birds nesting. Summer days are hot and humid, and insect repellent should be brought along any time of the year. Canoeing is the favorite way to explore the swamp. Several trails are available depending upon your time frame and interest. Canoes and equipment can be rented by contacting the above numbers. Early reservations, up to 2 months in advance, are a necessity. Boat tours guided by naturalists are available, as well. Or you just may use the boardwalk, trails, and observation tower for limited access into the swamp. Fishing holes and the canal contain largemouth bass, warmouth, chain pickerels, sunfish, and others. A Georgia fishing license is required.

Hampton
Clayton Co. Tara Field (4A7)

Airport is located 3 miles west of town.

☞ *Airport Information:*

Location: Atlanta sectional N33.23.35 W84.19.94
Attended: 1300-0100Z*
Elevation: 873 feet
Fuel: 100LL, Jet A
TPA: 1900 feet msl lgt acft
2400 feet msl hvy acft
Runway: 06-24: 4503 x 75 asph
FBO: 770/946-3153

☞ *Communication:*

CTAF:	122.725
Unicom:	122.725
App/Dep:	Atlanta 119.8

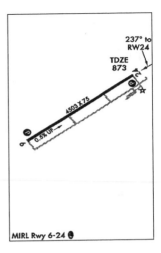

☞ *Transportation:*
Car Rental: South Lake Ford
770/471-7801

☞ *Lodging:*
Atlanta: **Hampton Inn** 770/968-8990;
Best Western 770/227-8400

BUCK BAKER RACING SCHOOL
(car racing adjacent to airport)
1613 Runnymede Lane, Charlotte, NC 28211; Tel: 800/529-2825 or
704/366-6224

Ever thought about racing a car? Buck Baker Racing School will
teach you how to "stand on it" in a Winston Cup Race Car. Complete
courses are available to learn fundamentals and racing techniques.
There is also a half-day "Ride & Drive Course" or "Hot Lap Rides" for
those that want to get the feel but not race themselves. Call for dates
available at the Atlanta Motor Speedway, a 1.5-mile super speedway
with 24-degree banked turns. Speedway is located adjacent to
airport.

Jekyll Island Airport (09J)
Airport is located 6 miles southeast of town.

☞ *Airport Information:*
Location:	Jacksonville sectional N31.04.47 W81.25.67
Attended:	Unattended
Elevation:	12 feet
Fuel:	Not available
TPA:	800 feet msl
Runway:	18-36: 3711 x 75 asph
FBO:	Not available

☞ *Communication:*
CTAF: 123.0
Unicom: 123.0
App/Dep: Jax Center 126.75

☞ *Transportation:*
Car Rental: Hertz 912/265-3645

☞ *Lodging:*
Jekyll Island: The **Jekyll Island Club Hotel** 912/635-2600 or 800/535-9547 is a turreted Victorian from the 1880s. **Ramada** 912/635-2111; **Holiday Inn** 912/635-3311

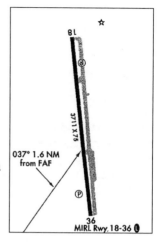

JEKYLL ISLAND GOLF CLUB

(approximately 1 mile from airport)
Captain Wylly Drive, Jekyll Island, GA 31527; Tel: 912/635-2368

Pleasant weather year-round adds to the attraction of gorgeous scenery in enjoying a game of golf. Three 18-hole courses are your choice, but the Oleander and Indian Mound courses seem to have more fans than the Pine Lake course. Jekyll Island was once a favored retreat for a group or "club" of millionaires, the Rockefellers, Macys, Morgans, Vanderbilts, Pulitzers, and other aristocrats who bought the island in 1887. The original "club" building has been turned into the Jekyll Island Club Hotel, and some of the mansions can still be seen.

WHILE YOU'RE THERE: Deep sea fishing, dolphin watching, sightseeing, and dinner cruises as well as water taxis to the other islands are available from **Jekyll Historic Wharf** 912/635-3152. **Summer Waves** 912/635-2074 is an 11-acre waterpark with wave pool, slides, and pools. Ride on beautiful Driftwood Beach and through maritime forest by contacting **Victoria's Carriages & Trail Rides** 912/635-9500.

Macon
Middle Georgia Reg.

GA

Airport (MCN)

Airport is located 9 miles south of town.

☞ *Airport Information:*

Location: Atlanta sectional
N32.41.57 W83.38.95

Airspace: Class D service 1200-0300Z*
Attended: 1000-0300Z*
Elevation: 354 feet
Fuel: 100LL, Jet A
TPA: 1154 feet msl
Runway: 05-23: 6501 x 150 asph/conc
13-31: 5001 x 150 asph/conc
FBO: Lowe Aviation 912/788-3491

REIL Rwys 13, 23, and 31
MIRL Rwy 13-31
HIRL Rwy 5-23

☞ *Communication:*

CTAF: 128.2
Unicom: 122.95
App/Dep: Macon 119.6 (above 5000'), 124.2 (5000' and below)
124.8 (3000' and below within 20 nm from Macon
VORTAC), 1000-0400Z* weekdays,
0300-1100Z* weekends and holidays
Atlanta Center 134.5 (0500-1100Z*)
Tower: Macon 128.2 (1200-0300Z*)
Ground; 121.65
ATIS: 118.95 (1200-0300Z*)

☞ *Transportation:*

Taxi: 912/781-7312
Car Rental: Budget 912/784-7130; Hertz 912/788-3600

☞ *Lodging:*

Macon: **Hilton Hotel** 912/746-1461

MUSEUM OF AVIATION

(approximately 8 miles from airport)
P.O. Box 2469, Robins AFB, GA 31099; Tel: 912/926-6870; Internet:
www.museum.robins.af.mil
Open daily, except major holidays. Free admission.

Approximately 90 aircraft are on display at this award-winning aviation museum, the fourth largest in the country. Four large buildings with more than 170,000 square feet of indoor exhibit space house historic aircraft and missiles from the U.S. Air Force collection. Several exhibits re-create scenes such as the Flying Tigers airfield in China in 1943 and a WWII airfield with a P-47 getting ready for takeoff. A theater with wrap-around screen features Smithsonian-produced films. A special Century of Flight Hangar displays famous Air Force aircraft such as the SR-71 Blackbird, B-29, F104, F-86, P-51, and U-2 Dragon Lady. The Hall of Fame honors men and women who significantly contributed to aviation in Georgia.

Monroe
Walton Co. Airport (D73)

Airport is located 1 mile southeast of town.

☞ *Airport Information:*
Location: Atlanta sectional N33.46.89 W83.41.61
Attended: 1400-2200Z*
Elevation: 867 feet
Fuel: 100LL, Jet A
TPA: 1700 feet msl
Runway: 03-21: 4112 x 60 asph
FBO: WHP Aviation 770/267-2343

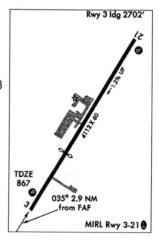

Rwy 3 ldg 2702'

4112 x 60

1.2% UP

TDZE
867

035° 2.9 NM
from FAF

MIRL Rwy 3-21

☞ *Communication:*
CTAF: 122.9
App/Dep: Atlanta 119.3
AWOS: 392.

☞ *Transportation:*
Taxi: 770/267-0447

☞ *Lodging:*
Monroe: **Days Inn** 770/267-3666

SKYDIVE MONROE
(located at airport)
P.O. Box 1204, Monroe, GA 30655; Tel: 770/207-9164

Skydive Monroe is dedicated to teaching sound skydiving skills through the most advanced methods of training, which are Tandem Progression and Accelerated Freefall. They recommend the tandem jump for those who only want to jump once and those who like hands-on training. There are nine jumps in the tandem progressions. The accelerated freefall method condenses the training period. Once you have mastered the skills of three tandem jumps, you will receive ground training, then complete the student program with only six freefall jumps. A souvenir video or photography (24 pictures) of your jump is possible on request. First weekend Tandem Jump starts at $150.

Pine Mountain
Callaway Gardens-
Harris Co. Airport (PIM)

Airport is located 2 miles southwest of town.

☞ *Airport Information:*

Location:	Atlanta sectional N32.50.44 W84.52.95
Attended:	Attended Mon-Fri 1600-2130Z*
	Unattended Tue-Thu
Elevation:	902 feet
Fuel:	100LL, Jet A
TPA:	1700 feet msl lgt acft
	1900 feet msl hvy acft
Runway:	09-27: 5001 x 100 asph
FBO:	706/663-5055

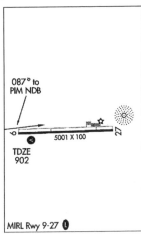

☞ *Communication:*

CTAF:	122.8
Unicom:	122.8
App/Dep:	Columbus 127.7; 126.55 (1200-0400Z*)
	Atlanta Center 120.45 (0400-1200Z*)
Clnc Del:	120.45

☞ *Lodging:*
Pine Mountain: A variety of rooms and cottages are available at **Callaway Gardens** 800/CALLAWAY. **Mountain Top Inn and Resort** 706/663-4719

CALLAWAY GARDENS
(gardens, golf and outdoor recreation approximately 4 miles from airport)
Box 2000, Pine Mountain, GA 31822; Tel: 800/CALLAWAY; Internet: www.callawaygardens.com
Admission to gardens is $13 for adults and $6.50 for children.

Discover nature and refresh your soul among stunning floral displays and 14,000 acres of natural woodlands. Visit the nation's largest tropical butterfly conservatory or the herb, vegetable, and flower gardens. Olden days come to life at the Log Cabin, and a large variety of plants and flowers may be enjoyed all year at the Sibley Center. Nature and bicycle trails invite for strolling and riding (bikes can be rented). Other recreational opportunities include tennis, racquetball, fishing, fly-fishing by appointment, and the gun club. The Mountain View golf course is home of the PGA Tour's prestigious Buick Challenge and was designed by Dick Wilson and Joe Lee. Tight, tree-lined fairways include four waterholes, three right and three left doglegs, plenty of bunkers, and two lakes presenting lateral hazards. In addition to this challenging course there are the Lake View, Garden View, and Skyview courses. Sunning and swimming are enticing at Robin Lake Beach but make sure you leave time for miniature golf, paddleboats, riverboat lake tours, and shuffleboard. Check for the times the "Flying High" Circus is in town.

PINE MOUNTAIN WILD ANIMAL PARK
(approximately 5 miles from airport)
1300 Oak Grove Road, Pine Mountain, GA 31822; Tel: 800/367-2751 or 706/663-8744
Open daily, except Christmas.
Admission is from $10.95 to $11.95.

This 500-acre park is home to hundreds of wild and exotic species from around the world. Most of these beautiful creatures roam and graze freely. Take a guided bus tour or drive through. Bus tours run daily during peak season, weekends only during the off-season.

Savannah Int'l Airport (SAV)

Airport is located 7 miles northwest of town.

☞ *Airport Information:*

Location:	Charlotte sectional N32.07.66 W81.12.13
Airspace:	Class C service 1100-0400Z*
Attended:	1100-0400Z*
Elevation:	51 feet
Fuel:	100LL, Jet A
TPA:	1550 feet msl conventional
	2050 feet msl overhead
Runway:	09-27: 9351 x 150 conc
	18-36: 7001 x 150 conc
	Warning: closed to some
	aircraft
FBO:	Signature Flight Support
	912/964-1557
FBO:	Savannah Aviation
	912/964-1022

```
                              245° 4.4 NM
                               from FAF
                                    109
                              81  A
              126         117
        A                        27
         0.5% UP
        9351 X 150         A    DZE
                          134   51
        7
        0
        0
        1
        x
        1
        5
        0
    36    A

TDZ/CL Rwy 9
REIL Rwy 27
REIL Rwy 18
HIRL All runways
```

☞ *Communication:*

CTAF:	119.1
Unicom:	122.95
App/Dep:	125.3 (011-109°), 120.4 (270-010°), 118.4 (110-269°)
	121.1 (1100-0400Z*), Jax Center 120.85 (0400-1100Z*)
Tower:	119.1 (1100-0400Z*)
Ground:	121.9
Clnc Del:	119.55
ATIS:	123.75 (1100-0400Z*)

☞ *Transportation:*

Taxi: 912/236-1133; 912/269-5586
Car Rental: Hertz 912/964-9595; Thrifty 912/966-2277

☞ *Lodging:*

Savannah: The **Days Inn** 912/236-4440 is located in the Historic District. Just 3 miles from the airport is the location of the **Comfort Inn** 912/748-5242.

☞ *Restaurants:*

Savannah: Indulge in gourmet cuisine prepared by a chef who won the "Best Chef in the Southeast" award at **Elizabeth's on 37th** 912/236-5547.

THE MIGHTY EIGHTH AIR FORCE MUSEUM
(approximately 5 miles from airport)
175 Bourne Ave, Poole, GA; Tel: 912/748-8888; Internet: www.
mighty8thmuseum.com
Open daily, except major holidays.
Admission is $7.50 for adults and $5.50 for children 6 to12 years old.

The Eighth Air Force was formed in Savannah and did become the
world's greatest air armada. By virtue of its size and scope of
operations it then became known as "The Mighty." The museum has
unique static displays as well as state-of-the-art visual displays.
History is covered from World War II through Desert Storm. You are
invited on a journey of sights and sounds, re-creating some of this
country's proudest moments at its darkest hours.

Valdosta Reg. Airport (VLD)
Airport is located 3 miles south of town.

☞ *Airport Information:*

Location: Jacksonville N30.46.95 W83.16.60
Airspace: Class D service 1200-0400Z*; other times Class G
Attended: Continuously
Elevation: 204 feet
Fuel: 100LL, Jet A
TPA: 1000 feet msl
Runway: 17-35: 6302 x 150 asph
04-22: 5596 x 100 asph
13-31: 3638 x 75 asph
FBO: 912/242-3175

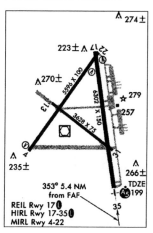

☞ *Communication:*

CTAF: 120.9
Unicom: 122.95
App/Dep: Valdosta 124.6 (8,000 feet
and above)
126.6 (below 8,000 feet)
Operations Mon-Fri 1200-0300Z*, Sat, Sun, Federal
holidays 1400-2200Z*
Jax Center 133.7
Tower: 120.9 (1200-0400Z*)
Ground: 121.7

☞ *Transportation:*
Taxi: 912/247-1150
Car Rental: Avis 912/242-4242; Hertz 912/242-7070

☞ *Lodging:*
Valdosta: The Fairfield Inn 912/253-9300 is located in the heart of the most progressive area of Valdosta and convenient to historic homes and other attractions. **Holiday Inn** 912/242-3881; **ClubHouse Inn** 912/247-7755 or 800/CLUBINN

WILD ADVENTURES
(theme park approximately 8 miles from airport)
3766 Old Clyattville Road, Valdosta, GA 31601; Tel: 800/808-0872 or 912/559-1330
Open seasonal, call to check.
Admission is $19.95 for adults and $17.95 for children 3 to 9 years old.

Experience a day full of fun and adventure for the whole family at the South's newest theme park. Wild Adventure features over 400 wild animals from around the world, an African safari ride, shows, keeper talks, petting zoo, and over 15 rides.

Anderson
Anderson Munic.-
Darlington Field (AID)

IN

Airport is located 3 miles east of town.

☞ *Airport Information:*

Location:	St. Louis sectional N40.06.52 W85.36.78
Airspace:	Class D service 1100-0300Z*
Attended:	1100-0300Z*
Elevation:	919 feet
Fuel:	100LL, Jet A
TPA:	1700 feet msl lgt acft
	1900 feet msl hvy acft
Runway:	12-30: 5401 x 100 asph
	18-36: 3399 x 75 asph
FBO:	Anderson Aviation
	765/644-1238

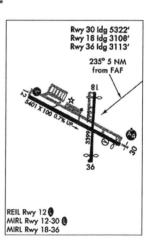

Rwy 30 ldg 5322'
Rwy 18 ldg 3108'
Rwy 36 ldg 3113'

235° 5 NM
from FAF

REIL Rwy 12 ●
MIRL Rwy 12-30 ●
MIRL Rwy 18-36

☞ *Communication:*

CTAF:	126.0
Unicom:	122.95
App/Dep:	Indianapolis Center 120.65
Tower:	126.0 (1100-0300Z)
Ground:	121.6
AWOS:	118.375

☞ *Transportation:*

Taxi: 765/644-7777
Car Rental: National 765/378-5757

☞ *Lodging:*

Anderson: **Motel 6** 765/642-9023; **Lees Inn Anderson** 765/649-2500

HOOSIER PARK RACETRACK
(horse racing approximately 5 miles from airport)
4500 Dan Patch Circle, Anderson, IN 47265; Tel: 800/526-RACE

Hoosier Park harness and thoroughbred horse racing year round.
Watch the trotters and pacers from April through August.
Thoroughbred racing is from September through November.
Highlights of the season are the Indiana Derby in October and the
Dan Patch Invitational Race in July.

French Lick Mun. Airport

(FRH)
Airport is located 3 miles southwest of town.

☞ *Airport Information:*

Location: St. Louis sectional N38.30.37 W86.38.22
Attended: 1400-2300Z*
Elevation: 792 feet
Fuel: 100LL, Jet A
TPA: 1600 feet msl lgt acft
2300 feet msl hvy acft
Runway: 08-26: 5500 x 100 asph
FBO: 812/936-2222

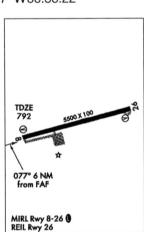

TDZE
792

5500 X 100

08

26

077° 6 NM
from FAF

MIRL Rwy 8-26 ●
REIL Rwy 26

☞ *Communication:*

CTAF: 122.8
Unicom: 122.8
App/Dep: Louisville 132.075 east
123.675 west

☞ *Transportation:*
Car Rental: B & O 812/295-2843

☞ *Lodging:*
French Lick: **French Lick Springs Resort** 800/457-4042 (see
below).

FRENCH LICK SPRINGS RESORT
(golf and spa resort approximately 4 miles from airport)
Highway 56, French Lick, IN 47432; Tel: 812/936-9300 or 800/457-
4042

This recently restored resort is located in the hills of the southern part of Indiana. Built in the early 1840s and modeled after the great spas of Europe, it attracted a wealthy elite who came from all over the country to "take the waters" in as many ways as they could. These days this elegant Victorian hotel with its verandahs that overlook formal gardens, lawns, and rolling woodlands attracts families and conventions. The spa can be enjoyed on a daily basis, with the spa director advising on exercise classes and body work. Golfers can challenge themselves on the Hill Course, host of several PGA and LPGA Championships, and the Valley Course, appealing to golfers of all skill levels. Facilities include a full health spa, in- and outdoor tennis, swimming, and horseback riding.

I N

Huntingburg Airport (HNB)
Airport is located 3 miles south of town.

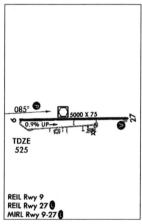

☞ *Airport Information:*

Location: St. Louis sectional N38.14.94 W86.57.22
Attended: Mon-Fri 1200-2300Z*
Sat-Sun 1300-2300Z*
Elevation: 529 feet
Fuel: 100LL, Jet A
TPA: 1500 feet msl lgt acft
2000 feet msl hvy acft
Runway: 09-27: 5000 x 75 asph
FBO: Jasper Flight Service
800/321-5391

085° → ☐ 5000 X 75
0.9% UP→
TDZE
525

REIL Rwy 9
REIL Rwy 27 ◐
MIRL Rwy 9-27 ◐

☞ *Communication:*

CTAF: 122.8
Unicom: 122.8
App/Dep: Evansville 126.4 (1200-0500Z*)
Indianapolis Center 128.3 (0500-1200Z*)
Clnc Del: 118.8
AWOS: 119.675

☞ *Transportation:*

Car Rental: Sternberg 812/482-5125; Ruxer 812/482-1200
contact FBO

☞ *Lodging:*
Santa Claus: The closest accommodation to Holiday World & Splashin' Safari is **Santa's Lodge** 812/937-1902 or 800/640-7895.
Huntingburg: **Best Western Dutchman Inn** 812/683-2334

☞ *Restaurants:*
Santa Claus: Family-style Mexican cuisine in a historic log building is served at **La Cantina Mexican Restaurant** 800/522-2684.

HOLIDAY WORLD & SPLASHIN' SAFARI
(theme and water park approximately 8 miles from the airport)
Jct. SR 162 & 245, Santa Claus, IN 47579; Tel: 800/GO SANTA
Open mid May to mid October.
Admission is $22.95 for adults and $16.95 for anybody under 54" tall.

Monsoon Lagoon, a huge interactive water play complex, will cool your body but not your spirit. A giant bucket drops 1,000 gallons of water every few minutes! With its 12 levels of "hands-on" fun, body slides and 60 different activities interconnected with bridges, cargo nets, and web crawls, Monsoon Lagoon will give your whole family an exciting day away.

Indianapolis
Speedway Airport (3SY)

Airport is located 4 miles west of town.

☞ *Airport Information:*
Location: St. Louis sectional N39.47.92 W86.21.33
Attended: 1300-2200Z*
Elevation: 870 feet
Fuel: 100LL
TPA: 1770 feet msl
Runway: 06-24: 2820 x 36 asph
FBO: 317/271-7040

☞ *Communication:*
CTAF: 122.7
Unicom: 122.7

☞ *Transportation:*
Taxi: 317/487-7777; 317/631-7521
Car Rental: Speedway Mazda National 317/844-9011

☞ *Lodging:*
Indianapolis: Amenities at the **Indianapolis Motor Speedway Brickyard Crossing Golf Resort & Inn** 317/241-2500 include the Hall of Fame Museum and golf course. **The Old Northside Bed & Breakfast** 317/635-9123 is a 4-room historic mansion with themed rooms. **Courtyard by Marriott Downtown** 317/635-4443; **Hampton Inn Downtown** 317/261-1200. Built in 1928, the **Canterbury Hotel** 317/634-3000 or 800/538-8186 is a landmark with a private entrance to Circle Center, a downtown shopping and entertainment complex.

I N

☞ *Restaurants:*
Indianapolis: Assemble a meal of ethnic and deli fare at **City Market** 317/634-9266, a renovated 19th-century building. "Hoosier" style food is served at the **Iron Skillet Restaurant** 317/923-6353. **St. Elmo's Steak House** 317/635-0636 has a satisfying steak, seafood, chicken, and chops menu.

INDIANAPOLIS MOTOR SPEEDWAY AND HALL OF FAME MUSEUM
(approximately 6 miles from airport)
4790 West 16th Street, Indianapolis, IN 46222; Tel: 317/481-8500
Museum is open daily except Christmas.
Admission to museum is $3.

The "Indy 500" is the most famous automobile race in the world. Generally scheduled during the month of May, following three weeks of practice and qualifying, it draws crowds of approximately 350,000 spectators. Watch 33 drivers compete for prize money in excess of $7.5 million! The Speedway has been the scene of automobile races since 1911, yet during the war years the infield became an aviation repair depot and landing field for military planes flying between bases in Dayton, Ohio, and Rantoul, Illinois. The landing strip became one of the country's first lighted aviation runways (according to the 1919 Indianapolis 500 race program). Former "500" driver and World War I flying ace Capt. Eddie Rickenbacker bought the Speedway in 1927 and expanded it to include an 18-hole public golf course in 1929. Golf course architect Pete Dye was in charge of the makeover, which was completed in 1993 for the course now called Brickyard Crossing. A senior PGA Tour event, the Brickyard Crossing Championship, now occurs every September. Of the total of 18 holes, holes 7,8,9,10 are inside the race track and the other 14 outside the back straightaway.

The Hall of Fame Museum enshrines Indy Racing Legends and houses one of the world's largest and most varied collections of cars, including more than 30 "500" winners.

Ticket orders are accepted by mail the day after each race for next years' race but sell out almost immediately.

WHILE YOU'RE THERE: The **Indianapolis Zoo** 317/630-2001 with its 3,000 animals and one of the world's largest enclosed whale and dolphin pavilions is an ideal place to take the kids. Rides on ponies, camels, and elephants are also available. Visit the **Imax 3D Theater** 317/233-4629 for dramatic 3D stories of human endeavors or astounding scenes of nature on a screen standing six stories tall by 80 feet wide. The **Eiteljorg Museum of American Indian and Western Art** 317/636-9378 displays both Native American art and Western paintings and bronzes. Works of art are by, among others, Georgia O'Keeffe, Frederic Remington, and Andy Warhol. One of the best and the largest in the country, the **Children's Museum of Indianapolis** 317/924-5431 or 800/208-KIDS boasts 5 floors of interactive fun and hands-on activities for the young and not-so-young alike.

Monticello
White Co. Airport (MCX)

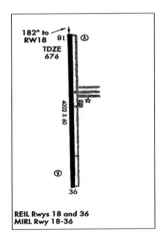

Airport is located 3 miles south of town.

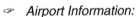

☞ *Airport Information:*

Location:	Chicago sectional
	N.40.42.53 W86.46.01
Attended:	1300-2200Z*
	Unattended major holidays
Elevation:	676 feet
Fuel:	100LL, Jet A
TPA:	1700 feet msl
Runway:	18-36: 4002 x 60 asph
FBO:	Tippecanoe Valley Aero
	219/583-9641

182° to RW18   8L

TDZE 676

4002 x 60

36

REIL Rwys 18 and 36
MIRL Rwy 18-36

☞ *Communication:*
CTAF: 122.8
Unicom: 122.8
App/Dep: Chicago Center 123.85

☞ *Lodging:*
Monticello: Sportsman Inn 219/583-5133

INDIANA BEACH AMUSEMENT RESORT
(approximately 7 miles from airport)
5224 E. Indiana Beach Road, Lake Shafer, Monticello, IN 47960;
Tel: 219/583-4141; Internet: www.indianabeach.com
Open May to September.
Admission is $23 for anybody over 44" and $12 for under 44"
(amusement and water park combination tickets).

Touting itself as Indiana's largest amusement resort and vacation playground, Indiana Beach Amusement Resort is home to the Hoosier Hurricane, Indiana's first and fastest roller coaster. Located on Lake Shafer, it features a sandy beach for swimming, a giant water park, 3 roller coasters, amusement rides, and other entertainment.

WHILE YOU'RE THERE: Just south of Indiana Beach is **Lake Shafer Boat Rentals** 219/583-5238, renting ski boats, pontoons, wave runners, runabouts, and fishing boats.

Bardstown
Samuels Field (BRY)

Airport is located 2 miles west of town.

☞ *Airport Information:*

Location: St. Louis sectional N37.48.94 W85.29.94
Attended: 1300-2300Z*
Elevation: 668 feet
Fuel: 100LL, Jet A
TPA: 1660 feet msl lgt acft
2160 feet msl hvy acft
Runway: 02-20: 4001 x 75 asph
FBO: Wings Aviation
502/349- 1996

☞ *Communication:*

CTAF: 122.8
Unicom: 122.8
App/Dep: Louisville 132.075 (east)
123.675 (west)

☞ *Transportation:*

Car Rental: Ford Rent A Car 502/348-3929
Wilson Bros 502/348-3964

☞ *Lodging:*

Bardstown: Old Kentucky Home Motel 502/348-5979; The
Talbott Tavern 502/348-3494 is a 1779 stagecoach stop turned into
a B & B. **Ramada Inn** 502/349-0363; **Holiday Inn** 502/348-9253

STEPHEN FOSTER - THE MUSICAL

(approximately 2 miles from the airport)
P.O. Box 546, Bardstown, KY 40004; Tel: 502/348-5971 or 800/626-
1563
Season is from mid-June to beginning of September.
Admission is from $15.

Go back in time to the 1850s with *Stephen Foster–The Musical.* Delightful entertainment for the whole family, this musical is about how Stephen Collins Foster, America's first great composer, wooed and won his Jeanie. Period costumes, lively choreography, and melodies of the composer make this an enjoyable evening under the stars. The amphitheater is located in My Old Kentucky Home State Park. Indoor theater available for inclement weather.

Frankfort
Capital City Airport (FFT)

Airport is located 1 mile southwest of town.

☞ *Airport Information:*

Location: St. Louis sectional N38.10.95 W84.54.28
Attended: 1000-0400Z*
Elevation: 804 feet
Fuel: 100LL, Jet A
TPA: 1800 feet msl
Runway: 06-24: 5005 x 100 asph
FBO: 502/564-3714

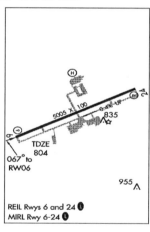

☞ *Communication:*

CTAF: 122.8
Unicom: 122.8
App/Dep: Lexington 120.75
Clnc Del: 118.1
ASOS: 119.275

☞ *Transportation:*

Taxi: 502/227-5000
Car Rental: Enterprise 502/695-5542; Rent-A-Car 502/875-7413

☞ *Lodging:*

<u>Frankfort:</u> **Days Inn** 502/875-2200, **Holiday Inn Capital Plaza** 502/227-5100; **Red Carpet Inn** 502/223-2041

CANOE KENTUCKY
(outdoor adventure approximately 8 miles from airport)
7323 Peaks Mill Road, Frankfort, KY 40601; Tel: 800/K-CANOE-1 or 502/227-4492

Whether you choose cycling along tree-shaded Bluegrass back roads or canoeing Elkhorn Creek, Canoe Kentucky can assist you. Packages include caving, fishing, horseback riding, hiking, and biking. Whitewater clinics and instruction for canoeing and kayaking round out their programs. Elkhorn Creek is called the "queen of Bluegrass streams," meandering more than 100 scenic miles through several counties. It's also an excellent fishing spot for smallmouth bass, largemouth bass, and rock bass.

Gilbertsville
Kentucky Dam State
Park (M34)

Airport is located 1 mile northwest of town.

☞ *Airport Information:*
Location: St. Louis sectional N37.00.57 W88.17.75
Attended: Daylight hours
Elevation: 349 feet
Fuel: 100LL, Jet A
TPA: 1200 feet msl
Runway: 09-27: 4000 x 100 asph
FBO: 502/362-4271

☞ *Communication:*
CTAF: 122.8
Unicom: 122.8
AWOS: 119.075

☞ *Transportation:*
Car Rental: West Key Leasing 502/527-0109

☞ *Lodging:*
Gilbertsville: **Ramada Inn** 502/362-4278

LAND BETWEEN THE LAKES NATIONAL RECREATION AREA
(recreation area visitor center approximately 5 miles from the airport) 100 Van Morgan Drive, Golden Pond, KY 42211; Tel: 502/924-2000; Internet: www.lbl.org.

Hours of operation vary by facility.
Admission is $3.50 for the Homeplace, $2.75 for the Planetarium, $3 per car for the Prairie. No charge for general admission to park.

Outdoor recreation opportunities abound on the uninhabited 40-mile long peninsula between Kentucky and Barkley Lakes. Visit the Golden Pond Visitor Center and Planetarium for a map. Some of Kentucky's most consistent fine bass fishing—with abundance of largemouth, small mouth, and spotted bass (the last two especially in Kentucky Lake)—can be found March through November. The area **KY** has also been called the "crappie capital of the world." Mountain bikes and canoes are available for rent during the summer months. Hiking trails get you close to wildlife. A gently winding road takes you through a prairie habitat restoration effort. Watch for elk and bison in an area that demonstrates how the region looked during the time of Daniel Boone. History comes alive at The Homeplace 1850, a working 19th-century farm. Interpreters in period clothing demonstrate the daily chores and activities of the 1850s. The farm consists of 16 original and restored log structures and is open March through November. The Nature Center has wildlife exhibits and many guided special events. Owl Prowls are just plain fun if you don't mind stumbling around in the dark. Winter is a great time to see bald eagles with counts of more than 150 during the past several years. Star gazers and amateur astronomers: the planetarium is open March-December and public observing sessions are presented by the West Kentucky Amateur Astronomers.
There is a great variety of special programs and demonstrations, including a photographer's workshop weekend. Call for a complete calendar.

Glasgow Mun. Airport

(GLW)
Airport is located 2 miles northwest of town.

☞ *Airport Information:*

Location:	St. Louis sectional N37.01.92 W85.57.16
Attended:	1400-2300Z*
Elevation:	715 feet
Fuel:	100LL, Jet A
TPA:	1700 feet msl
Runway:	07-25: 4586 x 75 asph

FBO:	Glasgow Aviation 502/678-4469

☞ *Communication:*
CTAF: 122.8
Unicom: 122.8
App/Dep: Memphis Center 132.1
AWOS: 118.525

☞ *Transportation:*
Taxi: 502/651-2118
Car Rental: Bailey Gibson 502/651-8851
Cave City 502/773-3174

☞ *Lodging:*
Mammoth Cave (inside the park): The **Mammoth Cave Hotel**
502/758-2225 is a clean and simple two-story inn inside the park
within steps of the visitor center. The **Woodland Cottages** 502/758-
2225 are for people favoring rustic lodgings.
Cave City: **Quality Inn** 502/773-2181; **Heritage Inn** 502/773-3121

☞ *Restaurants:*
Mammoth Cave: The **Mammoth Cave Hotel Restaurant** 502/758-
2225 inside the park is a busy place featuring southern fare such as
country ham.

JESSE JAMES RIDING STABLE
(approximately 6 miles from the airport)
Route 70W, Cave City, KY 42127; Tel: 502/773-2560

Rent horses by the half-hour or hour or for half-day guided rides
through the back country. Three hundred acres of property adjoin the
stables for your outings.

MAMMOTH CAVE NATIONAL PARK
(approximately 10 miles to entrance of park from airport)
Mammoth Cave, KY 42259; Tel: 502/758-2328; Internet: www.nps.
gov/maca/macahome.htm
Open daily except Christmas.
Cave tours run from $3.50 to $35 for adults. Youth and senior
discounts.

Mammoth Cave, lying below Mammoth Cave National Park, is the most extensive cave system on earth. With more than 350 miles of surveyed passageways, 14 miles open to the public, and 130 forms of life (albeit most of them quite small) it is not just a haven for spelunkers. Vast hanging draperies of multicolored limestone, glistening stalactites and stalagmites, underground rooms with snow-white gypsum-crystal flowers will impress even the layman. Depending on your stamina and interest, you can choose from 10 different tours. You will need reservations for the tours. But it's not all underground. Fishing for muskie, white berch, bass, and catfish await anglers in the Green and Nolin Rivers. Hiking trails are abundant, and one-hour scenic boat cruises can be undertaken on the Miss Green River from April through October. Buy tickets in advance at the visitor center—call 502/758-2243 for info. Birders will be especially delighted by the variety of common and rare birds. Poisonous snakes and plenty of other unpleasant creatures are found throughout the park, so be careful! Don't forget to bring a sweater and don't wear sandals.

Lexington
Blue Grass Airport (LEX)

Airport is located 4 miles west of town.

☞ *Airport Information:*

Location: Cincinnati sectional N38.02.22 W84.36.32
Airspace: Class C
Attended: Continuously
Elevation: 980 feet
Fuel: 100LL, Jet A
TPA: 1800 feet msl lgt acft
                  2300 feet msl hvy acft
Runway: 04-22: 7002 x 150 asph
                  08-26: 3501 x 150 asph-
                          conc
FBO: TAC Air 606/255-7724

☞ *Communication:*

Unicom: 122.95
App/Dep: Lexington 120.75, 120.15
                  (040-220º), 125.0
Tower: 119.1

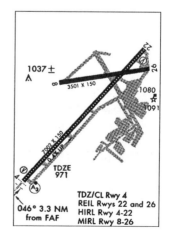

KY

Ground: 121.9
Clnc Del: 132.35
ATIS: 126.3

☞ *Transportation:*
Taxi: 606/231-8294
Car Rental: Avis 606/252-5581; National 606/254-8806

☞ *Lodging:*
Lexington: Stay at **Marriott's Griffin Gate Resort** 606/231-5100 to be surrounded by lush horse pastures bordered by miles of white rail fences. The **Brand House B & B** 606/226-9464 is a restored antebellum house near the center of Lexington. The signature garden-like courtyard distinguishes the **Courtyard by Marriott** 606/253-4646. For a rural retreat on a 300-acre horse farm, book your stay at the **Homewood B & B** 606/255-2814.

☞ *Restaurants:*
Lexington: Wood-oven pizzas, German sausage and of course, some excellent brews are a treat at the **Lexington City Brewery** 606/259-2739. A popular downtown meeting spot, the **Cheapside Bar and Grill** 606/254-0046 also serves good food. If you are into international cuisine or vegetarian dishes frequent the **Alfalfa Restaurant** 606/253-0014.

AVIATION MUSEUM OF KENTUCKY
(located on field)
P.O.Box 4118, Lexington, KY 40544; Tel: 606/231-1219; Internet: www.dynasty.net/users/rawham/KYAirMus.HTM
Open Tuesdays, Thursdays, Fridays, Saturdays and Sundays. Admission is $3 for adults.

The Aviation Museum of Kentucky is located right at Blue Grass Airport. Featuring a hangar full of aircraft for close-up viewing, it is also home to the Kentucky Aviation History Roundtable and the Kentucky Aviation Hall of Fame.

GRIFFIN GATE GOLF CLUB
(approximately 6 miles from airport)
1800 Newtown Pike, Lexington, KY 40511; Tel: 606/231-5100

Experience the challenge of a Rees Jones–designed 18-hole championship golf course on the rolling hills of Kentucky's famous bluegrass country. Opened in 1981, it hosts the Kentucky Johnny

Owens Intercollegiate Invitational and the Bank One PGA Senior Golf Classic. Water comes into play on 12 of the 18 holes, and 65 sandbunkers add to the fun. The course is part of Marriott's Griffin Gate Resort, which invites an overnight stay with the usual resort amenities and a 130-year-old mansion.

KEARNEY HILL GOLF LINKS

(approximately 7 miles from airport)
3403 Kearney Road, Lexington, KY 40511; Tel: 606/253-1981

Kearney Hill's open, Scottish-links style was designed by Pete and P.B. Dye and has their railroad ties trademark on No. 16. It's an 18-hole, par-72 course on bentgrass greens and fairways, only a few of which exist in Kentucky. Nestled in between horse farms, the course is rated among the top five in the state and hosts the Bank One Classic.

KENTUCKY HORSE PARK

(approximately 8 miles from airport)
4089 Iron Works Pike, Lexington, KY 40511; Tel: 800/678-8813
Open daily from mid-March to end of October. After October closed Mondays and Tuesdays. Closed major holidays.
Admission is $9.95 for adults, $4.95 for children 7 to 12 years old.

Lexington's legacy is clearly defined: the Horse Capital of the World...where fences and green fields seem to extend forever. The Kentucky Horse Park, a showplace of the Bluegrass, has extensive equine facilities, 40 different breeds of horses, and the International Museum of the Horse. Live horse tours and horse-drawn vehicle tours are included in the price of admission. On the Walking Farm Tour you can see a farrier and a harnessmaker and learn about horses' day-to-day care. Riders and horses are in full costume and tack in the Parade of Breeds Show. From June to October, polo is played on any one of the park's six polo fields.

WHILE YOU'RE THERE: The **Keeneland Race Course**

606/254-3412 is across the street from the airport. Horse races are October and April.

Louisville International Standiford Field (SDF)

Airport is located 4 miles south of town.

☞ *Airport Information:*

Location: St. Louis sectional N38.10.45 W85.44.16
Airspace: Class C
Attended: Continuously
Elevation: 500 feet
Fuel: 100LL, Jet A
TPA: 1500 feet msl lgt acft
2000 feet msl hvy acft
Runway: 17R-35L: 10000 x 150 conc
17L-35R: 8580 x 150 conc
11-29: 7249 x 150 conc
FBO: Johnson Control Aviation
Center 502/368-1515

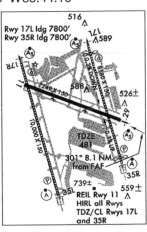

☞ *Communication:*

Unicom: 122.95
App: 132.325; 132.075 (east)
123.675 (west)
Dep: 132.075 (east); 123.675 (west)
Clnc Del: 126.1
Tower: 124.2 (east); 132.2 (west)
Ground: 121.7 (east); 119.825 (west)
ATIS: 118.15

☞ *Transportation:*

Taxi: 502/957-5977; 502/636-5511
Car Rental: Alamo 502/361-1606; Budget 502/363-4300
Thrifty 502/367-0231

☞ *Lodging:*

Louisville: If you prefer a 1901 Victorian mansion in the historic district stay at the **Old Louisville Inn** 502/635-1574. **Doubletree Downtown** 502/585-2200; **Holiday Inn Downtown** 800/626-1558

☞ *Restaurants:*

Louisville: An imaginative menu and good selection of microbrews are served at the **Baxter Station Bar and Grill** 502/584-1635. Venture to **Lilly's** 502/451-0447 for upscale Kentucky fare (closed

Sunday and Monday). Oyster lovers need to visit **Mazzoni's Oyster Cafe** 502/451-4436 .

KENTUCKY DERBY MUSEUM
(approximately 4 miles from airport)
704 Central Avenue, Louisville, KY 40208, Tel: 502/637-1111
Open daily.
Admission is $6.

The hands-on Kentucky Derby Museum captures the thrill and grandeur of the Kentucky Derby, the world's premier horse race, every day in an exciting 360-degree multimedia show. Expect memorabilia, exhibits, and art.
A walking tour of Churchill Downs, the home of the Derby, located next door, is included in the price of admission. The Kentucky Derby Festival precedes Derby Day and lasts 2 weeks. Apart from $20 tickets on race day, with no chance of a view, tickets are sold out months in advance for this spectacular day. The Festival has daily activities and fireworks. Call 800/928-FEST for info.

LOUISVILLE SLUGGER MUSEUM
(baseball museum approximately 6 miles from airport)
800 West Main Street, Louisville, KY 40202; Tel: 502/588-7228
Open Monday through Saturday.
Admission is $5 for adults and $3 for children 6 to 12 years old.

A giant baseball out front leads you to a nostalgic tribute to baseball's greatest hitters. See the actual bats swung by legendary sluggers like Henry Aaron. Or experience how fast a 95mph baseball coming at you really is. Also included is a guided tour of Hillerich & Bradsby, where the famous bats are made.

SIX FLAGS KENTUCKY KINGDOM - THE THRILL PARK
(amusement and water park approximately 2 miles from airport)
937 Phillips Lane, Louisville, KY 40209; Tel: 502/366-2231
Open daily during the summer, weekends pre- and postseason.
Admission is $28.99 for adults, $14.50 for children under 48" tall.

Twisted Sisters is the name of the newest addition to the roller coasters here. It's actually two coasters blasting out of the stations in different directions only to swing around and give you the feeling of hitting head-on. What a rush!! In all, there are more than 70 rides and attractions for all ages. Plus Hurricane Bay, a tropically themed water park with wave pool, slides, and river tubing adventure.

WHILE YOU'RE THERE: The J.B. Speed Art Museum
502/634-2700 has masterworks by Rembrandt, Rubens, Picasso,
Henry Moore and many others, as well as contemporary artists.
Louisville Zoo 502/459-2181

Owensboro
Daviess Co. Reg.
Airport (OWB)

Airport is located 3 miles southwest of town.

☞ *Airport Information:*

Location: St. Louis sectional N37.44.41 W87.10.00
Airspace: Class D service 1200-0400Z*; other times class G
Attended: Continuously
Elevation: 407 feet
Fuel: 100LL, Jet A
TPA: 1200 feet msl lgt acft
1500 feet msl hvy acft
Runway: 18-36: 6499 x 150 conc
05-23: 5000 x 100 conc
FBO: Martin Aviation 502/683-3475
Million Air Owensboro
502/926-6700
Owensboro Aviation
502/684-2044

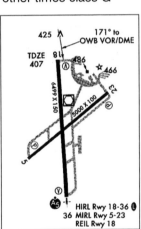

☞ *Communication:*

CTAF: 120.7
Unicom: 122.95
App/Dep: Evansville 126.4 (1200-0500Z*)
Indianapolis Center 128.3 (0500-1200Z*)
Tower: 120.7 (1200-0400Z*)
Ground: 121.7

☞ *Transportation:*

Taxi: 502/683-6262
Car Rental: Enterprise 502/926-4477

☞ *Lodging:*

Owensboro: The **Helton House** 502/926-7117 is a bed and breakfast with 4 guest rooms and 1 suite. **Hampton Inn** 502/926-2006; **Motel 6** 502/686-8606; **Days Inn** 502/684-9621

☞ *Restaurants:*

Owensboro: **Applebees Neighborhood Restaurant** 502/926-3472

RAMEY TENNIS SCHOOL AND RIDING STABLES

(approximately 3 miles from the airport)
5931 State Route 56, Owensboro, KY 42301; Tel: 502/771-5590

A stay at the close-by Best Western is included in the tennis or riding camp. Camps are held for youth and adults, 2-day weekends to up to 4-week summer camps. There are three of each indoor and outdoor tennis and racquetball courts and plenty of trails if you choose the equestrian camp. Tennis players will be able to take advantage of videotape analysis and computer stroke charting.

Stanton Airport (I50)

Airport is located 1 mile east of town.

☞ *Airport Information:*

Location: Cincinnati sectional N37.51.00 W83.50.75
Attended: Continuously
Elevation: 651 feet
Fuel: 100LL
TPA: 1700 feet msl
Runway: 06-24: 3000 x 70 asph
FBO: 606/663-4125

☞ *Communication:*

CTAF: 122.8
Unicom: 122.8

☞ *Transportation:*

Taxi: 606/663-5112

☞ *Lodging:*
Slade: The **Natural Bridge State Park Resort** 606/663-2214 has
35 rooms and 10 cottages. **Red River Gorgeous Cabin Rentals**
513/245-0025
Stanton: **Abner's Motel** 606/663-4379

☞ *Restaurants:*
Stanton: **Cottons Restaurant** 606/663-2142

KY

DANIEL BOONE NATIONAL FOREST
(approximately 10 miles from the airport)
1700 Bypass Road, Winchester, KY 40391; Tel: 606/745-3100
or 606/663-2852
Admission is free.

Daniel Boone was one of Kentucky's earliest fur-trapping pioneers.
The Red River Gorge Geological Area takes up part of the Daniel
Boone National Forest. It is a spectacular landscape with more than
80 natural arches sculpted by wind and water for 70 million years.
The gorge has the largest concentration of rock shelters and arches
east of the Rockies and is a favorite for day hikers. Extreme caution
is advised on hiking the Red River Gorge National Recreation Trail,
a 36-mile system of loop trails.
Adjoining the Red River Gorge is Clifty Wilderness, with steep
canyons, rugged cliffs, and rock arches.
Natural Bridge is a half-mile stretch of 900 tons of ancient rock
suspended across a mountainside. Located within the Natural Bridge
State Park Resort, it is also accessible via a sky lift from mid-April to
October.

MAINE

Bar Harbor
Hancock Co. Airport (BHB)
Airport is located 8 miles northwest of town.

ME

☞ *Airport Information:*

Location: Halifax sectional N44.26.99 W 68.21.69
Attended: 1200Z* to dusk
Elevation: 84 feet
Fuel: 100LL, Jet A
TPA: 1100 feet msl
Runway: 04-22: 5200 x 100 asph
17-35: 3364 x 75 asph
FBO: Acadia Air 207/667-5534

☞ *Communication:*

CTAF: 123.0
Unicom: 123.0
App/Dep: Bangor 124.5
Clnc Del: 119.9
AWOS: 118.025

☞ *Transportation:*

Taxi: 207/667-5995
Car Rental: Budget 207/667-1200; Hertz 207/667-5017

☞ *Lodging:*

Bar Harbor: The **Golden Anchor Inn and Pier** 800/328-5033 or 207/288-5033 is located on the waterfront in downtown Bar Harbor. Rated with three diamonds by the AAA Mobile Guide, the **Bar Harbor Inn** 800/248-3351 or 207/288-3351 is a full-service oceanfront resort with heated outdoor pool. Located one mile from Bar Harbor, the **Acadia Inn** 800/638-3636 or 207/288-3500 is fairly new and minutes from the National Park. **Holiday Inn's Sunspree Resort** 207/288-9723 features stunning vistas overlooking Frenchman's Bay with marina and outdoor heated pool. The **Bar Harbor Hotel - Bluenose Inn** 800/445-4077 or 207/288-3348 is Bar

Harbor's only 4-star Mobil Guide property.
Trenton: The **Sunrise Motel** 207/667-8452 is located next to the airport.

☞ *Restaurants:*
Bar Harbor: The **Fish House Grill** 207/288-3070 is a family restaurant serving great seafood, including lobster bakes. An advance ticket is necessary to eat lobster bakes at **Bar Harbor Lobster Bakes** 207/288-4055, evenings only from June to mid-October in Hulls Cove. Visit **Fisherman's Landing** 207/288-4632 for pick-your-own lobster dinner on the dock below town. Closes at 8:30 p.m. Known for its fabulous chowder is the **Island Chowder House** 207/288-4905.

ACADIA BIKE & COASTAL KAYAKING TOURS
(kayaking and biking approximately 8 miles from airport)
48 Cottage Street, Bar Harbor, ME 04609; Tel: 207/288-9605 or 800/526-8615

Get close to nature and enjoy the incredible beauty of Acadia National Park and its surrounding waters, which are ideally suited to travel and exploration by sea kayak. Paddling opportunities abound with miles of protected coastline and many off-shore islands. The natural beauty of Mt. Desert Island's granite cliffs side by side with sand and cobblestone beaches comes into full view from the ocean. Large, stable, one- and two-person kayaks equipped with foot-controlled rudders make paddling easy and fun. First-timers are welcome as everyone receives expert instruction before setting off. Trips from a few hours to multi-day camping trips are offered. Bikers can take advantage of more than 50 miles of car-free carriage paths, originally built for horse-drawn carriages. These wide, gravel-packed paths wind through peaceful forest and along the spectacular coastline. Or you may enjoy bicycling the Park Loop Road, which has many famous sights alongside, as well as cars! Reservations are essential, especially during the summer.

ACADIA NATIONAL PARK – HULLS COVE VISITOR CENTER
(visitor center approximately 8 miles from airport)
P.O. Box 177, Bar Harbor, ME 04609; Tel: 207/288-3338; Internet: www.nps.gov/acad
Visitor center is open mid-May through mid-October.
Park entrance fee is $10 per vehicle. Bikers and hikers pay $5 for a 4-day pass.

Spectacular Mt. Desert Island is the third largest island on the East Coast. Its beauty resulted from Ice Age glaciers that pushed through its existing mountains, carving valleys and a fjord, while studding offshore waters with ledges and islands. Stop by the visitor center to view a 15-minute introductory film shown every half hour to help you with your planning. Free maps and literature give details about hiking, biking, and their ranger-led activities. When the visitor center is closed you may obtain information at park headquarters on Rte. 233. Acadia offers about 120 miles of hiking trails ranging in difficulty from easy to strenuous. Climb Mount Cadillac, at 1,530 feet high, for a gorgeous view (early risers may watch the sun come up). If you are planning to visit in winter, don't forget that the carriage trails make for excellent cross-country skiing trails. However, you can't count on snow during the winter, so call in advance.

ME

BAR HARBOR WHALE WATCH CO.
(whale watching and nature cruises approximately 7 miles from airport)
39 Cottage Street, Bar Harbor, ME 04609; Tel: 207/288-2386; Internet: www.whalesrus.com
Season is from mid-May to late October.

Although the objective is to see some whales, keep your eyes open for seals, porpoises, and a variety of seabirds not seen ashore, on your way to the area where most whales are seen. Trips last 2 to 3 hours, during which a naturalist describes whale behavior. Tours leave from the Regency Holiday Inn one mile before you reach Bar Harbor and are conducted on a catamaran, which provides a more stable ride than single-hull craft. Although the catamaran is heated, bring warm clothing if you would like to take advantage of outside viewing decks. Special cruises devoted to nature study, seals, and puffins are in the company's cruise repertoire.

SEA BIRD WATCHER
(whale and puffin cruises approximately 8 miles from airport)
52 West Street, Bar Harbor, ME 04609; Tel:800/247-3794 or 800/421-3307
Season runs from May to October.

Visit Petit Manan Island to see those cute little puffins bobbing in the ocean water as they search for their food, as well as a variety of other seabirds. The Sea Bird Watcher does have a heated cabin but it would be wise to bring warm clothing, maybe even a poncho. And don't forget to bring binoculars! An experienced naturalist is on board to narrate the tour and answer questions. This company also has combination puffin/whale watching cruises.

WHILE YOU'RE THERE: See the full-size skeleton of a Minke whale at the **Bar Harbor Whale Museum** 207/288-2025. Displays include a dolphin and harbor seal skeleton, bird displays, information on whales, and much more. Four-hour deep-sea fishing trips leave from the **Bar Harbor Inn Pier** 207/288-4585. Trolley tours with stops for walks and pictures with an historical view of things are conducted by **Acadia & Island Tours** 207/288-9899. **Acadia Mountain Guides Climbing School** 207/288-8186 gives climbing instruction and guiding for all levels, half-days to multiple days. Listen to the sound of wind in the rigging as you glide through Frenchman Bay with **Bay Lady Schooner Cruise** 207/288-3322. The **National Park Canoe Rentals** 207/244-5854 provides canoes for rent on Long Pond, Acadia's largest lake. **Wildwood Stables** 207/276-3622, near Jordan Pond, organizes horse-drawn carriage rides during the season.

Carrabassett
Sugarloaf Reg. Airport (B21)

Airport is located 1 mile north of town.

☞ *Airport Information:*

Location: Montreal sectional N45.05.17 W70.12.97
Attended: Unattended
Elevation: 885 feet
Fuel: Not available
TPA: 2885 feet msl
Runway: 17-35: 2800 x 75 asph
FBO: 207/235-2288 (airport manager)

☞ *Communication:*

CTAF: 122.8

☞ *Lodging:*

Carrabassett: Slope-side lodging from one to five bedrooms is available through **Sugarloaf/USA Condominiums** 800/THE-LOAF.

☞ *Restaurants:*
Carrabasset: Located at the base of the lifts in Village West is **Gepetto's** 207/237-2192 with a menu of fish, steaks, Cajun specialties, pizzas, and sandwiches. The **Seasons Restaurant** 207/237-6834 is located in the Sugarloaf Inn and is an upscale, family restaurant. **Shuck's Grill & Bar** 207/237-2040 calls itself a "fishy operation with a little bit of bull." **Tufulio's Restaurant** 207/235-2010 is located in the heart of Carrabasset Valley and serves Italian specialties as well as chicken, steak, and seafood.

SUGARLOAF/USA

(skiing and golfing approximately 6 miles from airport)
R.R. 1, Box 5000, Carrabassett Valley, ME 04947; Tel: 800/THE-LOAF; Internet: www.sugarloaf.com

A 1997 *Snow Country* reader poll put Sugarloaf as the #1 resort in the East. A resort for all abilities, it offers a vertical drop of 2,820 feet, 125 trails and glades, and 60 miles of cross-country skiing at the Outdoor Center. The Fun Center organizes moonlight ski tours, snowshoe safaris, turbo tubing, and skating. Snowboarders can join clinics or give the halfpipe a try.
Summertime activities include golfing on their 18-hole, Robert Trent Jones–designed championship golf course, fishing, hiking, and mountain biking. Moose can frequently be seen in this area.

WHILE YOU'RE THERE: Guided mountain bike tours are offered through **Bigelow Bikes** 207/237-6830. For snowmobile rentals and guided service call **Flagstaff Rentals** 207/235-3333.

Fryeburg
Eastern Slopes Regional
Airport (IZG)

Airport is located 3 miles southeast of town.

☞ *Airport Information:*
Location: New York sectional N43.59.47 W70.56.87
Attended: 1200-2300Z*
Elevation: 452 feet

Fuel:	100LL
TPA:	1450 feet msl
Runway:	14-32: 4200 x 75 asph
FBO:	Fryeburg Aviation
	207/935-2800

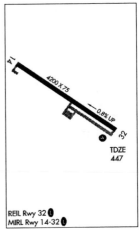

☞ *Communication:*

CTAF:	122.8
Unicom:	122.8
App/Dep:	Portland 125.5 (1100-0500Z*)
	Boston Center 128.2 (0500-
	1100Z*)
ASOS:	135.775

ME

☞ *Transportation:*

Taxi: 207/743-5444; 603/356-5577
Car Rental: McDonald's Motors 603/356-9341

☞ *Lodging:*

Fryeburg: **The Oxford House Inn** 207/935-3442 or 800/261-7206 is an elegant country inn overlooking the White Mountains. Another option is the **Admiral Peary House Bed & Breakfast** 207/935-3365 or 800/237-8080. Once the residence of Arctic explorer Robert E. Peary, it has been restored and was awarded the AAA-Mobil award. *North Conway:* The **White Mountain Hotel & Resort** 800/533-6301 is surrounded by White Mountain National Forest and offers tennis, bicycles, heated pool, and sauna.

☞ *Restaurants:*

North Conway: Colonial atmosphere and a French-American menu can be had a the **1785 Inn** 603/356-9025. For Scottish specialties such as Scottish trifle, Highland game pie, and steak and mushroom pie, visit the **Scottish Lion** 603/356-6381.

EMS CLIMBING SCHOOL
(approximately 10 miles from airport; actual climbing area is more than 10 miles from the airport)
Main Street, North Conway, NH 03860; Tel: 603/356-5433; Internet: www.emsclimb.com

EMS Climbing School has been in the business for more than 25 years and the White Mountains are the venue for their New Hampshire programs. They offer a large variety of instruction for all levels of expertise. The Basic Rock Lesson lasts only one day but an intermediate lesson the following day is advised to reinforce all the techniques learned. Specialized courses are taught as well. Rock climbing programs are held from April through November and winter programs run November through April. All necessary technical gear will be provided by the school.

SACO BOUND
(canoeing approximately 10 miles from the airport)
P.O. Box 119, Center Conway, NH 03813; Tel: 603/447-2177
Internet: www.sacobound.com

Canoeing the Saco River is one of New England's more unique recreational activities. The Saco is scenic with clear, calm water and miles of sandy beaches. During the summer the water is relatively warm, on average 3 to 4 feet deep, and there are many deeper waterholes that invite for a swim. Saco Bound specializes in guided family canoe trips with eleven different options, from the introductory to overnight trips. Canoe rentals available as well.

WHILE YOU'RE THERE: **Great Outdoors Hiking and Walking Vacations** 603/356-3113 or 800/525-9100 leads outings for various ages and abilities. Trails from the **Echo Lake State Park** 603/356-2672 (in summer) lead up to the White Horse and Cathedral ledges. Both are 1,000foot cliffs overlooking North Conway.

Jackman
Newton Field (59B)
Airport is located 1 mile west of town.

☞ *Airport Information:*
Location: Montreal sectional N45.37.92 W70.14.84
Attended: Unattended
Elevation: 1176 feet
Fuel: Not available
TPA: 2170 feet msl
Runway: 14-32: 2900 x 60 asph
FBO: 207/668-2111 (airport manager)

☞ *Communication:*
CTAF: 122.9

☞ *Lodging:*
Jackman: **Jackman Motel** 207/668-5051 has free pickup from the airport. **Sky Lodge** 207/668-2171 (see below).

WINDFALL OUTDOOR CENTER
(approximately 5 miles from airport)
P.O. Box 505, Route 201, Moose River, ME 04945; Tel:800/683-2009; Internet: www.windfallrafting.com
Season is from May to September.

A pristine wilderness location awaits you for whitewater rafting and kayaking. The town of Jackman/Moose River was selected by the producers of ESPN's Extreme Games as the starting point for their televised outdoor adventure race. Windfall's most popular adventure is the Kennebec Gorge trip in guided rafts on class III to V whitewater. Those interested in class III whitewater can board the boats below the gorge. Book early, as the state of Maine limits the number of passengers to preserve this wild resource from overuse. Spring offers the biggest water and lowest rates. Summer is the most popular season, offering warm water and big waves. Fall brings brilliant colors and lower rates again. Kayakers can try the Kennebec East in inflatable kayaks. Day and weekend trips are available.

WHILE YOU'RE THERE: Recreational activities such as mountain biking, hiking, canoeing, hunting, fishing, snow mobiling, and cross-country skiing can be arranged at the **Sky Lodge** 207/668-2171.

Rockland
Knox Co. Reg. Airport (RKD)
Airport is located 3 miles south of town.

☞ *Airport Information:*
Location: Montreal sectional N44.03.61 W69.05.96
Attended: Mon-Fri 1200-2300Z*, Note: Airport may be unattended after dark and on weekends.
Elevation: 56 feet
Fuel: 100LL, Jet A
TPA: 1100 feet msl

Runway: 13-31: 5000 x 100 asph
03-21: 4000 x 100 asph
FBO: Downeast Air 888/594-2171
Penobscot Air Service
207/596-6211

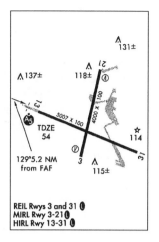

☞ *Communication:*
CTAF: 122.8
Unicom: 122.8
App/Dep: Brunswick 123.8
(1100-0300Z*)
Boston Center 128.2
(112-292º)
124.25 (293-111º);
(0300-1100Z*)
AWOS: 119.025

ME

☞ *Transportation:*
Taxi: 207/594-4000
Car Rental: Budget 207/594-0822; Enterprise 207/596-6211

☞ *Lodging:*
Camden: Enjoy panoramic views from the **Camden Harbour Inn** 207/236-4200 or 800/236-4266, a historic landmark inn. Quiet accommodations in a wooded setting just north of Camden Harbor are offered at **The Lodge** 207/236-8478 or 800/832-7058. Located in the heart of Camden is **The Blue Harbor House** 207/236-3196 or 800/248-3196, a restored 1810 Cape. **Best Western** 207/236-0500.
Rockland: The **Beech Street Guest House** 207/596-7280 is located on a quiet residential street in the heart of Rockland, a short walk to museums, restaurants, and the waterfront. For views overlooking Lake Chickawaukie, stay at the **Lakeshore Inn** 207/594-4209, a 1767 B&B with four guest rooms. Harbor views and a historic district location are yours at the **Old Granite Inn** 207/594-9036 or 800/386-9036.
Rockport: **Samoset Resort** 207/594-2511 or 800/341-1650 (see below). The **Sign of the Unicorn** 207/236-8789 is a quiet B&B.

☞ *Restaurants:*
Camden: **Zaddik's Pizza** 207/236-6540 serves pizza as well as Italian and Mexican style fare. Seafood at a good location is the trademark of **The Waterfront** 207/236-3747.
Rockland: **Miller's** 207/594-7406 is a traditional lobster pound

serving succulent lobsters and steamers on Wheelers Bay at Spruce Head. The **Harbor View Tavern** 207/354-8173 specializes in seafood and pasta and features outdoor dining with a harbor view.

MAINE SPORT OUTFITTERS
(sea kayaking and bicycling approximately 9 miles from airport)
P.O. Box 956, Route 1, Rockport, ME 04856; Tel: 207/236-7120; Internet: www.midcoast.com/~mainespt

Kayak tours and bicycling excursions are the best way to discover the real Maine Coast. Paddle for two hours in Camden's beautiful harbor, past lobster boats, windjammers, and a lighthouse or island. Or take a longer trip from four hours to six days. Discover the islands of Maine, paddling between them, and spend the night either camping or at a private island cottage. Wildlife along the coast includes harbor seals, common eiders, loons, and the occasional bald eagle and peregrine falcon, as well as ubiquitous cormorants and gulls. Single- or multi-day instruction is available.
Rockport is a picturesque village that draws artists and musicians. What a better way to explore the area than on bikes? Rent a bicycle for two-wheeling fun on the islands or along the coast. Rentals available for all ages.

OWLS HEAD TRANSPORTATION MUSEUM
(adjacent to airport)
P.O. Box 277, Owls Head, ME 04854; Tel: 207/594-4418; Internet: www.ohtm.org
Open daily.
Admission is $6 for adults, and $5 for children under 12 years old.

A collection of pioneer era (pre-1930) aircraft is complemented by historically significant automobiles, bicycles, motorcycles, and engines. Most of them are in operating condition and demonstrated at special events held from end of May through October. Call for exact dates. Spark your imagination by viewing a World War II vintage Stearman military training biplane next to a classic 1937 Mercedes 540K.

SAMOSET RESORT GOLF CLUB
(approximately 9 miles from the airport)
220 Warrenton Street, Rockport, ME 04856; Tel: 207/594-2511 or 800/341-1650; Internet: www.samoset.com

This course has been described of having the potential of being the

"Pebble Beach of the East" with its 18 par-70 holes and distracting views. Designed by Bob Elder and opened in 1972, it has ocean vistas from thirteen holes, and seven fairways actually border Penobscot Bay. At Samoset Resort, overnight guests may take advantage of other facilities including pools, tennis courts, bike rentals, and a racquetball court. Cross-country skis are available for rent during wintertime.

SCHOONERS *OLAD* & *NORTH WIND*
(windjammer cruises approximately 10 miles from the airport)
P.O. Box 432, Camden, ME 04843; Tel: 207/236-2323

The town of Camden nestles beneath the Camden Hills, which rise almost 1,400 feet above the harbor. It is a popular place to take a cruise aboard large schooners, known as windjammers. The company specializes in two-hour sails from Camden Harbor. The season is from late May through mid-October and they carry either 21 or 40 passengers. Remember it's always colder out on the water and to bring binoculars.

THE MAINE WINDJAMMER ASSOCIATION
(windjammer cruises approximately 10 miles from airport)
P.O. Box 1144, Blue Hill, ME 04614, Tel: 800/807-WIND; Internet: www.sailmainecoast.com

The Maine Windjammer Association represents the largest fleet of traditional sailing vessels in North America. Contact them to receive information on 13 vessels, all sailing from Camden, Rockland, or Rockport. Imagine a quiet adventure, relaxation, and the majestic coast of Maine. Sail by day and anchor at night with plenty of time on shore, including an island lobster bake. Three-, four- and six-day cruises will take you past birds, wildlife, and scenic villages.

WHILE YOU'RE THERE: Rockland is the self-proclaimed lobster capital of the world and celebrates the **Maine Lobster Festival** 207/596-0376 the first weekend in August. In addition to the previously mentioned companies **Schooner Appledore** 207/236-8353 also specializes in daysails, and **North End Shipyard Schooners** 800/648-4544 offers extended sails aboard historic wooden schooners. Hike a trail or drive up the paved road to the 900 foot summit of Mt. Battie to take in panoramic views of Penobscot Bay and the surrounding areas. For information call the **Camden Hills State Park** 207/236-3109.

MARYLAND

Annapolis
Lee Airport (ANP)

Airport is located 5 miles southwest of town.

☞ *Airport Information:*

Location: Washington sectional N38.56.57 W76.34.13
Attended: Apr-Oct 1200-0000Z*; Nov-Mar 1200-2200Z*
Airport closed after 0300Z*
Unattended on major holidays.
Elevation: 30 feet
Fuel: 100LL
TPA: 1030 feet msl
Runway: 12-30: 2505 x 48 asph
FBO: Chesapeake Aviation Service 410/956-4129
Annapolis Flying Service 410/956-2114

☞ *Communication:*
CTAF: 122.9

☞ *Transportation:*
Taxi: 410/268-3737
Car Rental: Enterprise 410/268-7751; Budget 410/266-5030

☞ *Lodging:*
Annapolis: The **Marriott Waterfront Hotel** 410/268-7555 has a
downtown location within easy walking distance of the Naval
Academy. Halfway between the airport and downtown Annapolis is
the location of the **Annapolis Courtyard** 410/266-1555. The **Prince
George Inn** 410/263-6418 and the **Two-O-One B & B** 410/268-8053
are located on a historic downtown cobblestone street.

☞ *Restaurants:*
Annapolis: Try some famous Maryland crabs right across the street
from the airport at **Hyman's Crabhouse** 410/956-2023. Watch the
boats go by from the **Chart House** 410/268-7166. Old time flair is
evident at **Middleton's Tavern** 410/263-3323, whose kitchen has

churned out food since 1750. **The Ramshead Tavern** 410/268-4545, a favorite with locals, brews its own brew.

ANNAPOLIS SAILING SCHOOL
(approximately 5 miles from airport)
601 6th Street, Box 3334, Annapolis, MD 21403; Tel: 410/267-7205
or 800/638-9192

America's oldest and largest sailing school is located in Annapolis. Enjoy a breeze on the Chesapeake Bay while learning the fundamentals or advanced techniques of sailing. Their choices are plenty—from 2-day basic weekend courses to extended 12-day courses that include one week of cruising. Boats range from 24 to 50 feet. Beginning students learn to sail aboard Annapolis Sailing School's famous Rainbows, the only boats ever designed and built for a sailing school to satisfy requirements for safety, comfort, and performance. The basic course starts at $250.

US NAVAL ACADEMY
(approximately 5 miles from airport)
Gate 1, King George Street, Annapolis, MD 21402, Tel: 410/293-1000;
Tours are $5.50 per person.
Admission is free.

The U.S. Naval Academy is beautiful just to walk around in, because of its location along the Severn River. Stop by the bronze-domed chapel, visit the small museum holding models of ships and naval memorabilia, or just watch the future naval officers. It is especially a thrilling sight during one of their full-dress parades. Excellent tours start every half hour at the visitor center.

WHILE YOU'RE THERE: Annual mega-events in Annapolis include the **United States Sailboat and Powerboat Show** 410/280-0445 on consecutive weekends in October. The **Maritime Museum** 410/268-5576 rents audio cassettes narrated by Walter Cronkite for self-guided walking tours of the historic district. Free 30-minute tours are offered at the **Maryland State House** 410/974-3400. It used to house the U.S. Congress and is the oldest state capitol in continuous legislative use. People interested in chartering for a cruise or renting a sailboat can contact **Schooner Woodwind** 410/263-8619.
Discover Annapolis Tours 410/626-6000 takes you through 350 years of history and architecture in the charming historic district. Let **Annapolis Bay Charters** 410/269-1776 or 800/292-1119 plan your

outing on the water under power or under sail. Interested in fishing charters? Contact the **American Powerboat Schools & Charters** 410/721-7517.

Baltimore-Washington Int'l Airport (BWI)

Airport is located 9 miles south of town.

MD

☞ *Airport Information:*

Location:	Washington sectional N39.10.52 W76.40.09
Airspace:	Class B
Attended:	Continuously
Elevation:	146 feet
Fuel:	100LL, Jet A
TPA:	1200 feet msl
Runway:	10-28: 10502 x 200 asph
	15R-33L: 9519 x 150 asph
	04-22: 6005 x 150 asph
	15L-33R: 5000 x 100 asph
	Check for runway closures!
FBO:	Signature Flight Support
	410/859-8393

☞ *Communication:*

Unicom:	122.95
App:	119.0 (020-100º), 124.55 (101-130º),
	119.7 (131-180º), 128.7 (181-019º)
Dep:	128.7, 133.75, 124.55
Tower:	119.4
Ground:	121.9
Clnc Del:	118.05
ATIS:	115.1; 127.8

☞ *Transportation:*

Taxi:	410/859-1100
Car Rental:	Thrifty 410/859-1136; Avis 410/859-1680
	Hertz 410/850-7400

94

☞ *Lodging:*
Baltimore: Centrally located to all the Inner Harbor attractions is the **Sheraton Inner Harbor** 410/962-8300. **Ramada Inner Harbor** 410/539-1188; **Hilton and Towers** 410/539-8400. For a location near the airport, stay at the **BWI Marriott Inn** 410/859-8300 or **BWI Holiday Inn** 410/859-8400.

☞ *Restaurants:*
Baltimore: Baltimore is famous for its seafood from the Chesapeake Bay, especially the crabs. **Faidley's** 410/685-6169 is located within Lexington Market and serves succulent oysters, clams and crabs on the go. The **Chart House** 410/539-6616 has a downtown location.

B & O RAILROAD MUSEUM
(approximately 9 miles from the airport)
901 W. Pratt Street, Baltimore, MD 21223; Tel: 410/752-2490
Open daily.
Admission is $6.50 for adults and $4 for children 3 to 12 years old.

History buffs will delight in the locomotives and ornate carriages. The museum sits on the site of the country's first railroad station and is one of the world's largest, with over 140 locomotives and rolling stock.

BABE RUTH BIRTHPLACE AND BASEBALL CENTER
(approximately 9 miles from airport)
216 Emory Street, Baltimore, MD 21230; Tel: 410/727-1539
Open daily.
Admission is $6 for adults and $3 for children 5 to 16 years old.

Birthplace of George Herman "Babe" Ruth, America's second largest baseball museum features a film and 26 exhibits on the famous home-run hitter.

BALTIMORE MARITIME MUSEUM
(ship displays approximately 9 miles from airport)
Pier 3 and 4, Pratt Street, Baltimore, MD 21202; Tel: 410/396-5528
Open daily.
Admission is $5 for adults and $3 for children under 12 years old.

Ever wondered what it feels like inside a submarine? Give it a try aboard the World War II submarine USS *Torsk*. It will increase your appreciation for submarine personnel really fast. Other ships to explore include a Coast Guard cutter and Chesapeake Bay light ship.

MARYLAND SCIENCE CENTER
(museum approximately 9 miles from airport)
601 Light Street, Baltimore, MD 21230; Tel: 410/685-5225
Open daily, except major holidays.
Admission is $9.75 for adults and $8 for teenagers 13 to 18 years old.

A museum that appeals to all ages, especially people who like to investigate things hands-on. The IMAX theater with its five-story screen shows films and documentaries.

MD

NATIONAL AQUARIUM
(approximately 9 miles from the airport)
Pier 3, Baltimore, MD 21202; Tel: 410/576-3800
Open daily, except major holidays.
Admission is $14 for adults and $7.50 for children 3 to 11 years old.

Even before the renovation of the shark exhibit and the addition of the new coral-reef exhibit, this aquarium was the jewel of Baltimore. Sharks, whales, dolphins, and plenty of other marine life add up to more than 5,000 species. Make sure you don't miss the dolphin show or a visit to the rainforest. Avoid busy summer weekends, as you will have to wait to enter.

WALTERS ART GALLERY
(approximately 9 miles from airport)
600 North Charles Street, Baltimore, MD 21201; Tel: 410/547-9000
Open daily, except Mondays.
Admission varies depending on exhibits.

Recognized internationally as one of the foremost art museums in the United States. Highlights include ancient art of Egypt, Greece and Rome; medieval armor; Baroque and Renaissance paintings and sculpture; crystal and porcelains; and the art of Japan, Thailand, China, India, and Southeast Asia. The gallery was formed by father and son William and Henry Walters. The Hackerman House located next door is home to fine pieces of Asian art.

WHILE YOU'RE THERE: The 27th floor observation deck of the **World Trade Center** 410/837-8439 offers a good view of the Inner Harbor and city. Works of Degas, Picasso, Matisse, Renoir,

Gaugin, Andy Warhol, and other artists are displayed at the
Baltimore Museum of Art 410/396-7101. Contact **Harbor Cruises**
410/727-3113 to take a look at the skyline from the water.

Clinton
Washington Exec.-
Hyde Field (W32)

Airport is located 2 miles southwest of town.

☞ *Airport Information:*
Location: Washington sectional N38.44.97 W76.55.95
Attended: Mon-Thu 1300-2300Z*; Fri-Sun 1300-0100Z*.
Unattended Thanksgiving and Christmas.
Elevation: 249 feet
Fuel: 100LL, Jet A
TPA: 1049 feet msl
Runway: 05-23: 3000 x 60 asph
FBO: Freedom Air 301/297-7556

☞ *Communication:*
CTAF: 122.8
Unicom: 122.8

☞ *Transportation:*
Taxi: 301/864-7700
Car Rental: Enterprise 301/868-8884

☞ *Lodging:*
See entries under *College Park Airport,* page 98.

☞ *Restaurants:*
See entries under *College Park Airport,* page 98.

PAUL E. GARBER FACILITY (SMITHSONIAN)
(aircraft museum approximately 5 miles from airport)
Suitland, MD 29746; contact the Smithsonian Institution at 202/357-1400.
Open daily.
Admission is free.

The Paul E. Garber Preservation, Restoration and Storage Facility houses the National Air and Space Museum's reserve collection of historically significant air and space craft. On display are approximately 160 aircraft as well as numerous spacecraft, engines, propellers, and other flight-related objects. Guided, behind-the-scenes tours lasting about two to three hours to look at the restoration workshop are available. There is no climate control in the warehouse type exhibit areas, so visitors should dress appropriately.

WHILE YOU'RE THERE: See entries under *College Park Airport* below. Distance to Washington, DC is approximately 10 miles.

✈ ✈ ✈

College Park Airport

(CGS)
Airport is located 1 mile east of town.

☞ *Airport Information:*

Location:	Washington sectional N38.58.84 W76.55.35	
Attended:	Mon-Thu 1130-0300Z*; Fri-Sun continuous	
Elevation:	50 feet	
Fuel:	80, 100LL	
TPA:	1050 feet msl	
Runway:	15-33: 2610 x 60 asph	
FBO:	301/864-5844	

Rwy 15 ldg 2197'
Rwy 33 ldg 2416'
TDZE 50
133° to MAP WP
2610 x 60
33
MIRL Rwy 15-33
REIL Rwys 15 and 33

☞ *Communication:*
CTAF: 123.0
Unicom: 123.0
App/Dep: Washington 119.85

☞ *Transportation:*
Taxi: 301/864-7700
Car Rental: Enterprise 301/345-6070

☞ *Lodging:*
Washington, DC: The **Hyatt Regency Washington** 202/737-1234 is an upmarket place near the Capitol. The **Hotel Washington** 202/638-5900 is famous for its roof-top bar overlooking the White

House.
College Park: The **Holiday Inn** 301/345-6700 and the **Best Western** 301/ 474-2800 are located near the airport.

☞ *Restaurants:*
Washington, DC: Southwestern influences are the flavor at the **Red Sage** 202/638-4444, an elegant place with a funky bar to spend an evening. **America** 202/682-9555 is located inside the Beaux Arts building of the wonderful Union Station, a train station with flair. The **Bombay Club** 202/659-3727 serves elegant Indian dishes in the vicinity of the White House. A trio to try among many.

BUREAU OF ENGRAVING AND PRINTING
(approximately 10 miles from airport)
14th and C Street, SW, Washington, DC 20228; Tel: 202/622-2000 or 202/874-3019
Closed weekends.
Admission is free.

A fun and interesting half-hour tour will lead you by printing presses that churn out huge sheets of money. You can watch from elevated walkways how the money is printed, checked for defects, and cut into single bills. Stamps and presidential invitations are printed here as well. Arrive early to pick up timed tickets during the summer months.

COLLEGE PARK AVIATION MUSEUM
(located on field)
1985 Cpl. Frank Scott Drive, College Park, MD 20740; Tel: 301/864-6029
Open daily.
Admission is $4 for adults and $2 for children.

Known as "The Oldest Continuously Operating Airport in the World," this museum was founded in 1909 by the Wright Brothers. You can follow many other significant "firsts" in this beautiful building, a combination of glass and bricks with a curved roof line reminiscent of an early Wright aeroplane. Exhibits include a 1911 Wright B Aeroplane, a 1918 Curtiss Jenny, a J-2 Cub, and an Ercoupe, among other displays and interactive components. A Wilbur Wright mock-up in his hangar, a flight simulator, interactive wind tunnel and much more are yours to experience and enjoy. Call for exact dates on special events and workshops.

FEDERAL BUREAU OF INVESTIGATION
(approximately 9 miles from airport)
10th Street and Pennsylvania Avenue, Washington, DC 20535; Tel:
202/324-3447
Open Monday through Friday.
Admission is free.

Hour-long tours get you a glimpse of the responsibilities and
activities of the FBI. Interesting facts are given about some
techniques used to catch criminals. An array of firearms is on
display, with a live-ammunition firearms demonstration at the
conclusion of the tour. One should try to arrive early in the day to
avoid waiting in lines, although they move fairly quickly.

GODDARD SPACE FLIGHT CENTER
(approximately 3 miles from airport)
Explorer Road, Mail Code 130, Greenbelt, MD 20771; Tel: 301/286-
8103; Internet: www.gsfc.nasa.gov
Open daily, except major holidays.
Admission is free.

The Goddard Space Flight Center was NASA's first center devoted
to the exploration of space and is still among the leaders in earth and
space sciences, astronomy, and space physics. Its visitor center
offers exhibits, tours, presentations and programs to show you what
NASA and the GSFC are all about. Call for special program dates
and times.

NATIONAL AIR AND SPACE MUSEUM
(approximately 10 miles from airport)
Jefferson Drive, Washington, DC 20560; Tel: 202/357-1300; Internet:
www.nasm.edu
Open daily, except Christmas.
Admission is free.

An absolute must for an aviator. Attracting almost 10 million people a
year, this museum is certainly one of a kind and not to be missed.
Here, the story of aviation is being told in an exceptional way. View
the handmade aircraft the Wright Brothers used for their first
powered flight and continue on with hundreds of historic aircraft all
the way to actual spacecraft. Schedule plenty of time to explore
twenty-three galleries. A giant IMAX screen features thrilling films. Or
visit the Albert Einstein Planetarium.

SMITHSONIAN INFORMATION CENTER
(approximately 10 miles from airport)
1000 Jefferson Drive, SW, Washington, DC 20560; Tel: 202/357-2700
Open daily.

The Castle, as the first museum built by the Smithsonian Institution is called, serves as the information center for the many museums and galleries in its organization. An orientation film will provide you with an overview of the offerings as well as updates on current exhibitions and events.

THE WHITE HOUSE

(approximately 9 miles from airport)
1600 Pennsylvania Avenue, Washington, DC 20501; Tel: 202/456-7041 or 202/619-7222

The White House, office and residence of the President of the United States, is generally open for tours Tuesdays through Saturdays. Try to come early to avoid long lines in winter. Tickets may be gone if you don't arrive early during the summer months. You will be rewarded with being shown through selected rooms such as the State Dining Room, the East Room—site of presidential news conferences, and other events.

U.S. CAPITOL
(approximately 8 miles from airport)
U.S. Capitol, Washington, DC 20510; Tel: 202/225-6827 or 202/224-3121
Open daily. No tours on Sunday.
Admission is free.

Visit the center of government, the home of the Senate and the House of Representatives. On days the lantern above the dome is lit, you may watch some legislative action from the gallery. Stroll through grand halls lined with statues and monuments and get a sense of the power wielded by the elected officials. You can take a tour or walk around on your own.

WHILE YOU'RE THERE: **Tourmobiles** 202/554-5100 let you jump on and off at attractions for convenient sightseeing. A very moving place, the **Vietnam Veterans Memorial** is located in Constitution Garden on The Mall. The **Lincoln Memorial** 202/426-6895 is especially beautiful during cherry blossom time in April or at night. The **Washington Monument's** 202/426-6839 elevators take you up inside the obelisk for an unrivaled view.

Easton
Newnam Field (ESN)

Airport is located 2 miles north of town.

☞ *Airport Information:*

Location: Washington sectional N38.48.25 W76.04.14
Attended: 1300-2300Z
Elevation: 74 feet
Fuel: 100LL, Jet A
TPA: 1100 feet msl lgt acft
1600 feet msl jet acft
Runway: 04-22: 5511 x 100 asph
15-33: 4002 x 100 asph
FBO: Maryland Air 410/822-0400

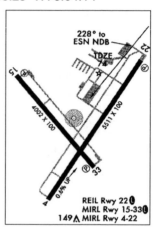

☞ *Communication:*

CTAF: 122.95
Unicom: 122.95
App/Dep: Baltimore 124.55
Clnc Del: 126.9
AWOS: 124.475

☞ *Transportation:*
Taxi: 410/822-1475
Car Rental: Thrifty 410/822-1676

☞ *Lodging:*
Easton: **Econo Lodge** 410/820-5555; **Tidewater Inn** 410/822-1300

☞ *Restaurants:*
Easton: **The Rustic Inn Restaurant** 410/820-8282 offers fine dining with an authentic historic interior. Visit the **Fiddle Leaf Cafe** 410/822-4353 for soups and sandwiches.

HOG NECK GOLF COURSE
(approximately 1 mile from airport)
10142 Old Cordova Road, Easton, MD 21601; Tel: 410/822-6079

You will get a look at this golf course from the air as you approach Newnam Field. This 18-hole course is not only conveniently located but also is ranked well by *Golf Digest*. It's a course for all skill levels and offers plenty of variety and challenge.

WHILE YOU'RE THERE: Easton is the only town in Maryland rated in the 100 Best Small Towns in America. Stroll tree-lined streets filled with unique shops and distinctive homes. The **Historical Society** 410/822-0773 offers walking tour maps or guided tours of three restored houses.

MD

Mitchellville
Freeway Airport (W00)

Airport is located 2 miles northwest of town.

☞ *Airport Information:*

Location: Washington sectional N38.56.48 W76.46.34
Attended: 1300Z* to dark. Unattended major holidays.
Elevation: 168 feet
Fuel: 100LL
TPA: 1000 feet msl lgt acft
1200 feet hvy acft
Runway: 18-36: 2425 x 30 asph
FBO: 301/390-6424

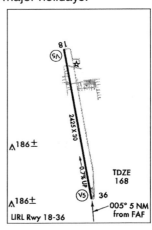

☞ *Communication:*
CTAF: 123.05
Unicom: 123.05
App/Dep: Andrews 119.3

☞ *Transportation:*
Taxi: 301/390-9091
Car Rental: Melvin 301/262-1313

☞ *Lodging:*
Bowie: **Comfort Inn** 301/464-0089; **Holiday Inn** 301/464-2200;

Rips Country Inn 301/805-5901
Largo: **Hampton Inn** 301/499-4600

☞ *Restaurants:*
Bowie: **Rips Country Inn** 301/805-5901

SIX FLAGS AMERICA
(amusement park approximately 9 miles from airport)
P.O. Box 4210, Largo, MD 20775; Tel: 301/249-1500;
Open during summer months and some pre/post-season weekends.
Admission is $29.99 for adults, $14.99 for children.

Six Flags America took over this amusement park from Adventure World and invested $30 million in new rides, shows and attractions. New for 99 are The Joker's Jinx, a half-mile ride with 4 upside-down loops, and Two Face, an inverted highspeed coaster that will leave you wondering which end is up! The region's largest waterpark, with a huge wave pool and many water rides, provides plenty of opportunities to cool off. October is the time for Hallow Scream during evenings.

Oakland (2G4)
Garrett Co. Airport

Airport is located 13 miles northeast of town.

☞ *Airport Information:*

Location:	Cincinnati sectional N39.34.82 W79.20.37
Attended:	1400-2300Z*
Elevation:	2933 feet
Fuel:	80, 100LL
TPA:	3733 feet msl
Runway:	08-26: 3000 x 75 asph
FBO:	Plane Aviation 301/387-4100

☞ *Communication:*

CTAF:	122.8
Unicom:	122.8
App/Dep:	Cleveland Center 124.4

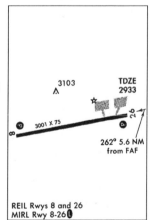

☞ *Transportation:*
Taxi: 301/387-4100
Car Rental: 301/387-6148

☞ *Lodging:*
Deep Creek Lake: **Wisp Resort** 800/462-9477 has slopeside lodging—see entry following; **Comfort Inn** 301/387-4200. Perched lakeside across from Wisp ski/golf is the **Lake Point Inn** 800/523-LAKE. The **Savage River Inn** 301/245-4440 is a fine B & B with fireplaces and mountain views.

☞ *Restaurants:*
Deep Creek Lake: Dine casually at **Uno's** 301/387-4UNO at the lakefront. The **Pizzaz Pizzeria** 301/387-YUMM is an ideal place for families staying at Wisp Resort. Seafood is the main fare at **Dr. Willy's Restaurant** 301/387-7380.

HIGH MOUNTAIN SPORTS
(outdoor activities approximately 6 miles from airport)
P.O. Box 85, McHenry, MD 21541; Tel: 301/387-4199

The area around Deep Creek Lake is very scenic and offers a multitude of recreational activities in the outdoors. Satisfy your needs for skiing, biking, in-line skating, and water-skiing at their store. They also offer lessons in water-skiing.

PRECISION RAFTING
(water sports approximately 7 miles from airport)
P.O.Box 185, Friendsville, MD 21531; Tel: 301/746-5290 or 800/477-3723

Garrett County is well known for its wild waters that challenge rafters and kayakers. Join Precision Rafting for awesome whitewater trips, family float trips, scenic kayak touring on Yough Lake, or lessons.

WISP RESORT
(resort approximately 3 miles from airport)
290 Marsh Hill Road, McHenry, MD 21541; Tel: 800/462-9477; Internet: www.gcnet.net/wisp

Golfing and skiing are the popular things to do here. The 18-hole golf course was ranked as one of the top 10 in Maryland by *Golf Digest* magazine in 1996. Mountain biking is done on secluded trails with panoramic views. There are twenty-three slopes for skiing.

Ocean City Mun. Airport (OXB)

Airport is located 2 miles southwest of town.

☞ *Airport Information:*

Location: Washington sectional N38.18.63 W75.07.44
Attended: May-Sep 1300-0100Z*
Mon-Thu 1300-2100Z*
Oct-Apr 1300-2200Z*
Unattended during some
holidays.
Elevation: 12 feet
Fuel: 100LL, Jet A
TPA: 800 feet msl
Runway: 14-32: 4070 x 75 asph-conc
02-20: 3200 x 75 asph-conc
FBO: 410/213-2471

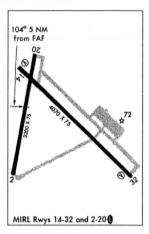

MIRL Rwys 14-32 and 2-20❶

☞ *Communication:*

CTAF: 122.8
Unicom: 122.8
App/Dep: Patuxent 127.95 (1200-0400Z*)
Washington Center 127.7 (0400-1200Z*)
Clnc Del: 121.75

☞ *Transportation:*

Taxi: 410/208-2828
Car Rental: Hertz 410/213-2400

☞ *Lodging:*

Ocean City: The customary Sheraton amenities are offered at the **Sheraton Fontainebleau Hotel** 800/638-2100 located directly on the beach. Half a mile from the beach is the **Francis Scott Key** 800/213-0088.

☞ *Restaurants:*

Ocean City: Typical American food is served while you watch the sunset over the Bay at **Fager's Island** 410/524-5500. For Mexican, drop in at the **La Hacienda Mexican Restaurant** 410/524-8080.

ASSATEAGUE ISLAND NATIONAL SEASHORE
(approximately 8 miles from airport)
Assateague Island, MD 21811; Tel: 410/641-1441
Entrance fee is $5 per vehicle.

For those of you trying to escape the hustle and bustle, Assateague
Island is the perfect place. Pristine, wide beaches invite to just sit
back and look at the waves. Wild ponies still roam the island. Stop
by the visitor center before you enter the park to pick up a booklet on
the nature trails. Displays will also inform you on the flora and fauna
you may see. This 20-mile stretch of beach is totally undeveloped, so
you need to bring your food/drinks and everything you need for the
day. Showers are available. Campsites can be booked in advance.
Assateague, being an unspoiled wilderness, is also a major
migratory stopover for birds. Scrub, salt marsh and mud flats are
refuges for the brown pelican, gulls, oystercatchers and the
endangered piping plover. All summer long, the back-bay shorelines
offer a panorama of pelagic and wading birds. Bring your binoculars
and search for terns, egrets, herons, ibis, cormorants, ospreys, and
many others. Winter is the time for harlequin ducks, canvasbacks,
purple sandpipers, and eiders. Bear in mind that winter also brings a
relief from mosquitoes and biting flies!

MD

EAGLE'S LANDING GOLF COURSE
(adjacent to airport)
12367 Eagles Nest Road, Berlin, MD 21811; Tel: 410/213-7277

Not only does this golf course have a very convenient location next
to the airport, it is also among the top-ranked courses in Maryland.
Some of the 18 holes offer an outstanding experience. The shots
through the marshes require care and thought. Yet don't miss the
wildlife and the pleasures of nature.

WHILE YOU'RE THERE: Sailboat rentals are available at
Sailing, Etc. 410/723-1144.

Stevensville   (W29)
Bay Bridge Airport

Airport is located 1 mile west of town.

☞ *Airport Information:*

Location:	Washington N38.58.58 W76.19.78
Attended:	1300-2200Z*
	Unattended major holidays
Elevation:	15 feet
Fuel:	100LL
TPA:	1000 feet msl
Runway:	11-29: 2910 x 60 asph
FBO:	Aero Source 410/643-6936

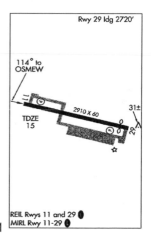

☞ *Communication:*

CTAF:	123.0
Unicom:	123.0
App/Dep:	119.0

☞ *Transportation:*

Taxi:	410/643-1500; 410/643-2361
Car Rental:	Discount Rent A Car
	410/643-7533

☞ *Lodging:*

Stevensville: The **Kent Manor Inn** 410/643-5757 is a restored 17th-century manor house half mile from the airport.
Grasonville: **Comfort Inn** 410/827-6767

☞ *Restaurants:*

Stevensville: **Hemingways** 410/643-2722 is located near the airport and overlooks the Chesapeake Bay and Bay Bridge.
Grasonville: **The Narrows Restaurant** 410/827-8113 serves delicious food in a waterfront setting. It is a favorite with locals and visitors. For casual crabhouse eating at its best, venture to **Harris Crab House** 410/827-9500 or the **Fisherman's Crab Deck** 410/410/827-6666. The latter is open only during the summer months. Both locations overlook the water.

CHESAPEAKE BAY BEACH CLUB
(approximately half mile from airport)
500 Marina Club Road, Stevensville, MD 21666; Tel: 410/604-1933

MD

Beach facilities open during summer season. Restaurant is open year-round.

Overlooking the Chesapeake Bay and Bridge, this beach club offers windsurfers, kayaks, and catamaran rentals for daytime entertainment and switches to an adult-only facility with dancing in the evening. Casual beach-style dining.

SEA DUX OUTFITTERS
(fishing and hunting approximately 5 miles from airport)
115 Pintail Road, Chestertown, MD 21620; Tel: 410/778-4362;
Internet: www.seadux.com

Operating out of the Kentmorr Marina, this charter boat operation specializes in sea duck hunting and charter fishing on the Chesapeake Bay. Full- and half-day trips are on the 40-foot yacht *Sea Dux*. Fishing season is approximately from April through November with bait, rods, reel and tackle provided. Generally duck hunting lasts from October through January. You shoot standing at the back of the boat anchored among a stool of decoys.

WHILE YOU'RE THERE: Catch a breeze on the Chesapeake. **B & B Charters** 410/643-1529 sails out of Castle Harbor Marina for day, weekend and full-week sails.

Falmouth Airpark (5B6)

Airport is located 4 miles northeast of town.

MA

☞ *Airport Information:*
Location: New York sectional N41.35.09 W70.32.47
Attended: Thu-Mon 1400-2200Z*
Elevation: 43 feet
Fuel: 80, 100LL
TPA: 1043 feet msl
Runway: 07-25: 2300 x 40 asph
FBO: 508/548-9617

☞ *Communication:*
CTAF: 122.8
Unicom: 122.8

☞ *Transportation:*
Taxi: 508/548-4100
Car Rental: U-Save 508/457-1700

☞ *Lodging:*
Falmouth: **Mostly Hall** 508/548-3786 is a six-room B & B. A wrap-around porch invites you to read a book from their library. You can also rent a bike to explore the neighborhood and work up an appetite for the complimentary afternoon refreshment. **Sea Crest Resort** 508/540-9400 is a 260-room property.

CAPE COD COUNTRY CLUB
(golf course approximately 3 miles from airport)
Theater Road, Falmouth, MA 02556; Tel: 508/563-9842

Designed by Donald Ross, this course is demanding enough to have hosted three Massachusetts Opens. The style is traditional, with tree-lined fairways and picturesque views of Coonamessett Pond. The course is rated par 71 and has 18 holes.

CAPE COD SOARING
(sailplane flights approximately 7 miles from airport)
114 Lovells Lane, Marston Mills, MA 02648; Tel: 508/420-4201

Soar with the birds and enjoy the quiet and peacefulness of a
sailplane. Cape Cod Soaring is New England's only year-round
soaring operation, weather permitting. Rides last from 20 to 40
minutes. Instruction is available.

NEW SEABURY RESORT
(resort approximately 5 miles from airport)
Box 549, New Seabury, MA 02649; Tel: 800/999-9033

Active people will enjoy this resort offering two 18-hole championship
golfcourses, a 5-star tennis club (rated by *Tennis Magazine*), and
paths for jogging and strolling. The private beach on Nantucket
Sound offers swimming, sunning, fishing, or just building sand
castles. Lessons for either golf or tennis are available daily by
appointment. Rent a sunfish from June through Labor Day. The
golfing is superb, with the Blue Championship course having hosted
the 1985 Women's NCAA championship. The Green Challenger
course has a shorter, easier layout but can be rather difficult when
the wind picks up from the ocean. Call in advance, as there are
restrictions on tee times for non-members.

MA

Nantucket
Mem. Airport (ACK)

Airport is located 3 miles southeast of town.

☞ *Airport Information:*

Location:	New York sectional N41.15.18 W70.03.61
Airspace:	Class D service (1100-0300Z*) May 15 - Sep 30
	(1130-0130Z*) Oct 1 - May 14
Attended:	Continuously
Elevation:	48 feet
Fuel:	100LL, Jet A
TPA:	900 feet msl
Runway:	06-24: 6303 x 150 asph
	15-33: 3999 x 100 asph
	12-30: 3125 x 50 asph

111

FBO: Grey Lady Aviation
508/228-5888

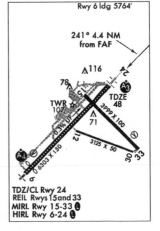

☞ *Communication:*
CTAF: 118.3
Unicom: 122.95
App/Dep: Cape 126.1 (1100-0400Z*)
May 15 - Sep 30
(1100-0300Z*)
Oct 1 - May 14
Boston Ctr 128.75
(0400-1100Z*)
May 15 - Sep 30
(0300-1100Z*)
Oct 1 - May 14

Tower: 118.3 (1100-0300Z*) May 15 - Sep 30
(1130-0130Z*) Oct 1 - May 14
Ground: 121.7
Clnc Del: 128.25
ATIS: 127.5 (1100-0200Z*) Oct 1 - May 14
(1100-0400Z*) May 15 - Sep 30

☞ *Transportation:*
Taxi: 508/325-5555
Car Rental: Budget 508/228-5666; Hertz 508/228-9421

☞ *Lodging:*
Nantucket: A collection of B & Bs in the heart of Old Historic Town can be reached at **800/588-0087**. The **Nantucket Resort** 800/ ISLANDS has 216 rooms and is located in the historic district, one block from Nantucket Harbor. It offers guided nature and island tours as well as nightly entertainment. The **Nantucket Inn** 800/321-8484 has 100 rooms and is situated next to the airport.

☞ *Restaurants:*
Nantucket: Classic French fare with the freshest island ingredients is prepared at **Chanticleer** 508/257-6231. Try lunch in the rose garden or dinner in the formal French manor style dining room with its trompe l'oeil painting. Reservations are essential and a jacket is required at dinner time. Call for opening times and days. Visit **Wauwinet** 508/228-0145 for fresh seafood in sophisticated surroundings. Open seasonally.

MA

NANTUCKET TOWN AND WHALING MUSEUM

(approximately 3 miles from airport)
Broad Street, Nantucket, MA 02554; Tel: 508/228-1736
Open seasonally.

Nantucket Town, an exquisitely preserved National Historic District, entices for a stroll on the cobblestone streets with their sea captains' houses and numerous antique, crafts, and specialty stores. It is well worthwhile to visit the whaling museum, which showcases the island's once thriving industry. Originally a 19th-century candle factory, it now houses whaling relics and memorabilia. Nantucket can get crowded with daytrippers from the mainland on summer weekends, so take advantage of the beautiful beaches surrounding the island. Watch for currents and riptides, which can make swimming extremely dangerous.

NANTUCKET WHALE WATCH

(approximately 3 miles from airport)
Straight Wharf, Nantucket, MA 02554; Tel: 800/WHALING
Cruises mid-July to mid-September from Hy-Line Dock.
Tickets are $75 for adults and $40 for children under 12 years.

Naturalists are on board to narrate most cruises. Trips depart at 9:30 a.m. and return approximately at 4:30 p.m. Bring enough warm clothing, as temperatures at sea can be much cooler than on land. Bird-watchers should bring binoculars to observe seabirds.

WHILE YOU'RE THERE: Take advantage of the **Daffodil Festival** 508/228-1700 in April or the **Cranberry Harvest Weekend** 508/228-1700 in October. The latter has bog tours and demonstrations, a harvest cookery contest, inn tours, and more. Kayaks are for rent at **Force 5 Watersports** 508/228-0700. **Barry Thurston's Fishing Tackle** 508/228-9595 rents equipment and can point out the best fishing spots. Mike Cody at **All Over It Charters** 508/325-6043 offers surf-casting and fly-fishing services.

Pittsfield Munic. Airport (PSF)

Airport is located 2 miles west of town.

☞ *Airport Information:*

Location: New York sectional N42.25.62 W73.17.58
Attended: Mon-Fri 1200-0100Z*, Sat 1300-2300Z*
Sun 1300-0100Z*
Elevation: 1194 feet
Fuel: 100LL, Jet A
TPA: 2200 feet msl
Runway: 08-26: 5001 x 100 asph
14-32: 3496 x 100 asph
FBO: Lyon Aviation 413/443-6700

☞ *Communication:*

CTAF: 122.7
Unicom: 122.7
App/Dep: Albany 125.0
Clnc Del: 128.6

☞ *Transportation:*

Taxi: 413/443-7111
Car Rental: Hertz 413/499-4153

☞ *Lodging:*

Pittsfield: **Comfort Inn** 413/443-4714; **White Horse Inn** 413/442-2512
Lenox: The **Cranwell Resort and Golf Club** 413/637-2580 offers cultural packages to Tanglewood. Eighty-five acres surround the Tudor style **Blantyre** 413/637-3556. Rooms in the main house are huge and lavishly decorated. **Quality Inn** 413/637-4244; **Howard Johnson** 413/442-4000

☞ *Restaurants:*

Lenox: Fireplaces warm you up on cool evenings at the **Gateways Inn** 413/637-2532. On the menu are continental and Italian cuisine of lamb, salmon, veal, and other dishes.

CANYON RANCH IN THE BERKSHIRES
(health resort approximately 7 miles from airport)
165 Kemble Street, Lenox, MA 01240; Tel: 800/726-9900

MA

Airport diagram:
259° 5.7 NM from FAF
1188, 1203
TDZE 1176
3496 X 100
5001 X 100
1261
1250
1190
1208
MIRL Rwys 8-26 and 14-32

An all-inclusive vacation spot that specializes in spa services. Minimum stay is 3 nights. Canyon Ranch promises a world of tranquility, healing, and renewal and was voted in the top 100 vacation destinations by Conde Nast readers in 1997. You can choose from massage and therapeutic bodywork, facials, skin care, herbal wraps, and seaweed treatments, to name just a few. Special packages for sleep disorders, smoking cessation, heart health, and many more are available for longer stays.

HANCOCK SHAKER VILLAGE
(museum approximatley 4 miles from airport)
Routes 20 and 41, Pittsfield, MA 01202; Tel: 413/443-0188; Internet: www.hancockshakervillage.org
Open daily from April to November.

MA

The village was founded in the 1790s by the Shakers, who sought perfection in themselves and in their work. Now turned into a museum, the twenty original buildings are attended by artisans and farmers who will help you explore and learn about the Shaker community. During July a hundred nationally acclaimed artisans show and sell folk art, furniture, ceramics, baskets, and other works in the 18th- and 19th-century tradition.

THE BOSTON SYMPHONY ORCHESTRA AT TANGLEWOOD
(outdoor concerts approximately 7 miles from airport)
Tanglewood, Lenox, MA 01240; Tel: 413/637-5165 after June 15th or 617/266-1492 before June 15th.

Tanglewood is the summer home of the Boston Symphony Orchestra from June through August. It is the best-known music festival in New England, with music director Seiji Ozawa presiding. Thousands flock to the 200-acre estate every summer weekend to enjoy a performance at the open-air stage. Make sure you call in advance for tickets.

WHILE YOU'RE THERE: Plaine's Cycling Center 413/499-0294 rents bikes for back-country-road exploration with magnificent views, especially during the beautiful fall foliage season. Expect hilly terrain.

Plymouth Munic. Airport (PYM)

Airport is located 4 miles southwest of town.

☞ *Airport Information:*

Location: New York sectional N41.54.59 W70.43.73
Attended: 1300Z* to dusk
Elevation: 149 feet
Fuel: 100LL, Jet A
TPA: 1150 feet msl
Runway: 06-24: 4350 x 75 asph
15-33: 2499 x 75 asph
FBO: Plymouth Airport 508/746-2020

REIL Rwy 24 ●
MIRL Rwys 6-24 and 15-33 ●

☞ *Communication:*

CTAF: 123.0
Unicom: 123.0
App/Dep: Cape 126.3
May 15 - Sep 30 (1100-0400Z*)
Oct 1 - May 14 (1100-0300Z*)
Boston Ctr 128.75 May 15 - Sep 30 (0400-1100Z*)
Oct 1 - May 14 (0300-1100Z*)
Clnc Del: 127.75

☞ *Transportation:*

Taxi: 508/746-2525
Car Rental: Thrifty 508/746-5240

☞ *Lodging:*

Plymouth: Across the street from the Plimouth Plantation is the **Pilgrim Sands Motel** 800/729-SANDS, with a private beach and pool facilites. The **Sheraton Inn** 508/747-4900 is within walking distance of the waterfront attractions such as the Mayflower II, Plymouth Rock, and Cranberry World. For a romantic retreat with spectacular views of Plymouth Bay, check into the **Plymouth Bay B & B** 800/492-1828. Five guest rooms are located in a grand shingle-style colonial home.

CAPTAIN JOHN BOATS

(whale watching approximately 5 miles from the airport)
Town Wharf, Plymouth, MA 02360; Tel: 800/242-2469
Cruises operate April to October.

Tickets are $25 for adults and $15 for children under 12 years old.

Captain John Boats has very successful whale watch cruises with 99% sightings. Also available are full- and half-day deep-sea fishing excursions. Listen to the most fascinating sea stories on a harbor cruise.

PLIMOUTH PLANTATION
(living history museum approximately 6 miles from airport)
P.O. Box 1620, Plymouth, MA 02362; Tel: 508/746-1622
Open daily April to November.
Admission is $19 for adults to visit the plantation and *Mayflower II*.

Plimouth Plantation offers you a chance to see Plymouth as it was when America's most famous immigrants — the Pilgrims — first colonized the New World. Costumed actors play roles of actual villagers carrying out their daily tasks. Two and a half miles away is the site of the *Mayflower II*, a 90-foot bark, a full-sized reproduction of the ship that carried the Pilgrims. Just a few steps away is Plymouth Rock, in itself a rather diminutive stone that has dubiously been identified as the actual rock the Pilgrims disembarked on. It served as a symbol of liberty during the American Revolution.

MA

WHILE YOU'RE THERE: Cranberry World 508/747-2350 exhibits the history and cultivation of the cranberry in a half-hour self-guided tour. Open during summer. **Billington Watercraft** 508/746-5644 provides kayaking tours and lessons.

Provincetown Munic. Airport (PVC)

Airport is located 2 miles northwest of town.

☞ *Airport Information:*
Location: New York sectional N42.04.32 W70.13.28
Attended: May-Oct during daylight hours
Elevation: 8 feet
Fuel: 100LL
TPA: 1000 feet msl
Runway: 07-25: 3498 x 100 asph
FBO: Cape Air 508/487-0241

☞ *Communication:*
CTAF: 122.8
Unicom: 122.8
App/Dep: Cape 118.2
　　　　May 15 - Sep 30 (1100-0400Z*)
　　　　Oct 1 - May 14 (0300-1100Z*)
App/Dep: Boston Ctr 128.75
　　　　Jun 15 - Sep 15 (0400-1100Z*)
　　　　Sep 16 - Jun 14 (0300-1100Z*)
Clnc Del: 120.65
AWOS: 119.025

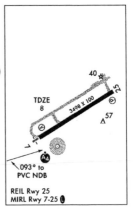

☞ *Transportation:*
Taxi: 508/487-7777
Car Rental: Thrifty 508/487-9418

☞ *Lodging:*
Provincetown: Guestrooms in the 1776 main house and other buildings of the **Fairbanks Inn** 508/487-0386 feature antiques, oriental rugs, and canopy beds on wide-board floors. **Masthead Cottages** 508/487-0523 offers unpretentious but cheerful seaside accommodations. Some of the decks overlook the beach. **Holiday Inn** 508/487-1711

☞ *Restaurants:*
Provincetown: Lobsters, chowders, and seafood are the specialty of **The Lobster Pot** 508/487-0842. Enjoy the view towards Provincetown Harbor and MacMillan Wharf. It's one of the busiest places in town during summer and not the place to go if you are in a hurry. **Moors Restaurant** 508/487-0840 specializes in seafood and Portuguese cuisine in a setting with a typical nautical theme.

ART'S DUNE TOURS
(dune tours approximately 2 miles from airport)
9 Washington Avenue, Provincetown, MA 02657; Tel: 508/487-1950
Tours run from May to October.
Tickets are $10 to $12 per person.

Dune tours depart from Town Wharf and proceed through the narrow streets of Provincetown before arriving on the dunes. Enjoy endless dunes with wispy beach grass, dark green and deep red beach plums nestled in hollows. Famous artists' beach shacks will be pointed out to you along the way to Pilgrim Lake and the Coast Guard station. Sunset tours available. Tours last about 1.5 hours.

PORTUGUESE PRINCESS WHALE WATCH
(approximately 3 miles from airport)
P.O. Box 1469, Provincetown, MA 02657; Tel: 508/487-2651

Board a 100-foot custom-designed high-speed vessel to watch whales in their natural habitat near the coast. Trips last 3-4 hours and depart from Provincetown Marina. Sightings are guaranteed.

PROVINCETOWN WHALE WATCH
(approximately 3 miles from airport)
132 Bradford Street, Truro, MA 02666; Tel: 508/487-3322
Tours run from April to November.
Tickets are $16 to $18 per person. Children under 10 are free with a parent.

Board the "Ranger V" for a narrated tour by a naturalist who also answers questions about the unique behaviour of whales. Cruises last about 2.5 hours depending on the location of the whales. A raincheck without an expiration date will be issued should no whales be sighted.

MA

WHILE YOU'RE THERE: Explore the area on two wheels from **Tim's Bicycle Shop** 508/487-6628. It's better to stick to the seashore's trails due to the heavy summer traffic. There are over 20 **galleries** east of MacMillan Wharf on Commercial Street representing a lively artist and artisan community. **Cap'n Bill & Cee Jay** 508/487-4330 operate fishing trips from MacMillan Wharf. **Nelson's Riding Stable** 508/487-1112 should be contacted by equestrians to take advantage of the trails.

Southbridge Munic. Airport (3B0)

Airport is located 2 miles north of town.

☞ *Airport Information:*

Location:	New York sectional N42.06.06 W72.02.30
Attended:	1300Z* to dusk
Elevation:	697 feet
Fuel:	100LL
TPA:	1700 feet msl

Runway: 02-20: 3500 x 75 asph
10-28: 1450 x 100 turf
  closed indefinitely
FBO: Jim's Flying Service
508/765-0226

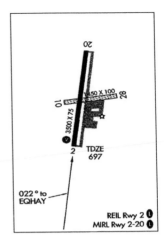

☞ *Communication:*
CTAF: 122.8
Unicom: 122.8
App/Dep: Bradley 123.95

☞ *Transportation:*
Taxi: 508/764-2551
Car Rental: Thrifty 508/764-8000

☞ *Lodging:*
Sturbridge: **Publick House** 508/347-3313 has been sheltering travelers for 220 years and is also popular for its food. The 100-room lodge has an outdoor pool, tennis court, and jogging course. **Old Sturbridge Village Lodges and Oliver Wight House** 508/347-3327 offer a range of lodging in the charm and tradition of early New England adjacent to the museum listed below. **Quality Inn** 508/347-3306

☞ *Restaurants:*
Sturbridge: Hungry people pour into **Publick House** 508/347-3313 for fresh fish and lobster pie.

STURBRIDGE VILLAGE
(living history museum approximately 3 miles from airport)
1 Old Sturbridge Village Road, Sturbridge, MA 01566; Tel: 508/347-3362

A working model of an early 1800s New England town with more than 40 buildings on a 200-acre site. Costumed "villagers" don't just give you the past — they live it. There are exhibits like a water-powered wool carding mill and an 1830s saw mill. Sturbridge is one of the most respected establishments of its type and the largest living history center in the Northeast.

Vineyard Haven
Martha's Vineyard (MVY)

Airport is located 3 miles south of town.

☞ *Airport Information:*

Location: New York sectional N41.23.58 W70.36.86

Airspace: Class D service
May 15 - Oct 31
(1100-0300Z*)
Nov 1 - May 14
(1200-2200Z*)

Attended: Continuously

Elevation: 68 feet

Fuel: 100LL, Jet A

TPA: 1068 feet msl

Runway: 06-24: 5500 x 100 asph
15-33: 3297 x 75 asph

FBO: Flywright Aviation
508/693-1067

☞ *Communication:*

CTAF: 121.4

Unicom: 122.95

App/Dep: Cape 124.7 May 15 - Sep 30 (1100-0400Z*),
Oct 1 - May 14 (1100-0300Z*)
Boston Ctr 128.75 May 15 - Sep 30 (0400-1100Z*)
Oct 1 - May 14 (0300-1100Z*)

Tower: Vineyard 121.4 May 15 - Oct 31 (1100-0300Z*)
Nov 1 - May 14 (1200-2200Z*)

Ground: 121.8

Clnc Del: 124.7 (when tower is closed)

ATIS: 126.25 May 15 - Oct 31 (1100-0300Z*)
Nov 1 - May 14 (1200-2200Z*)

☞ *Transportation:*

Taxi: 508/693-2929; 508/693-0003

Car Rental: Budget 508/693-7322; Hertz 508/693-2402

☞ *Lodging:*

Martha's Vineyard: The **Oak Bluffs Inn** 508/693-7171 is open May to October. The whimsical Victorian architecture reminds one of bygone days, but present-day conveniences assure comfort. The

121

Hob Knob Inn 508/627-9510 offers outstanding guest service with any activities you might enjoy. The inn has its own Boston Whaler for fishing trips, and harbour and sunset cruises. Advance coordination required. Children over 12 years are welcome. The **Up Island Country Inn** 508/645-2720 is located on Gay Head, the least developed township of the island. Here at the westernmost end you will find mile-long cliffs, exquisite beaches, and wonderful sunsets. The Greek Revival house has three guest suites, and you will receive a pass to those beaches restricted to Gay Head residents. Two-day minimum stay required. Vineyard Haven is the location of the **Tisbury Inn** 508/693-2200 with its 30 guest rooms.

☞ *Restaurants:*

Martha's Vineyard: Be prepared to wait for a table at the **Black Dog Tavern** 508/693-9223. But the glassed-in porch overlooking the harbor will reward you for your patience. Chowders, pastas, steak, and fish will satisfy your appetite.

FARM NECK GOLF CLUB
(approximately 5 miles from airport)
Oak Bluffs, MA 02557; Tel: 508/693-3057
Access restrictions apply during summer!

This oceanside course makes it a pleasure to play. The tight, well-trapped front nine is a 1976 Ted Robinson–Geoffrey Cornish design. It was joined in 1979 by the longer and more open back nine. A local rule requires any ball moved or stolen by seagulls to be moved back or replaced at the original point! It is an 18-hole par 72 course.

WHILE YOU'RE THERE: Rent bikes from **Cycle Works** 508/693-6966 or **Martha's Bike Rentals** 508/693-6593. Two miles west of the airport is the **Arrowhead Farm** 508/693-8831 which rents out horses. There are numerous businesses on the island renting boats of all sizes. Following is just a small selection: **Ayuthia Charters** 508/693-7245 (sailboats); **Dockside Watersports** 508/693-8852 (jet skis, boat rentals); **Shenandoah–Coastwise Packe Co.** 508/693-1699 (square topsail schooner cruises); **Wind's Up** 508/693-4252 (windsurfing and sailboats).

MICHIGAN

Beaver Island (SJX)

Airport is located 4 miles southwest of town.

☞ *Airport Information:*

Location:	Green Bay sectional N45.41.54 W85.33.98
Attended:	Irregularly
Elevation:	669 feet
Fuel:	Unavailable
TPA:	1500 feet msl
Runway:	09-27: 4000 x 50 asph
	14-32: 3300 x 120 turf
	05-23: 2130 x 120 turf
	Check for runway closures!
FBO:	616/448-2750

Rwy 14 ldg 2767'
Rwy 23 ldg 1336'
Rwy 32 ldg 2990'

280° to SJX NDB

4000 X 50

TDZE
669   3300 x 120

MIRL Rwy 9-27 ◗
REIL Rwys 9 and 27 ◗

MI

☞ *Communication:*

CTAF:	122.8
Unicom:	122.8
App/Dep:	Minneapolis Center 134.6

☞ *Transportation:*

Taxi: 616/448-2415; 616/448-2317
Car Rental: Erin Motel 616/448-2240; Auto Clinic 616/448-2438

☞ *Lodging:*

Beaver Island: On Lake Michigan, **Beaver Island Lodge** 616/448-2396 is a hotel with beautiful views. The **Bluebird B & B** 616/448-2600 is a 120-year-old farmhouse and the island's only B & B.

☞ *Restaurants:*

Beaver Island: The **Beachcomber Restaurant** 616/448-2469 offers fine dining overlooking the harbor. **Baileys** 616/448-2396 is located at the *Beaver Island Lodge.* The scenery overlooks the lake with elegant dining. Visit the **Stoney Acre Grill** 616/448-2560, a family restaurant, for Sunday breakfast buffet.

LAKESPORTS
(recreational rentals approximately 5 miles from airport)
P.O. Box 512, Beaver Island, MI 49782; Tel: 616/448-2166

Beaver Island is the most remote inhabited island in the *Great Lakes*, with a year-round population of only 450 people. Relax and enjoy the slow pace or try a variety of outdoor activities. Lakesport rents canoes, kayaks, sailboats, mountain bikes, pedal-boats, windsurfers, tents, and fishing supplies. Two lighthouses, the Mormon Print Shop, and Marine Museum add to the natural attractions.

Bellaire
Antrim Co. Airport (ACB)

Airport is located 1 mile northeast of town.

☞ *Airport Information:*

Location: Green Bay sectional N44.59.32 W85.11.90
Attended: Jun-Sep 1300-2300Z*; Oct-May 1200-2200Z*
Elevation: 623 feet
Fuel: 100LL, Jet A
TPA: 1600 feet msl
Runway: 02-20: 5000 x 100 asph
FBO: 616/533-8524

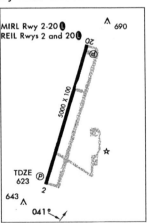

☞ *Communication:*

CTAF: 122.7
Unicom: 122.7
App/Dep: Minneapolis Center 132.9
AWOS: 119.275

☞ *Transportation:*
Taxi: 616/533-8644
Car Rental: Kaskinen 616/533-8651

☞ *Lodging:*
Bellair: **Windward Shore Inn** 616/377-6321

☞ *Restaurants:*
Bellair: **Sonny Pizza** 616/533-6844

SHANTY CREEK RESORT

(golfing, skiing and other outdoor activities approximately 4 miles from airport)
Bellair, MI 49615; Tel: 616/533-8621 or 800/678-4111; Internet: www.shantycreek.com

Arnold Palmer, the legend of golf players, has created The Legend, an award-winning course and one of his star creations, receiving excellent comments. Overlooking Lake Bellaire, it has no parallel holes and it stretches across 600 acres of pine forest. A member of the prestigious Audubon Cooperative Sanctuary System, the course is as natural as they come, with a design to enhance the wildlife environment as well as making the game enjoyable — and enough challenges along the way to keep you focused. The Schuss Mountain Golf Club challenges players with 38 bunkers and nine water hazards strategically placed by Mother Nature herself, yet it's a player-friendly course designed by Warner Bowen. The original course, the Shanty Creek Golf Club, is the resort's most forgiving course. A new addition will be a course designed by Tom Weiskopf, who received *Golf World's* "1996 Golf Course Architect of the Year Award." To improve your game, choose from half-day to 5-day sessions at the Jack Seltzer Golf Academy.

MI

Shanty Creek is also popular for its skiing on Schuss Mountain. Improvements include 12 new slopes, 40 feet of new vertical drop, 4 new quad chairlifts, night skiing, and snow-making capacity.
Perch lures fisherman to Lake Bellaire, and trout to area streams. Rollerblade and bike on smooth paths covering rolling hills, frequent the tennis courts, or set sail on the lake.

Detroit
Detroit Metropolitan
Wayne Co. Airport (DTW)

Airport is located 15 miles south of town.

☞ *Airport Information:*
Location: Detroit sectional N42.12.72 W83.20.93
Airspace: Class B
Attended: Continuously
Elevation: 640 feet

Fuel:	100LL, Jet A
TPA:	1400 feet msl
Runway:	03L-21R: 12001 x 200 conc
	03R-21L: 10000 x 150 conc
	09L-27R: 8700 x 200 asph
	03C-21C: 8500 x 200 asph
	09R-27L: 8500 x 150 conc
FBO:	Signature Flight Support
	734/942-4855

HIRL all runways

RAIL Rwy 21C
TDZ/CL Rwys 3L and 3R
REIL Rwys 3C, 9L and 21C

☞ *Communication:*

Unicom:	122.95
App:	125.15, 118.575 (east)
	124.05 (west)
Dep:	132.025 (turbojets-east), 134.3 (turboprops-east)
	125.525 (turbojets-west), 118.95 (turboprop-west)
	118.575 (east)
Tower:	Metro 135.0 (west), 118.4 (east)
Ground:	132.72 (south), 121.8 (west), 119.45 (east)
Clnc Del:	120.65, pre-taxi clearance: 120.65
ATIS:	133.675

☞ *Transportation:*
Taxi: 734/942-4690; 734/946-5700
Car Rental: Hertz 734/941-4747

☞ *Lodging:*
Dearborn: Holiday Inn Crown Plaza 734/729-2600; **Ramada Inn**
734/729-6300

HENRY FORD MUSEUM AND GREENFIELD VILLAGE
(approximately 10 miles from airport)
20900 Oakwood Blvd., Dearborn, MI 48124; Tel: 313/271-1620
Closed on major holidays. Village buildings closed January-March.
Admission is $12.50.

America's largest indoor-outdoor museum, the Henry Ford Museum
and Greenfield Village covers the industrial revolution with exhibits
about communications, industry, agriculture, and domestic life. In
addition to a large "Automobile in American Life" exhibition, it also
houses aircraft and trains in the transportation section. Among the
displays are the first aircraft to fly over the North and South Pole and
the first Sikorsky helicopter. The Wright Brothers' bicycle shop,
where they built their first airplane, is part of Greenfield Village,

among a total of about 80 historic structures.

Detroit
Willow Run Airport (YIP)
Airport is located 3 miles east of town.

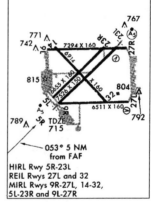

MI

☞ *Airport Information:*

Location: Detroit sectional N42.14.28 W83.31.82
Airspace: Class D
Attended: Continuously
Elevation: 716 feet
Fuel: 100LL, Jet A
TPA: 1700 feet msl lgt acft
2200 feet msl hvy acft
Runway: 05R-23L: 7526 x 150 asph
09L-27R: 7294 x 160 asph
14-32: 6914 x 160 asph
05L-23R: 6655 x 160 asph
09R-27L: 6511 x 160 asph
FBO: Signature Flight Support
734/482-2621
Active Aero Service
734/483-7833

☞ *Communication:*

Unicom: 122.95
App/Dep: Detroit 118.95
Tower: 120.0
Ground: 121.75
ATIS: 127.45

☞ *Transportation:*

Taxi: 734/699-1222
Car Rental: Avis 734/482-2621 (Signature Flight Support)

☞ *Lodging:*

Detroit: **Red Roof Inn** 734/697-2244

127

YANKEE AIR MUSEUM
(located on field)
P.O. Box 590, Belleville, MI 48112; Tel: 313/483-4030
Closed Mondays and holidays.
Admission is $5 for adults, $4 for children.

Historic aircraft are on display in an indoor/outdoor setting with the
B-24 "Liberator" bombers being the focal point. Many of the aircraft
are flyable, with the others on static display. Ongoing restoration
work can be observed. Display room topics include WW I and II,
Korean, and Vietnam wars, Women in Aviation, and the B-24
Liberator Bomber.

Drummond Island Airport
Airport is located 1 mile southwest of town.   (Y66)

MI

☞ *Airport Information:*

Location: Lake Huron sectional N46.00.56 W83.44.64
Attended: Mon-Sat 1300-2200Z*
Elevation: 668 feet
Fuel: 100LL, Jet A
TPA: 1470 feet msl
Runway: 08-26: 4000 x 75 asph
  18-36: 2500 x 150 asph-turf
FBO: Bailey's Services
  906/493-5411

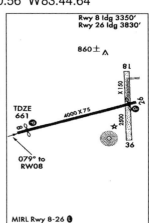

☞ *Communication:*
CTAF: 122.8
Unicom: 122.8
App/Dep: Toronto Center 132.65

☞ *Transportation:*
Car Rental: Bailey's Services 906/493-5411

☞ *Lodging:*

Drummond Island: **Woodmoor Resort** 800/999-6343 offers a
variety of accommodations from the hotel to waterfront cottages and
log homes. See entry following. **Arnold's Landing Resort** 888/252-
2650 or 906/493-5654

☞ *Restaurants:*
Drummond Island: **Bayside Dining** 800/999-6343 at *Woodmoor Resort*; **Bear Track Inn** 906/493-5090

WOODMOOR RESORT
(year-round recreational resort approximately 4 miles from airport)
33494 S. Maxton Road, Drummond Island, MI 49726; Tel: 800/999-6343; Internet: www.drummondisland.com

Originally the site of a private hunting and fishing preserve and purchased in the mid-80s as a corporate retreat, Woodmoor Resort now offers a long list of activities throughout the year. The Rock, Woodmoors' Harry Bowers–designed golf course, appears on Michigan's top ten lists. The course covers over 400 acres and each fairway is lined by hardwood and cedar woods. Participating in the Audubon Cooperative Sanctuary System, it is a wildlife habitat as well as scenic course. The long-standing tradition of hunting and fishing continues on the island. Hunters can choose from both wild game and preserve hunts. The island is rich in woodcock, grouse, and ducks. Small fishing boats, pontoons, kayaks, and canoes are available for rent to enjoy the protected waters of Potagannissing Bay. Trails invite hiking, biking, cross-country skiing, and snow shoeing. Ice-skate rentals are available during winter. Summer offers tennis, swimming, or lounging on the sandy beach. A sporting clays course, sauna, and 8-lane bowling alley round out the activities.

MI

Empire Airport (Y87)

Airport is located 3 miles southeast of town.
CAUTION: Watch for airport closure!

☞ *Airport Information:*

Location:	Green Bay sectional N44.47.25 W86.00.26
Attended:	Unattended
Elevation:	944 feet
Fuel:	Unavailable
TPA:	1720 feet msl
Runway:	17-35: 2600 x 50 asph
	09-27: 2275 x 150 turf
FBO:	Airport manager 616/326-5194

☞ *Communication:*
CTAF: 122.9

☞ *Transportation:*
Taxi: Not available

☞ *Lodging:*
Empire: **Lakeshore Inn Motel** 616/326-5145

☞ *Restaurants:*
Empire: **Daves Place** 616/326-5199

SLEEPING BEAR DUNES NATIONAL LAKESHORE
(outdoor recreation with visitor center approximately 2 miles from airport)
9922 Front Street, Empire, MI 49630; Tel: 616/326-5134; Internet: www.nps.gov/slbe

Sleeping Bear Dunes National Lakeshore protects 71,000 acres of sand hills that edge the Leelanau Peninsula. The preserve takes its name from an Ojibwe legend of a mother bear that collapsed after swimming across Lake Michigan. The tribe saw her shape in the dunes. The dunes are the highest outside the Sahara Desert and rise 460 feet above the lake. Climb atop the Dune Climb for a rewarding view or hike the Dunes Trail. The Pierce Stocking Scenic Drive offers panoramic views over 7.1 miles but is closed during the winter. The visitor center has exhibits, a slide program, trail maps, and book sales. During the winter about 50 miles of trails are marked for cross-country skiing. The park's lakes and rivers offer opportunities for swimming, boating, and fishing. Anglers with a license can fish for trout, pike, bass, and salmon. Canoes can be rented on the Platte and Crystal Rivers. Deer, rabbit, squirrel, ruffed grouse, and waterfowl hunting is possible in season, observing state regulations.

Gaylord
Otsego Co. Regional
Airport (GLR)

Airport is located 1 mile southwest of town.

☞ *Airport Information:*
Location: Lake Huron sectional N45.00.81 W84.42.19
Attended: Mon-Fri 1230-0130Z*, Sat-Sun 1300-0100Z*
Closed on major holidays.
Elevation: 1328 feet
Fuel: 100LL, Jet A
TPA: 2200 feet msl lgt acft
2400 feet msl hvy acft
Runway: 09-27: 6500 x 100 asph
18-36: 3000 x 75 apsh
Check for runway closures!
FBO: North County Aviation
517/732-6192

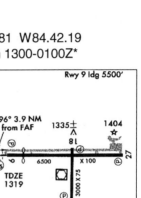

☞ *Communication:*
CTAF: 122.8
Unicom: 122.8
App/Dep: Minneapolis Center 134.6
ASOS: 118.375

☞ *Transportation:*
Taxi: 517/732-1232
Car Rental: Gaylord Ford 517/732-6737

☞ *Lodging:*
Gaylord: See **Treetops** 888/TREETOPS or 517/732-6711 entry below.

TREETOPS SYLVAN RESORT
(golfing and skiing approximately 7 miles from airport)
3962 Wilkinson Road, Gaylord, MI 49735; Tel: 888/TREETOPS;
Internet: www.treetops.com

Choose from four golf courses at this resort. Robert Trent Jones designed the Masterpiece course to have the highest slope rating in Michigan. It features dramatic elevation changes and a wide diversity of design. Views of the Pigeon River Valley are breathtaking anytime but especially so when fall foliage is at its peak. It is considered the most difficult of the courses here and opened in 1987. The Premier course was designed by Tom Fazio and is touted as a "user-friendly" tree-lined course with rolling fairways. It is the only Fazio–designed course in the state. An astonishing combination of holes can be played on the Signature course. The diversity of tees on this course offers players options to play each hole, yet creates a challenging course for all levels of play. The Tradition, the newest addition to Treetops, traverses gentle terrain and has short distances from green to tee. The latter two courses are Rick Smith designs. If you wish to improve your game, Rick Smith's Golf Academy provides insightful analysis.

During wintertime, enjoy 19 downhill runs at the Alpine Village of Gaylord, which is served by 7 lifts. Nordic enthusiasts will find the Midwest's best terrain for cross-country skiing, with 12 miles of groomed and tracked trails. Instructors at the Alpine Ski School are available for lessons.

✈ ✈ ✈

Hancock
Houghton Co. Mem. Airport (CMX)

Airport is located 4 miles northeast of town.

☞ *Airport Information:*

Location: Green Bay sectional N47.10.11 W88.29.34
Attended: 0900-0500Z*
Elevation: 1095 feet
Fuel: 100LL, Jet A
TPA: 1900 feet msl lgt acft
2300 feet msl hvy acft
Runway: 13-31: 6501 x 150 asph
07-25: 5196 x 100 asph
FBO: 906/482-3970

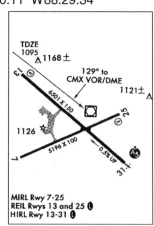

☞ *Communication:*

CTAF: 122.7
Unicom: 122.7
App/Dep: Minneapolis Center 127.2

MIRL Rwy 7-25
REIL Rwys 13 and 25 ◑
HIRL Rwy 13-31 ◑

☞ *Transportation:*
Taxi: 906/482-5515
Car Rental: Avis 906/482-1200; National 906/482-6655

☞ *Lodging:*
Hancock: The **Ramada Inn Waterfront** 906/482-8400 is located on Portage Lake. **Copper Crown Motel Best Western** 906/482-6111

☞ *Restaurants:*
Hancock: Whether you feel like eating steaks, chops. seafood, Italian, or pizza, it all can be had at **Gino's Restaurant** 906/482-3020.

QUINCY STEAM HOIST, SHAFTHOUSE, TRAM RIDE & UNDERGROUND MINE
(mining museum approximately 3 miles from airport)
201 Royce Road, Hancock, MI 49930; Tel: 906/482-3101
Open mid-May through mid-October.
Admission charged.

MI

Keweenaw Peninsula was the site of extensive copper mining from the 1840s to the 1960s and the Quincy Mining Company, one of the first commercially successful, is the longest operating mine there. You can ride a tram to an underground tour that gives a firsthand view of the mine's operation, or you can explore the mine's surface area.

WHILE YOU'RE THERE: The **Coppertown USA Museum** 906/337-4354 provides an introduction of the story of Copper Country. Tools, equipment, and early mining techniques are on display.

Harbor Springs Airport(D87)
Airport is located 3 miles east of town.

☞ *Airport Information:*
Location: Lake Huron sectional N45.25.53 W84.54.80
Attended: 1300Z to dusk
Elevation: 686 feet
Fuel: 100LL, Jet A
TPA: 1700 feet msl

Runway: 10-28: 4157 x 75 asph
FBO: 616/347-2812

☞ *Communication:*
CTAF: 122.8
Unicom: 122.8
App/Dep: Minneapolis Center 134.6

☞ *Transportation:*
Taxi: 616/348-3125
Car Rental: Budget 616/347-7441

☞ *Lodging:*
Harbor Springs: Best Western 616/347-9050; See **Boyne Highlands Resort** 616/526-3000 below.

Rwy 10 ldg 3712'
Rwy 28 ldg 3712'

4157 X 75

047° 5.6 NM
from FAF

MIRL Rwy 10-28 ◖

☞ *Restaurants:*
Harbor Springs: **Blue Corn Grill** 616/526-8000

BOYNE HIGHLANDS RESORT
(golfing and skiing approximately 4 miles from airport)
600 Highlands Drive, Harbor Springs, MI 49740; Tel: 616/526-3000;
Internet: www.boyne.com

Three 18-hole and one 9-hole course are yours to play on at this resort. It's a casual place with top-notch golf. The Heather course features wooded fairways consisting of birch, maple, beech, and cedar trees with imposing water hazards, ridges, and hollows. It is an award-winning Robert Trent Jones–designed course and remains one of the best loved courses in the state. Individual holes of the Donald Ross Memorial course are re-creations of the master's most famous holes from Oakland Hills, Seminole, Royal Dorchnoch, and Iverness. Test your versatility on Moor's doglegs with rolling bunkers and a great par-5 finishing hole. Yet don't overlook their newest addition, the 9-hole Arthur Hills course. Jim Flick, who was recently named one of three "Master Teachers of America" by *Golf* magazine, is available for personalized instruction by appointment during July and August.
Ski the 42 runs with a 550-foot vertical drop during winter time. A family-friendly ski area, it also has a snowboard half pipe and terrain park. Cross-country skiers are invited on 13 miles of groomed trails. The resort has hallmarks of a quaint European village, with hiking, fishing, and charter boat trips available.

Kalamazoo/Battle Creek Int'l Airport (AZO)

Airport is located 3 miles southeast of town.

☞ *Airport Information:*

Location: Chicago sectional N42.14.09 W85.33.12
Airspace: Class D service 1100-0400Z*, Terminal Radar Service; Other times class G
Attended: Continuously
Elevation: 874 feet
Fuel: 80, 100LL, Jet A
TPA: 1670 feet msl lgt acft
2070 feet msl hvy acft
2370 feet msl turbine acft
Runway: 17-35: 6500 x 150 asph
05-23: 3999 x 100 asph
09-27: 3350 x 150 asph
FBO: Kal-Aero 616/343-2548

☞ *Communication:*

CTAF: 118.3
Unicom: 122.95
App/Dep: 121.2 (173-352º), 119.2 (353-172º),
123.8 (1100-0400Z*)
Chicago Center 127.55 (0400-1100Z*)
Tower: 118.3 (1100-0400Z*)
Ground: 121.9
Clnc Del: 121.75
ATIS: 127.25

☞ *Transportation:*
Taxi: 616/345-0177
Car Rental: Avis 616/381-0555; National 616/382-2820

☞ *Lodging:*
Kalamazoo: The **Lee's Inn** 616/382-6100 is adjacent to the airport.
Quality Inn 616/388-3551

☞ *Restaurants:*
Kalamazoo: **Bilbos Pizza In A Pan** 616/382-5544

MI

KALAMAZOO AVIATION HISTORY MUSEUM

(adjacent to airport)
3101 East Milham Road, Kalamazoo, MI 49002; Tel: 616/382-6555
Open daily, except major holidays.
Admission is $10 for adults and $5 for children 6 to 15 years old.

Also called the Air Zoo, this museum has preserved and restored to
air-worthy conditions many of the world's greatest aircraft. The
aircraft on display played a major role in America's effort to restore
peace in World War II, the Korean War, the Vietnam War, and the
battle over the Persian Gulf. Aircraft restoration in progress can be
viewed at the Flight Center. More than 50 aircraft are on display as
well as original photographs, scale models, paintings, and other
paraphernalia. A 64-seat theater regularly presents classic military
feature films and award-winning documentaries.

WHILE YOU'RE THERE: The third weekend in July,
Kalamazoo flowers during the **County Flowerfest** 616/381-3597 in
Bronson Park downtown. Volunteers plant 155,000 annuals or join
the Bicycle Club for rides over country roads with stops at greenhouses and nurseries.

Mackinac Island Airport

(MCD)
Airport is located 1 mile northwest of town.

☞ *Airport Information:*

Location: Lake Huron sectional N45.51.90 W84.38.24
Attended: Jun-Aug 1200-0100Z*
Sep-May 1230-2230Z*
Elevation: 740 feet
Fuel: Not available
TPA: 1900 feet msl
Runway: 08-26: 3501 x 75 asph
FBO: 906/847-3231

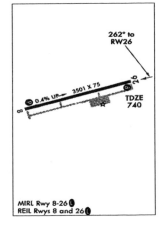

☞ *Communication:*

CTAF: 122.7
Unicom: 122.7
App/Dep: Minneapolis Center 134.6
AWOS: 128.325

☞ *Transportation:*
Taxi: 906/847-3323 for horse-drawn carriage
Car Rental: No cars are allowed on the island.

☞ *Lodging:*
Mackinac Island: Be aware that most lodging is seasonal and closed during the winter! See the **Grand Hotel** 906/847-3331 entry following. The **Chippewa Hotel** 800/241-3341 or 906/847-6414 is a downtown Victorian charmer. **Mission Point Resort** 800/833-7711 features 18 acres of waterfront property. **Haan's 1830 Inn** 906/847-6244 during summer and 414/248-9244 during winter, was the first B & B on this island and is located three blocks from downtown. **Lake View Hotel** 906/847-3384

☞ *Restaurants:*
Mackinac Island: **Chuck Wagon Restaurant** 906/847-3775

FORT MACKINAC
(approximately 2 miles from the airport)
E. Bluff Road, Mackinac Island, MI 49757; Tel: 906/847-3328
Open mid-May to mid-October.
Admission is $6.95.

MI

Fourteen original restored buildings that are more than 200 years old and a location on a bluff overlooking the village and straits draw visitors to explore this fort. Costumed "soldiers" re-enact life in the late 1880s with blacksmith demonstrations and exhibits. Children can try on period clothing and "fire" muskets in a "Discovery Room."

GRAND HOTEL
(resort hotel approximately 2 miles from airport)
Mackinac Island, MI 49757; Tel: 800/33-GRAND or 906/847-3331;
Internet: www.grandhotel.com
Open May through October.

Mackinac Island is steeped in history, and the Grand Hotel dominates the island in a fine example of tradition. Explore the quaint 19th-century Victorian village by foot and indulge in some famous fudge-tasting and antique browsing. Old world hospitality and charm beckon in a hotel that originally opened in 1887. Indulge in carriage tours, musical entertainment, golf, tennis, swimming, and hiking and strolling the car-less surroundings. Historic points of interest are *Fort Mackinac, Arch Rock* overlooking Lake Huron, *Skull Cave,* and *Surrey Hill.*

MACKINAC ISLAND CARRIAGE TOURS
(horse-drawn tours approximately 2 miles from airport)
Main Street, Mackinac Island, MI49757; Tel: 906/847-3573 or
906/847-3325

Under Mackinac's most unusual law, cars are prohibited, giving the
island a romantic and timeless tranquillity. A horse-drawn carriage
will take you to historic points of interest, including Surrey Hill, Arch
Rock, Fort Mackinac, and the Grand Hotel.

WHILE YOU'RE THERE: The **Indian Dormitory** 906/847-3328
with its native American culture displays and live interpretations of life
in the 1800s is included in the admission to the fort. It is located on
Main Street. Nature enthusiasts can stop by the **Butterfly House**
906/847-3972 for a display of several hundred live butterflies
encompassing more than 80 different species from all over the world.
Use the eight miles of paved, car-less road that circle the island to
explore its natural beauty. The **Information Kiosk** 906/847-3783 on
Main Street provides full details on bike rental and horseback rides
as well as free detailed maps. Bike rental shops can be found at the
ferry docks on Main Street.

Oscoda
Wurtsmith Airport (OSC)

Airport is located 3 miles northwest of town.

☞ *Airport Information:*

Location: Lake Huron sectional N44.27.16 W83.22.82
Attended: Dawn to dusk. Unattended major holidays
Elevation: 634 feet
Fuel: 100LL, Jet A
TPA: 1634 feet msl
Runway: 06-24: 11800 x 300 conc
FBO: Oscoda Wurtsmith Airport Services 517/739-8486

☞ *Communication:*

CTAF: 123.0
Unicom: 123.0
App/Dep: Minneapolis Center 118.525
Awos: 116.1

☞ *Transportation:*
Car Rental: Rent-a-ride 517/362-8541

☞ *Lodging:*
Oscoda: See **Lakewood Shores Resort**
800/882-2493 or 517/739-2073 below;
Huron House B & B 517/739-9255 is a
retreat on Lake Huron with beach and
fireplaces.

☞ *Restaurants:*
Oscoda: Seafood baked in parchment is
a specialty at **The Pack House** 517/739-
0454, a 1878 home turned restaurant.

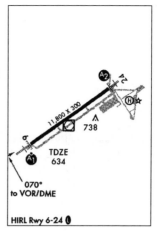

LAKEWOOD SHORES RESORT
(golfing approximately 2 miles from airport)
7751 Cedar Lake Road, Oscoda, MI 48750; Tel: 800/882-2493 or
517/739-2073; Internet: lakewoodshores.com

MI

Located on the shores of Cedar Lake, this family resort offers a golf
course with Scottish flavor. The Gailes was rated "The Number One
Public and Resort Course in the State of Michigan" by *Golf Digest* in
1996. Designed to recreate the actual look of the famed seaside
course in Scotland, it has large double greens and meandering
burns. Non-golfers may enjoy swimming on the private beach, jet
skiing, canoeing, or fishing.

Traverse City
Cherry Capital Airport (TVC)

Airport is located 2 miles south of town.

☞ *Airport Information:*
Location: Green Bay sectional N44.44.45 W85.34.95
Airspace: Class D service 1200-0200Z*, 1100-0100Z* EDT
              Other times Class E
Attended: Oct-May 1200-0200Z*, Jun-Sep 1100-0400Z*
Elevation: 624 feet
Fuel: 100LL, Jet A
TPA: 1420 feet msl lgt acft, 2120 feet msl multiengine acft

Runway: 10-28: 6501 x 150 asph
18-36: 5107 x 150 asph
5-23: 3204 x 75 asph
FBO: Harbour Air 616/929-1126

☞ *Communication:*
CTAF: 124.2
Unicom: 122.95
App/Dep: Minneapolis Center 132.9
Tower: 124.2 (1200-0200Z*,
1100-0200Z* EDT)
Ground: 121.8
ATIS: 126.0

684± 81 706 701 TDZE 675± 617 6501 X 150 736 36 279° 5.8 NM from FAF 705±
MIRL Rwy 18-36
HIRL Rwy 10-28
REIL Rwys 18 and 36

☞ *Transportation:*
Taxi: 616/929-7433
Car Rental: Avis 616/946-1222; Budget 616/947-3883;
National 616/947-1560

MI

☞ *Lodging:*
Acme: See **Grand Traverse Resort Village** 800/748-0303 or
616/938-2100 below.
Traverse City: **Park Place Hotel** 616/946-5000; **Days Inn** 616/941-
0208; The **Bayshore Resort** 800/634-4401 or 616/935-4400 is
located on sandy West Grand Traverse Bay beachfront and features
indoor pool and spa.

GRAND TRAVERSE RESORT VILLAGE
(golfing and other outdoor activities approximately 6 miles from
airport)
100 Grand Traverse Village Boulevard, P.O.Box 404, Acme, MI
49610; Tel: 800/748-0303 or 616/938-2100; Internet: www.gtresort.
com

Grand Traverse is located on 1,400 acres of spectacular Northern
Michigan landscape and is a full-service, year-round resort. Golfing
is a highlight of the resort, with Jack Nicklaus's Bear course being
ranked among the "Top 50 Resort Courses in America" by *Golf
Digest*. It's a rather challenging course with heather-covered
mounds, cavernous pot bunkers, and terraced fairways. Spruce Run
accommodates most skill levels and mid-handicappers will find it
more enjoyable than the Bear course. Golfers and non-golfers alike
can test their luck on the area's streams and rivers with guided tours
or battle lake trout, Coho, and Chinook salmon on local charter

fishing expeditions. Also available are a cross-country ski center and beach club. Snowmobilers are invited on 200 miles of groomed trails through scenic state forest. The health club features spa facilities, in- and outdoor swimming pools, weight room, saunas, and tennis and racquetball courts.

WHILE YOU'RE THERE: The area around Traverse City claims to be the "Cherry Capital of the World." Thousands of acres of cherry orchards surround the town. The annual **National Cherry Festival** 616/947-1120 is held during the first full week in July with fireworks, concerts, parades, and of course, cherries in all shapes and forms. May is the time to visit to enjoy a countryside decorated with the pink blossoms of the cherry trees. Savor the scenery of the bay area aboard the **Grand Traverse Dinner Train** 616/933-3768. Dinner and luncheon tours run all year in addition to special events such as "Mysteries" and "Train Robberies."

MI

NOTES:

NEW HAMPSHIRE

Claremont Munic. Airport
(CNH)
Airport is located 1 mile west of town.

☞ Airport Information:
Location: New York sectional N43.22.23 W72.22.12
Attended: Irregularly
Elevation: 545 feet
Fuel: 100LL
TPA: 1550 feet msl
Runway: 11-29: 3100 x 100 asph
FBO: Fryman Air 603/543-1180

NH

☞ Communication:
CTAF: 122.7
Unicom: 122.7
App/Dep: 134.7

☞ Transportation:
Car Rental: Paul & Son Ford
603/543-1281

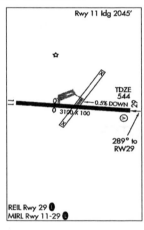

☞ *Lodging:*
Claremont: The **Wes Budget Motel** 603/542-9567 is located downtown. A 1900s English Manor, the **Goddard Mansion B & B** 603/543-0603 has 10 guest rooms.

MORNINGSIDE FLIGHT PARK
(hang- and paragliding center approximately 3 miles from airport)
357 Morningside Lane, Charlestown, NH 03603; Tel: 603/542-4416;
Internet:www.cyberportal.net/morningside
Open from approximately April to Thanksgiving. Lessons by appointment only.

Morningside is known as one of the premiere sites in the USA for hang gliding. Its centerpiece is a 250-foot gently sloping hill wide enough to accommodate 20 gliders side by side. All-terrain vehicles shuttle you and your glider up the hill between flights. In business since 1975, they offer certified instruction for both hang gliding and paragliding. Introductory lessons start in the classroom with presentations of history, flight principles, and safety considerations. Hang gliding students are suspended in a simulator to become familiar with weight shift and correct posture before moving on to level ground training. On-site camping, swimming, and hiking are available for non-flying guests. Four-hour bunny-slope lessons in hang gliding start at $95. Paragliding introductory course starts at $125.

NOTE: A grass runway is on site for single engine aircraft. By appointment only. (CTAF 122.75)

Nashua
Boire Field (ASH)

Airport is located 3 miles northwest of town.

☞ *Airport Information:*

Location: New York sectional N42.46.91 W71.30.89

Airspace: Class D service
Apr1-Oct31 (1200-0200Z*)
Nov1-Mar31 (1200-2300Z*)

Attended: 1200-0200Z*

Elevation: 200 feet

Fuel: 100LL, Jet A1

TPA: 1200 feet msl lgt acft
1700 feet msl heavy acft

Runway: 14-32: 5500 x 100 asph

FBO: Keyson Airways
603/598-4526

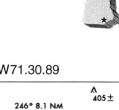

☞ *Communication:*

CTAF: 133.2

App/Dep: Manchester 124.9

Clnc Del: 121.8

Ground: 121.8

Tower: 133.2 Apr 1-Oct 31 (1200-0200Z*)
Nov 1-Mar 31 (1200-2300Z*)

ATIS: 125.1

☞ *Transportation:*
Taxi: 603/882-7444
Car Rental: Budget 603/883-5650; Thrifty 603/883-1935

☞ *Lodging:*
Nashua: **Comfort Inn** 603/883-7700; **Holiday Inn** 603/888-1551;
Nashua Marriott 603/880-9100

SKY MEADOW COUNTRY CLUB
(golf approximately 5 miles from airport)
2 Sky Meadow Drive, Nashua, NH 03062; Tel: 603/888-9000

Pick a clear day to play at Sky Meadow and you will be rewarded with incredible views from the highest elevation in Nashua. Don't be distracted too much, though, as this course is not forgiving, with its water hazards and steep hills. Featuring 18 holes at par 72, No. 11 plays 75 feet downhill from tee to green. Sky Meadow was designed by William Amick and opened in 1989. This course is ranked 3rd in New Hampshire by *Golf Digest.*

NH

Portsmouth
Pease Int'l Tradeport (PSM)
Airport is located 1 mile west of town.

☞ *Airport Information:*

Location:	New York sectional N43.04.68 W70.49.40
Airspace:	Class D
Attended:	Mon-Fri 1100-0330Z*
	Sat-Sun 1100-0230Z*
Elevation:	101 feet
Fuel:	100LL, Jet A
TPA:	1100 feet msl lgt acft, rectangular tfc pattern:1600 feet msl; overhead tfc pattern: 2100 feet msl
Runway:	16-34: 11318 x 150 asph/ conc
FBO:	Seacoast Aviation 603/427-0350

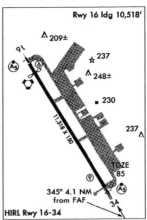

☞ *Communication:*
Unicom: 122.95
App/Dep: Manchester 125.05
Ground: 120.95
Tower: 128.4
ATIS: 132.05 (1000-0500Z*)

☞ *Transportation:*
Taxi: Taxi stand at airport
Car Rental: National 603/334-6000

☞ *Lodging:*
Portsmouth: The **Sheraton Harborside Portsmouth** 603/431-2300 is on the harbor in historic downtown. An elegant Queen Anne Inn, the **Sise Inn**, 603/433-1200 is within walking distance of shops, entertainment, and the waterfront; 34 rooms are decorated in Victorian style. **Hampton Inn** 603/431-6111
Rye: Across from the ocean and a sandy beach, you can rent housekeeping cottages at **Atlantic Four Winds** 603/436-5140. Closed during winter.

NH

☞ *Restaurant:*
Portsmouth: **Margarita's Mexican Restaurant and Watering Hole** 603/431-5828. Go European at the **Dinnerhorn Restaurant & Bratskellar** 603/436-0717.

STRAWBERY BANKE MUSEUM
(approximately 3 miles from airport)
Marcy Street, Portsmouth, NH 03802; Tel: 603/433-1100; Internet: www.strawberybanke.org
Open daily mid April to end of October, plus special holidays.
Admission is $12 for adults, $8 for youths (7 to 17), $28 for families.

Tour historic homes and period gardens dating from 1695. Also visit craftspeople and costumed roleplayers at this 10-acre, 40-building village museum.

WATER COUNTRY
(approximately 3 miles from airport)
Route 1, Portsmouth, NH 03801; Tel: 603/436-3556; Internet: www.watercountry.com
Open during summer.
Admission is charged.

Play the waves of the biggest wave pool in New England, or tube down the Raging Rapids and the Plunge. Water Country offers fun for the young and not-so-young.

WENTWORTH BY THE SEA GOLF CLUB
(approximately 5 miles from airport)
Wentworth Road, Route 1B, Rye, NH 03870; Tel: 603/433-5010

Water, water, water... Half the holes of this 18-hole, par-70 course are either on or overlook the Atlantic ocean. No. 7 is a gorgeous par 3 that extends into the Atlantic. Witches Creek and ponds add even more water to the layout and about hundred sand bunkers add variety.

WHILE YOU'RE THERE: Portsmouth Harbor Cruises
603/436-8084 offers cruises to view the bird life of the Inland Waterways, to the Isles of Shoals (a colonial fishing settlement), and also has narrated harbor cruises. Rentals and charters are available from **Atlantic Fishing Fleet** 603/926-2469 in Rye Harbor. Also from Rye Harbor, take whale-watching trips with **New Hampshire Seacoast Cruises** 603/964-5545.

Twin Mountain Airport (8B2)
Airport is located 1 mile southwest of town.

☞ *Airport Information:*

Location: Montreal sectional N44.15.84 W71.32.85
Attended: Feb-Sep 1300-0100Z*, Oct-Jan 1300-2100Z*
Elevation: 1459 feet
Fuel: Not available
TPA: 2300 feet msl
Runway: 09-27: 2640 x 60 asph
FBO: 603/846-5505

☞ *Communication:*

CTAF: 122.8
Unicom: 122.8

☞ *Transportation:*

Taxi: 603/444-0407
Car Rental: Crosstown Motors 603/444-6922 (call ahead)

☞ *Lodging:*
Bretton Woods: Mt. Washington Hotel & Resort 603/278-1000 (see below).

☞ *Restaurant:*
Bretton Woods: The **Mt. Washington Hotel & Resort** 603/278-1000 (see below) features five restaurants and seven lounges. Located across the street from the ski area, a renovated railroad station, **Fabyan's Station Restaurant** 603/278-2222, serves lunch and dinner daily.

MT. WASHINGTON HOTEL & RESORT
(golf resort approximately 5 miles from airport)
Route 302, Bretton Woods, NH 03575; Tel: 603/278-1000 ext. 8540

Golfers will love the 27 holes of PGA championship golf at this historic grand resort. At the center is the Donald Ross–designed Mt. Washington Course, with one of the most spectacular settings in the Northeast. The historic 9-hole Mount Pleasant Course was first opened in 1895 and restored in 1989 by Cornish-Silva. But golfing is not the only leisure attraction available here. Horseback riding, tennis, swimming at the in- or outdoor pools, hiking, and horse-drawn carriage rides can be pursued. Or just lounge on the 900-foot wraparound veranda and enjoy the spectacular vistas of the White Mountains.

NH

WHILE YOU'RE THERE: Bretton Woods Ski Area 800/232-2972 has alpine, cross-country and snowboarding facilities. The **Twin Mountain Fish and Wildlife Center** 603/846-5108 has informative fishing-related displays and information.

NEW JERSEY

Atlantic City Int'l Airport (ACY)
Airport is located 9 miles northwest of town.

☞ *Airport Information:*

Location: Washington sectional N39.27.45 W74.34.63
Airspace: Class C
Attended: Continuously
Elevation: 76 feet
Fuel: 100LL, Jet A
TPA: 1500 feet msl non-turbo
2000 feet msl turbo
Runway: 13-31: 10000 x 180 asph
04-22: 6144 x 150
concrete/asph
FBO: Midatlantic Jet Aviation
609/383-3993

☞ *Communication:*
Unicom: 122.95
App/Dep: 134.25 (310-129°); 124.6 (130-309°)
Tower: 120.3
Ground: 121.9
Clnc Del: 127.85
ATIS: 108.6

☞ *Transportation:*
Taxi: 609/344-1221
Car Rental: Avis 609/383-9595; Budget 609/383-0682
Hertz 609/646-7733

☞ *Lodging:*
Absecon: **Marietta's Seaview Resort** 609/652-1800 see entry
below; **Comfort Inn North** 609/641-7272; **Days Inn Absecon**
609/652-2200; **Hampton Inn** 609/652-2500
Atlantic City: See entry under Atlantic City Munic., Bader Airport.

☞ *Restaurants:*
Atlantic City: see entry under Atlantic City Munic., Bader Airport.

EDWIN B. FORSYTHE NATIONAL WILDLIFE REFUGE'S BRIGANTINE DIVISION
(bird-watching approximately 10 miles from airport)
Box 72, Great Creek Road, Oceanville, NJ 08231; Tel: 609/652-1665
Open daily sunrise to sunset.
Admission is $4 per vehicle.

One of the great bird sights of the East Coast, this Wildlife Refuge has an 8-mile wildlife drive, two short circular foot trails and observation towers. Diverse coastal habitat such as salt marshes, tidal bays, freshwater marshes, and coniferous brushland are popular with migrating as well as nesting birds. The Holgate Unit on Long Beach Island is home to nesting colonies of oystercatchers, skimmers, and terns. Beginning of November is best for watching spectacular concentrations of ducks, geese, and brants. Teals are best seen during September and ruddy turnstones during May and June. Watch for glossy ibises end of April. Mid-March to mid-April is the time for waterfowl migrations. This place is not just liked by a large variety of birds but also by insects, so don't forget your repellent.

MARRIOTT'S SEAVIEW RESORT
(golf and golfschool approximately 5 miles from airport)
Route 9, Absecon, NJ 08201; Tel: 800/932-8000; For golf school reservations call 888/554-3737.

Improve your game of golf with John Jacob's Golf School at Marriott's Seaview Resort, a truly elegant bayside retreat. Two 18-hole championship courses are regarded as legendary by serious golfers. The Bay Course is a Donald Ross–designed course featuring rolling terrain, small greens, pot bunkers and panoramic views. The Pines is a newer and tougher track through heavy woods inter-spersed by azaleas and dogwoods. Bunkers (110 of them) mingle with the fairways and greens. Choose from John Jacob's weekend or three-day programs which include a stay at the resort. Instruction only is available as well—or just enjoy a good round of golf on these outstanding courses.
The Seaview Resort, a full service resort, also has tennis courts, sauna, steam room, and a pool. Atlantic City's famous casinos and boardwalk are a short drive away.

WHILE YOU'RE THERE: The **Towne of Historic Smithville** 609/652-7777 is a restored authentic 18th-century village set around Lake Meone with restaurants and shops. The **Village Greene** 609/652-7777 has an around-the-village train ride, miniature golf, and paddle boats. Whale watching, sports fishing trips and charter service are available through **The Atlantic Star** 609/348-0669 at the Kammerman's Marina.

Atlantic City Munic./Bader Field (AIY)

NOTE: Airport CLOSED to jet aircraft!!
NOTE: Check for airport closure times.
Airport is located 1 mile west of town.

☞ *Airport Information:*

Location:	Washington sectional N39.21.60 W74.27.37
Attended:	Unattended
Elevation:	9 feet
Fuel:	Not available
TPA:	800 feet msl
Runway:	11-29: 2830 x 100 asph
	04-22: 2596 x 100 asph
	Check for runway closures!
FBO:	Not available

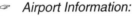

☞ *Communication:*

CTAF:	123.0
Unicom:	123.0
App/Dep:	Atlantic City 134.25 (north)
	124.6 (south)
Clnc Del:	121.7

☞ *Transportation:*

Taxi:	609/345-1105; 609/344-1221
Car Rental:	Hertz 609/298-8585

☞ *Lodging:*

Atlantic City: Choose among the many casino resorts such as **Harrah's** 609/441-5000 or 800/2-HARRAH. **Caesars** 609/348-4411 or 800/524-2867; **Sands Hotel** 609/441-4000 or 800/AC-SANDS;

Trump Plaza 609/441-6000 or 800/677-7378; and **Trump Taj Mahal** 609/449-1000 or 800/825-8786; **Econo Lodge Boardwalk** 609/344-9093; **Days Inn** 609/344-6101; **Holiday Inn Boardwalk** 609/348-2200; **Quality Inn** 609/345-7070

☞ *Restaurants:*
Atlantic City: Seafood is the specialty at the **Flying Cloud Cafe** 609/345-8222, a waterfront restaurant with outdoor deck (limited hours during winter!). The **Hard Rock Cafe** 609/441-0007 and **Planet Hollywood** 609/347-STAR are represented with their familiar themes and food. For ethnic flavors try **Little Saigon's** 609/347-9119 Vietnamese or **Los Amigos'** 609/344-2293 Mexican. The **White House Sub Shop** 609/345-1564 is fast and famous for sandwiches. All-you-can-eat buffets are available at the large casinos. Check the lodging listings for phone numbers.

ATLANTIC CITY BOARDWALK
(approximately 1 mile from airport)
Tel: 609/348-7100

The world's first boardwalk was built in 1870 as a temporary walkway raised above the beach so that holiday guests could stroll along the beach without tracking sand into the grand hotels. Now you'll find landmark hotels and famous casinos along the wooden walkway. Central Pier offers rides and games, and of course the beach beckons for a swim. Bikes may be rented from vendors along the boardwalk, but you will have to dodge the masses of people. (Be careful in this area at night!)

NJ

Gamblers are drawn to the 24-hour operating casinos that dominate the city. Donald Trump's Taj Mahal has the second largest casino floor in the world and occupies nearly twenty acres. Ostentatious and humongous, it is a showplace of kitsch with minarets and onion domes. Caesars is the East Coast version of the famous casino with the same name in Vegas. It's done in a Roman theme with columns, Greek gods, and laurel wreaths. In between gambling you can take in entertainment from Broadway shows to championship boxing.

Belmar - Farmingdale
Allaire Airport (BLM)
Airport is located 5 miles west of town.

☞ *Airport Information:*
Location: New York sectional N40.11.22 W74.07.49
Attended: Jun-Sep 1200-0200Z*
Oct-May 1200-2300Z*
Elevation: 159 feet
Fuel: 100LL, Jet A
TPA: 1000 feet msl
Runway: 14-32: 7300 x 80 asph
03-21: 3707 x 50 asph
FBO: Allaire Airport Authority
732/938-4800

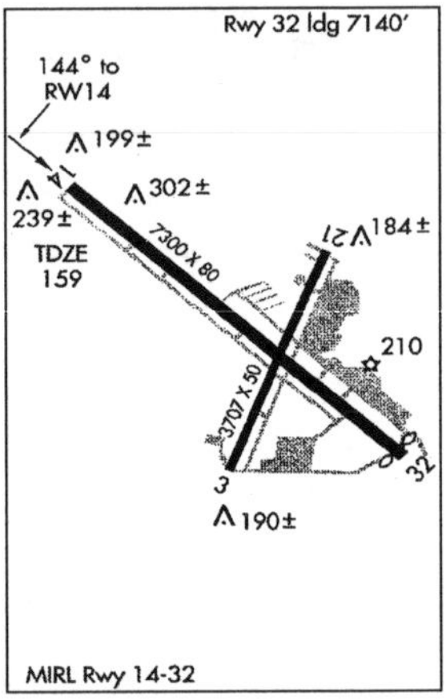

☞ *Communication:*
CTAF: 123.0
Unicom: 123.0
App/Dep: McGuire 120.25
Clnc Del: 120.95
AWOS: 121.625

☞ *Transportation:*
Taxi: 732/223-1114
Car Rental: Enterprise 908/223-6400
Olympic Limousine 800/822-9797

☞ *Lodging:*
Colts Neck: **Village Inn** 732/294-8666; **Colts Neck Inn Hotel**
732/409-1200
Belmar: **Down the Shore B & B** 732/681-9023; **The Inn at the
Shore** 732/681-3762

HOMINY HILL GOLF COURSE
(approximately 7 miles from airport)
92 Mercer Road, Colts Neck, NJ 07722; Tel: 732/462-9222

Consistently ranked as one of the best public courses since it opened
in 1964, it was laid out by Trent Jones. Its features are rolling hills
with lots of bunkers. An outstanding long and tough course with 18
holes requiring accurate shots.

WHILE YOU'RE THERE: The **Belmar Municipal Marina**
732/681-2266 is home to some 25 party and charter boats, all of
which make daily ocean trips in search of fluke, blackfish, blues,
albacore, shark, and other local fish.

Sussex Airport (FWN)

Airport is located 1 mile southwest of town.

☞ *Airport Information:*

Location: New York sectional N41.12.01 W74.37.38
Attended: Dawn to 0200Z*
Elevation: 421 feet
Fuel: 80, 100LL
TPA: 1200 feet msl lgt acft
                  1400 feet msl hvy acft
Runway: 03-21: 3499 x 75 asph
FBO: Aerobatex 201/875-7337

☞ *Communication:*
CTAF: 122.7
Unicom: 122.7
App/Dep: New York 127.6

☞ *Transportation:*
Taxi: 201/875-7337 Aerobatex will arrange taxi
Car Rental: Franklin Sussex Motors 201/875-3188

☞ *Lodging:*
McAffee: **Days Inn** 201/827-4666
Sussex: **Sussex Motel** 201/875-4191

GREAT GORGE COUNTRY CLUB

(golf approximately 5 miles from airport)
Route 517, McAffee, NJ 07428; Tel: 201/827-5757
Closed during winter.

George Fazio designed three 9-hole courses; the Quarry Nine,
featuring actual stone quarries, seems to be the favorite one. The
Lake Nine is the longest one and the Rail Nine offers nice views,
especially in fall.

WHILE YOU'RE THERE: **Vernon Valley/Great Gorge Ski Area/Alpine Slide** 201/827-2000 and **Hidden Valley** 973/764-6161 are New Jersey's largest ski areas.

Teterboro Airport (TEB)
Airport is located 1 miles southwest of town.

☞ *Airport Information:*

Location: New York sectional N40.51.01 W74.03.65
Airspace: Class D
Attended: Continuously
Elevation: 9 feet
Fuel: 100LL, Jet A
TPA: 1000 feet msl lgt acft
1500 feet msl hvy acft
Runway: 01-19: 7000 x 150 asph
06-24: 6013 x 150 asph
FBO: Air Charters Inc.
201/288-9000
Million Air 201/288-5040

NJ

☞ *Communication:*

App: New York 127.7
Dep: New York 126.7, 119.2
Tower: 119.5; 125.1
Ground: 121.9
Clnc Del: 128.05
ATIS: 132.025

☞ *Transportation:*
Taxi: 201/288-1950
Car Rental: Enterprise 201/641-7565; Hertz 201/641-5122

☞ *Lodging:*
Hasbrouck Heights: Holiday Inn 201/2889600

AVIATION HALL OF FAME OF NEW JERSEY
(located on field)
400 Fred Wehran Drive, Teterboro, NJ 07608; Tel: 201/288-6344
Open daily, except Mondays.
Admission is $5 for adults and $3 for children.

New Jersey's aviation and space heritage is manifested here. The Hall of Fame honors men and women who significantly contributed to aviation. The Aviation Educational Center, part of the museum, displays aircraft piston, helicopter, and jet and rocket engines.

Wildwood
Cape May Co. Airport (WWD)

Airport is located 4 miles northwest of town.

☞ *Airport Information:*

Location: Washington sectional N39.00.51 W74.54.50
Attended: Mon-Fri 1330-2130Z*
Elevation: 23 feet
Fuel: 100LL
TPA: 823 feet msl single engine acft
1023 feet msl twin engine acft
Runway: 01-19: 4998 x 150 asph
10-28: 4998 x 150 asph
14-32: 4000 x 150 asph
FBO: Flight Services Inc.
609/889-0300

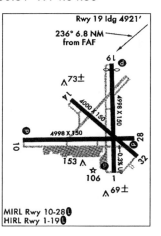

☞ *Communication:*

CTAF: 122.7
Unicom: 122.7
App/Dep: Atlantic City 124.6
Clnc Del: 121.7
AWOS: 118.275

☞ *Transportation:*

Taxi: 609/884-5711; 609/886-9600
Car Rental: Airport Auto 609/889-1100

☞ *Lodging:*

Cape May: In the heart of the historic district and two blocks from the beach is the **Manor House** 609/884-4710. The **Mainstay Inn** 609/884-8690 originally was a 1870s men's gambling club. Now a B & B, it still has the feel of the good old times. **Summer Cottage**

Inn 609/884-4948; **Queen Victoria** 609/884-8702
Wildwood Crest: The **Armada** 800/399-3001, **Reges** 609/729-9300, **Ocean Holiday** 800/321-6232, and **Lotus Inn** 609/522-6300 are just a few of the many hotels near the beach.

☞ _Restaurants:_
Cape May: For seafood patronize either **The Lobster House** 609/884-8296 or **A & J Blue Claw** 609/884-5878. **Louisa's** 609/884-5882 is called the best place in town by some people. Cheap pizzas and burgers can be had along Beach Avenue.

CAPE MAY BIRD OBSERVATORY
(approximately 6 miles from airport)
701 E. Lake Drive, Cape May Point, NJ 08212; Tel: 609/884-2736

Due to its location on the Atlantic Flyway, Cape May is famous for its concentration of migrating birds. Birders, pick up your binoculars and experience birds in their beautiful breeding plumage during May or join the Hawkwatch for the hawk count from September through November. Seventeen different species of hawks and eagles are seen regularly. Over one million seabirds such as scoters, loons, cormorants and gannets were counted in the fall of 96. The Observatory sponsors educational programs throughout the year.

NJ

VICTORIAN CAPE MAY – CENTER FOR THE ARTS
(tours and activities approximately 5 miles from airport)
1048 Washington Street, P.O.Box 340, Cape May, NJ 08204; Tel: 609/884-5404

Cape May, the oldest U.S. seashore resort, charms the visitor with more than 600 Victorian houses built in competitive splendor after the town burned down in the late 1800s. It's Gingerbread-by-the-Sea! You can walk brick sidewalks on tours, or take a trolley. There's a lighthouse to climb, and a cruise around the Cape will show you yet another view of the town. Victorian Week (October) and Christmas season attract off-season visitors to special events.

WHILE YOU'RE THERE: Pick up a bike to pedal around town form the **Village Bike Shop** 609/884-8500. If you are up to a dolphin or whale watching voyage, or just a trip around Cape May, contact the **Cape May Whale Watcher** 609/884-5445. Wave runners, kayaks, and boats can be rented from **Cape May Water Sports** 609/884-8646. Daily sails on an 80-foot-tall ship are scheduled by the **Yankee Schooner** 609/884-1919 from May to September .

NEW YORK

Cooperstown
Westville Airport (NY54)
Airport is located 4 miles southeast of town.

☞ *Airport Information:*
Location: New York sectional N42.37.75 W74.53.46
Attended: May-Nov 1300-0100Z*; Dec-Apr 1300-2100Z*
Elevation: 1260 feet
Fuel: 80, 100LL
TPA: 2050 feet msl
Runway: 02-20: 2320 x 125 turf
FBO: 607/286-9013

☞ *Communication:*
CTAF: 122.8
Unicom: 122.8

☞ *Transportation:*
Taxi: 607/547-8811
Car Rental: Cooperstown - Westville Airport 607/286-9013
Smith Ford 607/547-9924

☞ *Lodging:*
Cooperstown: **Best Western Inn at the Commons** 607/547-9439;
Cooperstown Motel 607/547-2301

NATIONAL BASEBALL HALL OF FAME
(approximately 8 miles from the airport)
Main Street, Cooperstown, NY 13326; Tel: 607/547-7200
Open daily, except major holidays.
Admission is $9.50 for adults and $4 for children 7 to 12 years old.

Baseball fans, this is your chance to buy baseball memorabilia, eat
in baseball-themed restaurants, and sleep in baseball-themed
motels. The museum displays memorabilia from the immortals,
including the bat with which Babe Ruth hit his famous "called shot"

NY

home run in the 1932 World Series. Paintings, displays, and audiovisual presentations trace the history of the game and recall the great moments. Ceremonies for new inductees are held at the Clarks Sports Center 10 minutes down the road in late July or early August.

THE FARMERS' MUSEUM AND VILLAGE CROSSROADS
(approximately 9 miles from the airport)
P.O. Box 800, Cooperstown, NY 13326; Tel: 607/547-1450; Internet: www. cooperstown.net/nysha
Open daily Apr-Oct.

Outdoor museum of rural life in early times. Founded in 1943, it is one of the oldest open-air sites in the USA. A dozen buildings were moved to the site from the surrounding region to recreate a 19th-century farm community. A print shop, school house, general store, pharmacy, doctor's and lawyer's office, church, tavern, and black-smith shop are filled with exhibits. Craftspeople work at broom making, cabinet making, weaving, and spinning. Special events, such as the Harvest Festival in the fall and a 19th-Century Fourth of July festival, are held throughout the year. Ask about a combination ticket with the National Baseball Hall of Fame.

NY WHILE YOU'RE THERE: **Corvette Hall of Fame and Americana Museum** 607/547-5135. The **Cooperstown Brewing Co.** 607/286-9330 is an English style microbrewery that offers tours.

East Hampton (HTO)
Airport is located 3 miles west of town.

☞ *Airport Information:*

Location:	New York sectional N40.57.58 W72.15.11
Attended:	1300Z* to sunset
Elevation:	56 feet
Fuel:	100LL, Jet A
TPA:	1100 feet msl
	1500 feet msl turbine acft
Runway:	10-28: 4255 x 75 asph
	04-22: 2501 x 100 asph
	16-34: 2223 x 75 asph

FBO: Sound Aircraft Services 516/537-2202

☞ *Communication:*
CTAF: 122.7
Unicom: 122.7
App/Dep: New York 132.25
Clnc Del: 132.25

☞ *Transportation:*
Taxi: 516/324-3377
Car Rental: Hertz 516/537-8119

☞ *Lodging:*
East Hampton: Hunting Inn 516/324-0410

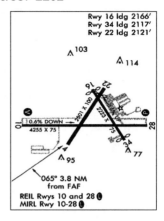

DUCK WALK VINEYARDS
(approximately 6 miles form the airport)
162 Montauk Highway, Water Mill, NY 11976; Tel: 516/726-7555
Open daily.

Though Long Island has about a dozen wineries, this one is the most spectacular. It reminds you of a Normandy chateau with its 17,000-square-foot copper-roofed building. Weekend tours and tastings are free at the tasting rooms and on a terrace overlooking the vineyards. Just remember the "bottle to throttle" rules!

Elmira
Harris Hill Gliderport
WARNING: This is a private airport.
Call ahead at 607/734-0641 or 607/733-3470 for details and permission to land.

NATIONAL SOARING MUSEUM
(located adjacent to field)
Harris Hill, 51 Soaring Hill Drive, Elmira, NY 14903; Tel: 607/734-3128; Internet: www.soaringmuseum.org
Open daily, except major holidays.
Admission is $4 for adults, $2.50 for youth.

Elmira hosted the first national soaring contests between 1930 and 1946 and now calls itself the "Soaring Capital of America." You can experience the science, history, and adventure of motorless flight at this museum, which also is home to the largest collection of gliders and sailplanes in the world. Watch experts bring older gliders back to life at the restoration facilities. You can also use a computer to design your own aircraft from wings, tails, and fuselages in the museum's collection and then test it in a "virtual" wind tunnel.

WHILE YOU'RE THERE: Take a sailplane ride at the **Harris Hill Soaring Corp.** 607/734-0641 or 607/739-7899.

Ellenville
Resnick Airport (N89)

Airport is located 1 mile northeast of town.

☞ *Airport Information:*

Location: New York sectional N41.43.67 W74.22.64
Attended: 1300Z* to dusk
Elevation: 292 feet
Fuel: 100LL
TPA: 1500 feet msl
Runway: 04-22: 3850 x 75 asph
FBO: Rondout Aviation
914/647-2100

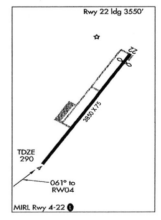

☞ *Communication:*

CTAF: 122.8
Unicom: 122.8
App/Dep: New York 32.75

☞ *Transportation:*
Taxi: 914/647-5757
Car Rental: Enterprise 914/374-5010

☞ *Lodging:*
Call the **American Country Collection of B & B's** 800/810-4948 for reservations throughout the Hudson Valley and Eastern New York.

PINEGROVE DUDE RANCH

(approximately 5 miles from airport)
Lower Cherrytown Road, Kerhonkson, NY 12446; Tel: 914/626-7345
or 800/346-4626; Internet: www.pinegrove-ranch.com

This all-inclusive ranch offers a complete program of sports, games, arts & crafts, and entertainment for all ages. Ever wanted to be a cowboy when you grow up? This is the place to fulfill your cattle driving dreams. Other activities include golf, fishing, skeet shooting, skiing, archery, dance lessons, basketball, and lots more. Birds and wildlife are abundant on the 600-acre preserve. No hunting on this property!

WHILE YOU'RE THERE: Contact **Mountain Wings** 914/647-3377 for hang gliding and para-gliding lessons.

Farmingdale
Republic Airport (FRG)

Airport is located 1 mile east of town.

☞ *Airport Information:*

Location: New York sectional N40.43.73 W73.24.81

NY

Airspace: Class D service
1200-0400Z*

Attended: Continuously
Elevation: 82 feet
Fuel: 100LL, Jet A
TPA: 1100 feet msl lgt acft
1600 feet msl turbine acft
Runway: 14-32: 6827 x 150 asph
01-19: 5516 x 150 asph
FBO: Million Air North
516/752-9022

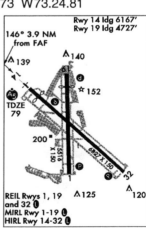

☞ *Communication:*
CTAF: 118.8
Unicom: 122.95
App/Dep: New York App 127.4, 132.4, 134.35, 123.7, 118.4
New York Dep 125.7, 134.35, 123.7
Clnc Del: 128.25

161

Tower: 118.8, 125.2 (1200-0400Z*)
Ground: 121.6
ATIS: 126.65 (1200-0400Z*)

☞ *Transportation:*
Taxi: 516/249-1212
Car Rental: Sears Car Rental 516/752-1867

☞ *Lodging:*
Huntington: **Huntington Hilton** 516/845-1000

BETHPAGE STATE PARK GOLF COURSE
(approximately 2 miles from airport)
Farmingdale, NY 11735; Tel: 516/249-0707

There are 5 public courses in this state park. The Black Course (18 holes, par 71) is rated 4½ stars and "super value" by *Golf Digest*. It is a regular site for major tournaments — as good as or better than some fine private courses in the area — and will host the 2002 U.S. Open. The style is traditional with narrow fairways and wooded, hilly terrain. Come early or expect a wait to play. Bethpage has four more 8-hole courses, all of them popular.

OLD WESTBURY GARDENS

(approximately 8 miles from airport)
P.O. Box 430, Old Westbury, NY 11568; Tel: 516/333-0048
Open from late April to Christmas. Closed on Tuesdays.
Admission is $10 for adults, $6 for children (combination house and garden ticket). Garden only tickets are $6 for adults and $3 for children.

With its elegant Charles II style mansion and outstanding gardens on 150 rolling acres, Old Westbury Gardens is a magnificent example of the finest landscape design. Wonderful garden benches offer lovely views of formal gardens, ponds, arbors, meadows, woodlands, and sweeping lawns. The Phipps family built the estate in 1904 and English furniture and paintings by Reynolds and Gainsborough furnish the rooms. Especially smashing is spring with its beds of bulbs in formal parterres. Old Westbury Gardens is rarely without color during the growing season. Separate fees admit visitors to the house or gardens. Workshops and "Talk & Tours" are scheduled throughout the season.

Glen Falls
Floyd Bennet Airport (GFL)

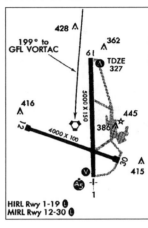

Airport is located 3 miles northeast of town.

☞ *Airport Information:*

Location: New York sectional N43.20.47 W73.36.62
Attended: 1200-0000Z*
Elevation: 328 feet
Fuel: 100LL, Jet A
TPA: 1128 feet msl
Runway: 01-19: 5000 x 150 asph
　　　　　12-30: 4000 x 100 asph
FBO: Empire East Aviation
　　　　518/798-3091

☞ *Communication:*

CTAF: 123.0
Unicom: 123.0
App/Dep: Albany 125.0

☞ *Transportation:*

Taxi: 518/793-4646; 518/793-9601
Car Rental: Maltbie Chevrolet 518/668-5736

NY

☞ *Lodging:*

Lake George: The **Clinton Inn** 518/668-2412 has a private sand beach and heated pool. Quiet lakeside accommodations can be found at the **Still Bay Resort** 518/668-2584 or 800/521-7511. **Holiday Inn** 518/668-5781

THE GREAT ESCAPE SPLASHWATER KINGDOM
(approximately 8 miles from airport)
Route 9, P.O. Box 511, Lake George, NY 12845; Tel: 518/792-3500
Open Memorial Day through Labor Day.
Admission is $25.99 for people taller than 48" and $18.99 for 48" and under.

Ride the world's #1 wooden coaster, Corkscrew Loop Coaster, or any of the 125 rides. Cool off at the 5-story water adventure or in the wave pool.

WHILE YOU'RE THERE: Rent wave runners or water skis from **Mike's Lake Sports** 518/668-4919. Contact **Lake George Shoreline Cruises** 518/668-4644 for sightseeing, sunset, or entertainment cruises. Take advantage of the scenic trails overlooking Lake George on horseback — **Saddle Up Stables** 518/668-4801.

Lake Placid Airport (LKP)

Airport is located 1 mile southeast of town.

☞ *Airport Information:*

Location:	Montreal sectional N44.15.87 W73.57.71
Attended:	Jul-Aug 1300-0100Z*; Sep-Jun 1400-2200Z*
Elevation:	1744 feet
Fuel:	100LL
TPA:	2700 feet msl
Runway:	14-32: 4200 x 60 asph
FBO:	Adirondack Flying Service 518/523-2473

☞ *Communication:*

CTAF:	122.8
Unicom:	122.8

☞ *Transportation:*

Taxi:	518/523-3333
Car Rental:	Hertz 518/523-3158

☞ *Lodging:*

Lake Placid: Located on the shores of the lake and within the Olympic Village is the **Wildwood On the Lake** 518/523-2624. Rowboats, canoes and paddleboats are free for guests. The *New York Times* called genteel **Mirror Lake Inn** 518/523-2544 "a classic." It's Lake Placid's only AAA 4-diamond resort. **Econo Lodge** 518/523-2817; **Ramada Inn** 518/523-2587; **Four Seasons Motor Lodge** 518/946-2247 or 800/4S-LODGE; or contact the Central Reservation Service 800/44-PLACID.

☞ *Restaurants:*

Lake Placid: **The Cottage** 518/523-9845, with a view of Mirror Lake, serves sandwiches and salads. Mirror Lake is where the U.S. canoe and kayaking teams practice. New American cuisine with

Adirondack flair is served at the **Lake Placid Lodge** 518/523-2700.

ADIRONDACK MOUNTAIN CLUB
P.O.Box 867, Lake Placid, NY 12946; Tel: 518/523-3441

This is the best source for information on hiking and other outdoor activities in the region. It's a non-profit organization with 22,000 members and a leader in teaching outdoor skills and promoting outdoor recreation. You don't have to be a member to participate in their workshops and programs: rock climbing and guided hikes during the summer and skiing, snowshoeing, winter hiking and camping during the winter. A fishing license is required for their ice fishing sessions.

HIGH FALLS GORGE
(waterfalls 9 miles from the airport)
Route 86, Wilmington, NY 12997; Tel: 518/946-2278; Internet: www. lakeplacid.ny.us/highfallsgorge
Daily from Memorial Day to Columbus Day.
Admission $5.50 for adults, $3.50 for juniors.

Self-guided scenic tours along the Ausable River as it cascades over three waterfalls, plunging 700 feet between high granite cliffs. Gift shop, restaurant, and picnic area.

HIGH PEAKS MOUNTAIN ADVENTURES
331 Main Street, Lake Placid, NY 12946; Tel: 518/523-3764 Internet: www.hpmac.com

This company offers guided rock climbing, sea kayaking, hiking, mountain biking, rafting, and horseback riding. Practice your rock climbing at their indoor gym first, if you like. Equipment rental and purchase available.

JONES OUTFITTERS
(fly-fishing, fishing, canoeing, and kayaking)
37 Main Street, Lake Placid, NY 12946; Tel: 518/523-3468

Big trout abound in a special section of the Ausable River for catch and release. Instruction in fly-fishing as well as canoeing and kayaking available. Rentals and sales of canoes, kayaks and fishing gear and bait. Fishing licenses are sold as well. Call the fishing hotline 518/891-5413 for straight talk on fishing hotspots. Jones Outfitters is the oldest Orvis shop in the country (since 1958)!

NY

OLYMPIC SPEED SKATING OVAL/OLYMPIC CENTER
(approximately 1 mile from the airport)
In front of the Olympic Center in center of village. Lake Placid, NY 12946; Tel: 518/523-1655

Skate outdoors where American speedskater Eric Heiden won a record five gold medals in the 1980 Games or watch training and competitions. Public skating in the early evening and afternoon sessions on the weekend. Lessons and skate rentals. A hockey box at the center of the oval is available for practice and pick-up games. The oval is used for in-line rollerblading during the summer months.

OLYMPIC SPORTS COMPLEX AT MT. VAN HOVENBERG
(Bobsled, luge, cross-country skiing, biathlon, firing range, and mountain biking approximately 6 miles from the airport)
Lake Placid, NY; Tel: 518/523-4436
NOTE: The bobsled and luge runs were recently under renovation. Call ahead to confirm operations before you go.

If you really want to get your blood flowing, try North America's only public bobsled and luge runs. A professional driver will be with you on the bobsled, but on the luge, the closet thing to supersonic sledding, you are on your own. Appointments are necessary. Training and competitions are held throughout the winter, so you may just watch during those times. The cross-country skier will find 50 kilometers of groomed trails that connect to the Cascade Cross Country Center and the Jackrabbit trail. Snowmaking, rentals, ski-school, and warming lodge — it's all there. Be sure to call ahead, as major national and international competitions affect operation times. During the summer, wheeled bobsleds begin the descent at the half-mile start. At speeds over 45 mph, they are nearly as fast as during the winter. Mountainbiking is a great experience on the cross-country trails during the summer for all ages and experience levels. Rent a bike or bring your own.

WHITE FACE MOUNTAIN SKI CENTER
(skiing, hiking, and biking approximately 8 miles from the airport)
Wilmington, NY 12997; Tel: 518/946-2223

According to *Skiing Magazine* White Face Mountain has the East's biggest vertical drop of 3,216 feet and also some of the East's most interesting intermediate terrain. You can ski down the same slopes used for the alpine events during the 1980 Olympic Winter Games.

Sixty-five trails, the longest run 3 miles, are accessed by 10 lifts. Snowboarders are welcome and instruction is available for both snowboarding and skiing. How about enjoying the thrill of downhill mountain biking during the summer? Take the mid-station chairlift to a variety of intermediate and advanced trails. Bike rentals available. For summertime picnics take the chairlift to Little Whiteface. An observation deck opens onto beautiful scenery. The Stag Brook Falls nature trail, descending from mid-station, offers a fascinating and relatively easy hike alongside waterfalls and pools of Stag Brook.

WHILE YOU'RE THERE: Watch America's best ski jumpers and freestylers train and compete year-round on the jumps at the **Olympic Ski Jumping Complex and Kodak Sports Park** 518/523-2202. Freestylers end up in a 750,000-gallon pool during the summer! A chairlift and elevator ride up to the tower will reward you with excellent views. The **Olympic Center** 518/523-1655 has four indoor ice rinks and a museum. Watch hockey players, speed skaters, and figure skaters practice and compete year-round. Guided tours are available. Toboggan rides at **Lake Placid Toboggan Chute** 518/523-2591 will give you a thrill on Mirror Lake. **Lake Placid Snowmobiling** 518/523-3596 offers scenic tours. Hunting, fly-fishing, and charter fishing is available through **Placid Bay Ventures Guide Service** 518/523-1744. Windsurfers can be rented from **Mountain Run** 518/523-9443. **Middle Earth Expeditions** 518/523-9572 offers whitewater rafting, hunting, fishing, and mountaineering.

NY

Millbrook
Sky Acres Airport (44N)

Airport is located 6 miles southwest of town.

☞ *Airport Information:*
Location: New York sectional N41.42.45 W73.44.28
Attended: Mon-Fri 1430Z* to dusk; Sat-Sun 11300Z* to dusk
Elevation: 700 feet
Fuel: 100LL
TPA: 1500 feet msl
Runway: 17-35: 3828 x 60 asph
FBO: Her Gin Aviation 914/677-5010

☞ *Communication:*
CTAF: 122.8
Unicom: 122.8
App/Dep: New York 132.75

☞ *Transportation:*
Taxi: 914/226-5773

☞ *Lodging:*
Call the **American Country Collection of Bed and Breakfasts** 800/810-4948 for reservations throughout the Hudson Valley and Eastern NY.

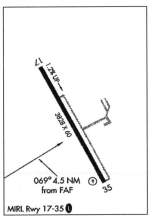

ORVIS SANDANONA FLY-FISHING AND SHOOTING SCHOOL
(approximately 7 miles from airport)
Millbrook, NY 12545; Tel: 800/235-9763

Orvis Sandanona is a 19th-century sporting preserve where you can improve your wing-shooting skills or fly-fishing. Their approach to shotgunning offers both the novice and the seasoned veteran a complete shooting system applicable to upland hunting, water-fowling, or sport clays. The program includes footwork, stance, gun handling, swing, visual concentration, proper gun mounting, and correct fit of the shot gun. Fly-fishing is taught in casting pools as well as classrooms. You'll learn essential knots, casting techniques, choosing gear and tackle, gamefish identification, proper fly selection, and how to read water and stream entomology. Two-day classes from April to August.

Montauk Airport (MTP)
Airport is located 3 miles northeast of town.

☞ *Airport Information:*
Location: New York sectional N41.04.59 W71.55.25
Attended: Apr-Oct daylight hours; other times irregularly
Elevation: 20 feet
Fuel: None available
TPA: 1000 feet msl
Runway: 06-24: 3480 x 85 asph

168

FBO: 516/668-3738

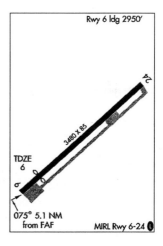

☞ *Communication:*
CTAF: 122.7
Unicom: 122.7
App/Dep: New York App 132.25
          Providence Dep 125.75
           (1100-0500Z*)
          Boston Ctr Dep 124.85
           (0500-1100Z*)

☞ *Transportation:*
Taxi: 516/668-3838
Car Rental: 516/668-2364

☞ *Lodging:*
Montauk: See **Gurney's Inn** 516/668-2345 below; **Daunts Albatross Resort Inn** 516/668-2729. **Montauk Manor** 516/668-4400 is an "all-suite" resort overlooking Gardiners Bay and Block Island, with unparalleled sunsets and heated pools.

☞ *Restaurants:*
Montauk: The freshest possible seafood is served in- or outdoors at **Gosman's Dock** 516/668-5330 at the entrance of Montauck Harbor. Expect a wait in season as reservations are not accepted. Restaurant is closed from mid-October to April.

NY

GURNEY'S INN
(International health and beauty spa 3 miles from airport)
290 Old Montauk Highway, Montauk, NY 11954; Tel: 516/668-2345; Internet: www.gurneysweb.com

Expect luxury pampering at Gurney's Inn, located at the tip of Long Island. The spa draws on the ocean for inspiration, and its diversity of seawater treatments makes Gurney's special on the East Coast. Additional therapies include massage, herbal and seaweed body wraps, seaweed baths and facials. Miles of wide sandy beaches invite you for a walk. Fishing is nearby. The spa building is a distance from the time-share buildings. The facilities can get crowded during the summer; two nights' minimum stay required on weekends.

MONTAUK DOWNS STATE PARK GOLF COURSE
(approximately 3 miles from the airport)
Fairview Ave., Montauk, NY 11954; Tel: 516/668-1100

Robert Trent Jones re-designed this public course in 1968; *Golf Digest* gave it four stars. Its sandy soil and rolling dunes make it close to a true course, although it has some parkland. It offers 18 holes at par 72 and of course beautiful views, thanks to its location at the eastern end of Long Island. Expect some wind to make things interesting.

WHILE YOU'RE THERE: Horseback riding through 4,000 acres of trails to the beach is possible at the **Deep Hollow Ranch** 516/668-2744. President George Washington ordered the **Montauk Point Lighthouse** 516/668-2428 to be built. On a clear day you may be able to see Rhode Island from the top after ascending 137 steps. **Viking Fishing Fleet Ferry Services** 516/668-5709 has fishing charters, cruises, and whale-watch trips.

Monticello
Sullivan County
Int'l Airport (MSV)

NY

Airport is located 6 miles northwest of field.

☞ *Airport Information:*

Location:	New York sectional N41.42.10 W74.47.70
Attended:	1300-2200Z*
Elevation:	1403 feet
Fuel:	100LL, Jet A
TPA:	2400 feet msl
Runway:	15-33: 6300 x 150 asph
FBO:	Woodstock Aircraft Services 914/583-5830

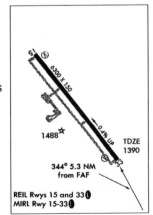

☞ *Communication:*

CTAF:	122.8
Unicom:	122.8
App/Dep:	New York 132.75
Clnc Del:	121.6

AWOS: 134.025

☞ *Transportation:*
Taxi: 914/292-8805; 914/794-4040
Car Rental: Budget 914/794-4424

☞ *Lodging:*
Kiamesha Lake: See **Concord Resort Hotel** 914/794-4000 below.

CONCORD RESORT HOTEL
(golf course approximately 10 miles from airport)
Concord Road, Kiamesha Lake, NY 12751; Tel: 914/794-4000

The famous "Monster" golf course received its name for a reason.
Unconscionably long (7,700 yards) and rather difficult, it is seldom
played full length and does not need to be. The course is already
very long if you start from the middle markers and demands strategic
ball placement on every shot. Don't expect a weak hole; you won't
get one. It is said to be one of the greatest courses of the Northeast,
with its challenge and beauty. It features 18 holes at par 72. First-
time visitors should use a yardage book or face a three-digit score.
The International and Challenger 9 are also on resort grounds. But
don't just visit this resort for good golfing. Tennis courts, jogging
trails, in- and outdoor swimming pools, horseback riding, bowling,
skeet shooting, shuffleboard, volleyball, miniature golf, hand- and
softball, exercise classes, and a health club chase boredom away.
Boating and fishing are excellent choices on Lake Kiamesha.
Outdoor ice-skating and four ski lifts are tempting during winter.
Children may enjoy a full program and their own supervised dining
room.

NY

WHILE YOU'RE THERE: Horse racing (harness racing) is
going on year-round at the **Monticello Raceway** 914/794-4100.

New Paltz
Stanton Airport (43N)

Airport is located 2 miles west of town.

☞ *Airport Information:*
Location: New York sectional N41.45.01 W74.06.98
Attended: Irregularly
Elevation: 303 feet
Fuel: None available
TPA: 1400 feet msl
Runway: 14-32: 2400 x 23 asph-gravel
FBO: Term Aviation 914/255-5687

☞ *Communication:*
CTAF: 122.9

☞ *Transportation:*
Taxi: 914/255-1550
Car Rental: Rent A Wreck 914/255-5666

☞ *Lodging:*
New Paltz: See **Mohonk Mountain House** 914/255-1000 below.
Days Inn 914/883-7373

☞ *Restaurants:*
New Paltz: Family-owned **Dominick's** 914/255-0120 menu features
Italian fare of seafood, poultry, and veal.

MOHONK MOUNTAIN HOUSE
(resort approximately 2 miles from airport)
Lake Mohonk, New Paltz, NY 12561; Tel: 914/255-1000
Admission charged.

Your rewards for landing on a 23-foot-wide runway are many. The
landscape is truly incredible: rocky cliffs rising above a crystal clear
lake surrounded by lush forest in the Shawangunk Mountains on the
edge of the Catskills. Mohonk was built in the late 1800s by two
Quaker brothers, who envisioned it as an unspoiled retreat where
visitors could enjoy the wonders of nature. Spectacular gardens (for
which the earth had to be trucked in), woodlands, and more than 100
gazebos can be enjoyed in every season. Early June rewards you

with mountain laurel in bloom. May offers old-fashioned favorites in the cultivated garden near the hotel. Victorian flower beds brim with annuals and fall colors are riotous. Trails for hiking and cross-country skiing are well marked. Golf, tennis, croquet, lawn bowling, swimming, boating, and ice skating round out your visit. Day passes are handed out for entrance to the gardens. Most weekends require a minimum of two nights' stay. Theme programs are held throughout the year. Call for details.

ROCKING HORSE RANCH RESORT
(approximately 4 miles from airport)
600 Route 44-55, Highland, NY 12528; Tel: 800/647-2624

All members of your family will find something to do at this all-inclusive resort. It's like the Club Med of Ranch Resorts and was voted "my favorite ranch resort" by readers of the *Family Circle Magazine*. The long list of activites includes: horseback riding, water skiing, paddle boats, fishing, tennis courts, handball courts, laser rifle range, archery range, croquet, miniature golf, private ski slope/lifts (100% snow making), ice skating, square dancing, sleigh rides, scavenger hunts, petting zoo, supervised day camp, 3 heated pools, hiking trails, nightly entertainment, and many scheduled activities. The atmosphere is casual and the scenery in the Shawangunk mountains glorious.

NY

WHILE YOU'RE THERE: Hiking, biking, mountain biking, horseback riding and boating (by permit), swimming, scuba, cross-country skiing, and rock climbing are possible at the **Minnewaska State Park Reserve** 914/255-0752. Contact the **Mountain Skills Climbing School** 914/687-9643 for rock and ice climbing. **Rivendale Vineyards and Winery** 914/255-2494 offers tours, tasting and wine sales.

Niagara Falls Int'l Airport (IAG)

Airport is located 4 miles east of town.
WARNING: FLIGHT RESTRICTIONS APPLY - Check current directories, sectionals and NOTAMS.

☞ *Airport Information:*

Location: Detroit sectional N43.06.44 W78.56.72
Airspace: Class D service 1200-0400Z*
Attended: Continuously
Elevation: 590 feet
Fuel: 100LL, Jet A
TPA: 1400 feet msl lgt acft
2100 feet msl jet acft
Runway: 10L-28R: 9125 x 140 asph-concrete
06-24: 5188 x 150 asph
10R-28L : 3973 x 75 asph
FBO: Niagara Frontier Transport Authority 716/297-4494

280° 4.1 NM from FAF
TDZE 588 624
9125 X 150
3973 X 75
101 10R 28L 28R
622 694
667 TWR 651

REIL Rwys 6, 10R, 24 and 28L
HIRL Rwy 10L-28R
MIRL Rwys 6-24 and 10R-28L

☞ *Communication:*

CTAF: 118.5
Unicom: 122.95
App/Dep: Buffalo 126.5
Tower: 118.5 (1200-0400Z*)
Clnc Del: 119.25
Ground: 121.7
ATIS: 120.8 (1200-0400Z*)

☞ *Transportation:*

Taxi: 716/285-9331; 716/284-8833
Car Rental: Budget 716/298-4258

☞ *Lodging:*

Niagara Falls: The top floors of the **Days Inn Falls View** 716/285-9321 offer views overlooking the upper rapids. Just steps away from the Falls, it features marble in the lobby and cathedral ceilings. Authentic Old English atmosphere and spectacular view of the upper rapids await you at the **Red Coach Inn** 716/282-1459. This 1923 inn has an outdoor patio for summer dining plus wood burning fireplaces. **Holiday Inn-Grand Island** 716/773-1111; **Quality Inn**

716/284-8801; **Ramada Inn** 716/282-1212; **Clarion Hotel** 716/285-3361

☞ *Restaurants:*
Niagara Falls: **Clarkson House** 716/754-4544 specializes in charboiled steak, seafood, and chicken. Open-hearth cooking. An Italian American menu is served at the **Como** 716/285-9341. **Hard Rock Cafe** 716/282-0007

AQUARIUM OF NIAGARA FALLS
(approximately 5 miles from airport)
701 Whirlpool Street, Niagara Falls, NY 14301; Tel: 716/285-3575;
Internet: www.niagaranet.com/niagara/aquarium.html
Open daily, except Christmas and Thanksgiving.
Admission is $6.50 for adults and $4.50 for ages 4 to 12 years old.

The world's first inland oceanarium has dolphin, electric eel, and sea lion shows. There are also shark and river otter feedings, as well as interactive Great Lakes fish displays and a New England tidal pool. Two thousand marine creatures!

ARTPARK
(summer theater approximately 5 miles from airport)
P.O. Box 371, Lewistown, NY 14092; Tel: 716/754-9000 or 800/659-7252
Shows from May-October.

A 200-acre state park and summer theater is located on Robert Moses Parkway. The Artpark is devoted to visual and performing arts and has a 2,300-seat theater with lawn seating. You can attend musicals, classical concerts by the Buffalo Philharmonic Orchestra, dance programs, and jazz and pop concerts.

CAVES OF WIND TOUR
(approximately 5 miles from airport)
Niagara Reservation State Park, P.O. Box 1132, Niagara Falls, NY 14303; Tel: 716/278-1770
Open May to mid-October, hours depending on season.

The Caves of the Wind Tour takes visitors into the spray of Bridal Veil Falls. You will be outfitted with yellow raincoats for a body-soaking trek that includes an option to walk to Hurricane Deck. This is as close to the falls as you'll ever (want to) get. Trip starts on Goat Island, which also has excellent hiking trails.

MAID OF MIST TOUR
(approximately 5 miles from airport)
151 Buffalo Avenue, Niagara Falls, NY 14303; Tel: 716/284-8897
Spring to late October.
Tickets are $8 for adults, and $4.50 for children.

This is the half-hour, world-famous boat tour that takes you to the
base of the Falls on the Niagara River. The American Falls are 180
feet high, 1,100 feet wide at the brink, with the Canadian Falls right
next to them. Rain ponchos are handed out, as the mist will cover
you. It is quite some sight, sound, and experience. Boats leave every
15 minutes from the base of the observation tower at Prospect
Point.

NIAGARA HISTORIC WALKING TOURS
(approximately 5 miles from airport)
Niagara Reservation State Park at Prospect Point, Niagara Falls, NY
14301; Tel: 716/278-1770
Daily April to October.

One-hour walking tours of the park highlighting views of the Falls,
geology, dare-deviltry, rescues, industry, and hydroelectricity.

RIVER OAKS GOLF CLUB
NY
(approximately 4 miles from airport)
210 Whitehaven Road, Grand Island, NY 14072; Tel: 716/773-3336
Closed during the winter months.

This course is located off scenic Niagara River and is one of the top-
ranked layouts in western New York State. It's a par 72, 18-hole
course surrounded by large oaks and maple trees and was designed
by Desmund Muirhead.

WHILE YOU'RE THERE: Use the Master Pass Niagara
716/278-1770 for savings at all State Park attractions. Can be
purchased at any park attraction.

Red Hook
Sky Park Airport (46N)

Airport is located 2 miles east of town.

☞ *Airport Information:*

Location: New York sectional N41.59.08 W73.50.16
Attended: 1330-2200Z*
Elevation: 323 feet
Fuel: 100LL
TPA: 1523 feet msl
Runway: 01-19: 2664 x 30 asph
FBO: Red Hook Air Service
914/876-1800

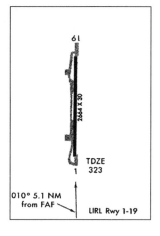

☞ *Communication:*

CTAF: 122.8
Unicom: 122.8
App/Dep: New York 132.75

☞ *Transportation:*
Taxi: 914/758-1478

☞ *Lodging:*
Red Hook: **Red Hook Inn** 914/758-8445

OLD RHINEBECK AERODROME
(aviation museum approximately 6 miles from airport)
Stone Church Road, Rhinebeck, NY 12572; Tel: 914/758-8610
Open mid-May through October.
Admission is $4 for adults, $2 for children 6 to 10 years old.

Cole Palen started to collect, restore, build, and fly antique airplanes over 40 years ago and is the founder of the museum. On display at the Aerodrome are 54 World War I and earlier aircraft as well as engines and cars. Weekend airshows are held from mid-June through October, flying original aircraft or accurate copies powered with original engines.

Saranac Lake
Adirondack Regional
Airport (SLK)

Airport is located 4 miles northwest of town.

☞ *Airport Information:*

Location: Montreal sectional N44.23.12 W74.12.37
Attended: 1200-0130Z*
Elevation: 1663 feet
Fuel: 100LL, Jet A
TPA: 2463 feet msl light acft
2663 feet msl heavy acft
Runway: 05-23: 6573 x 150 asph
09-27: 3998 x 100 asph
FBO: 518/891-4600

☞ *Communication:*

CTAF: 123.0
Unicom: 123.0
App/Dep: Boston Center 120.35
ASOS: 124.175

229° 5.9 NM
from FAF

TDZE
1663

6573 X 150

3998 X 100

0.4% UP

1642

1700

HIRL Rwy 5-23
MIRL Rwy 9-27

NY

☞ *Transportation:*

Taxi: 518/891-2444
Car Rental: Hertz 518/891-9044

☞ *Lodging:*

Saranac Lake: Onetime home of William Avery Rockefeller, **The Point** 518/891-5674 or 800/255-3530 is an exclusive hideaway resort located on a 10-acre wooded peninsula on Upper Saranac Lake. The buildings are made of local stone and wood. **Land's End** 518/891-4059 was built in 1932 as a hunting camp for the Du Pont family. A non-smoking-only facility, it is furnished in Adirondack style. **Sara-Placid Motor Inn** 518/891-2729 or 800/794-2729; **Adirondack Comfort Inn** 518/891-1970 or 800/221-2222

☞ *Restaurants:*

Saranac Lake: The **Owl's Nest** 518/891-5500 features pizza with fresh toppings on homemade dough.

LAKE PLACID RANCH
(outdoor activities approximately 3 miles from airport)
RR#1 - Box 282, Lake Clear, NY 12983; Tel 518/891-5684, 800/613-6033; Internet: www.dude.dude-ranches.com

Outdoor activity is the name of the game at this ranch. During the summer you can experience the Adirondacks on horses for cattle drives or just riding. Located on a 150-acre private estate, Lake Placid Ranch is the Tri-Lakes' largest riding stable. During winter try Yamaha snowmobiles, sleigh rides, or even dogsledding. Free boots and helmets for snowmobiling, hot chocolate, and free childcare make things easy.

WHILE YOU'RE THERE: The Willard Hanmer Guideboat, Canoe, & War Canoe Races are held annually on Lake Flower and Saranac River in early July. The 90-mile Adirondack Canoe Classic from Old Forge to Saranac Lake is held the 2nd week in September. The Saranac Lake Winter Carnival is the oldest annual winter carnival in the Eastern USA. The hallmark of the Carnival is the Ice Palace, built in the village on the shore of Lake Flower, which can attain heights of over 60 feet. Call the **Chamber of Commerce** 518/891-1990 for more information.

Saratoga Springs
Saratoga County
Airport (5B2)

NY

Airport is located 3 miles southwest of town.

☞ *Airport Information:*

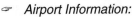

Location:	New York sectional N43.03.08 W73.51.67
Attended:	1230Z* to dusk
Elevation:	433 feet
Fuel:	100LL, Jet A
TPA:	1200 feet msl
Runway:	05-23: 4700 x 100 asph-conc
Runway:	14-32: 4000 x 100 asph-conc
FBO:	Richmor Aviation
	518/885-5354

☞ *Communication:*
CTAF: 122.8
Unicom: 122.8
App/Dep: Albany 118.05
Clnc Del: 132.025
AWOS: 132.025

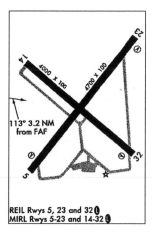

113° 3.2 NM
from FAF

REIL Rwys 5, 23 and 32 ❶
MIRL Rwys 5-23 and 14-32 ❶

☞ *Transportation:*
Taxi: 518/584-2700
Car Rental: Hertz 518/792-8525

☞ *Lodging:*
Saratoga Springs: **Gideon Putnam
Hotel** 518/584-3000 or 800/732-1560

☞ *Restaurants:*
Saratoga Springs: A local favorite, **Eartha's Kitchen** 518/583-0602, is a small bistro serving an eclectic, ever-changing menu. Open Wed-Sat only.

SARATOGA PERFORMING ARTS CENTER
(approximately 5 miles from airport)
Saratoga Springs, NY 12866; Tel: 518/587-3330;
Internet:www.spac.org
Summer only.

Saratoga Springs is the home of the giant amphitheater hosting the New York City Opera, New York City Ballet, the Philadelphia Orchestra, Saratoga Jazz Festival, and Saratoga Chamber Music Festival. All performances are rain or shine.

WHILE YOU'RE THERE: Thoroughbred and harness racing goes on from March to November at the **Saratoga Harness Raceway** 518/584-2110. The season for thoroughbred racing at the **Saratoga Race Course** 518/584-6200 starts in mid-July and lasts six weeks.

Schenectady Co. Airport (SCH)

Airport is located 3 miles north of town.

☞ *Airport Information:*

Location: New York sectional N42.51.16 W73.55.77
Airspace: Class D service 1230-0330Z*
Attended: 1230-0000Z*
Elevation: 378 feet
Fuel: 100LL, Jet A
TPA: 1300 feet msl lgt acft
1500 feet msl hvy acft
Runway: 04-22: 7000 x 150 asph
10-28: 4840 x 150 asph
FBO: Fortune Air 518/374-7815
Richmor Aviation
518/399-8171

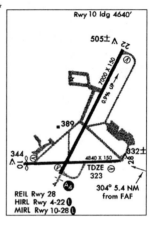

Rwy 10 ldg 4640'

REIL Rwy 28
HIRL Rwy 4-22
MIRL Rwy 10-28

☞ *Communication:*

CTAF: 121.3
Unicom: 122.95
App/Dep: Albany 118.05
Tower: 121.3 (1230-0330Z*)
Ground: 121.9
AWOS: 119.275

NY

☞ *Transportation:*
Taxi: 518/382-8231

EMPIRE STATE AEROSCIENCES MUSEUM
(located on field)
130 Saratoga Road, Scotia, NY 12302; Tel: 518/377-2191
Open year-round Tuesday to Saturday. Open Sundays from May to October.
Admission is $3 for adults, $1 for children.

The outdoor area of the museum features a display of fighter planes, helicopters, and aircraft dating from WW II. Films are shown in the 30-seat theater. There's a space flight simulator you can try. An aviation research library, historical artifacts, memorabilia, and a restoration center are part of the museum as well.

Watertown Int'l Airport

(ART)
Airport is located 5 miles west of town.

☞ *Airport Information:*

Location: New York sectional N43.59.52 W76.01.30
Attended: 1300Z* to dusk
Elevation: 325 feet
Fuel: 100LL, Jet A
TPA: 1225 feet msl
Runway: 07-25: 5000 x 150 asph
Runway: 10-28: 4997 x 150 asph
FBO: Brouty Aircraft Services
315/639-3783

☞ *Communication:*

CTAF: 123.0
Unicom: 123.0
App/Dep: Wheeler-Sack 128.2

☞ *Transportation:*

Taxi: 315/782-2121
Car Rental: 315/788-8412

☞ *Lodging:*

Watertown: **Longway's Motel** 315/788-2910

ADIRONDACK RIVER OUTFITTERS

(approximately 5 miles from airport)
P.O. Box 649, Old Forge, NY 13420; Tel: 800/525-RAFT; Internet:
www.aroaadventures.com
Open May to October. Reservations required.

Raft the Black River for eight miles with no less than 14 sets of
rapids. Bring an adventurous attitude for a day of exhilarating
whitewater. Be aware that melting snow creates high water and the
intensity of the Black River quadruples at that time. The class III to IV
rapids in the spring are powerful and continuous. Unexpected swims
are definitely a possibility. Previous rafting experience is
recommended in the spring, with the age minimum set at 16 years.
The rest of the year the age minimum is 14 years and experience is
not required. Trips originate in Watertown.

Asheboro Munic.
Airport (W44)

Airport is located 6 miles southwest of town.

☞ *Airport Information:*

Location: Charlotte sectional N35.39.23   W79.53.70
Attended: 1300Z* to dusk.
Closed Christmas.
Elevation: 673 feet
Fuel: 100LL, Jet A
TPA: 1500 feet msl
Runway: 03-21: 5001 x 75 asph
FBO: Asheboro Air Service
910/625-6120

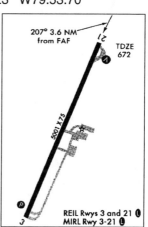

☞ *Communication:*

CTAF: 122.8
Unicom: 122.8
App/Dep: Greensboro 118.5
AWOS: 119.275

NC

☞ *Transportation:*
Taxi: 910/672-8294
Car Rental: Enterprise 910/625-0560

☞ *Lodging:*
Asheboro: **Hampton Inn** 910/625-9000; **Days Inn** 910/629-2101

☞ *Restaurants:*
Asheboro: The **Prime Sirloin** 910/626-3769 is a good choice for steak lovers.

PFAC FLYING MUSEUM
(located on field)
P. O. Box 1814, Asheboro, NC 27204; Tel: 336/625-0170
Open daily.

Admission is $5 for adults, children under 10 years free.

Step back into aviation past to see the planes that preserved our freedom. The PFAC - Peddycord Foundation for Aircraft Conservation Flying Museum has a unique collection of military memorabilia and aircraft. On display are a B-25 Mitchell Bomber, Republic F84-F Jet, Vultee BT-13A, North American A-T6G Texan, Grumman TBM Avenger, Piper Flitfire, Cessna O-2A Navy, PT 13D Stearman, and Cessna Birddog L19A. The foundation is also the sponsor of the Warbird Air Show during the first weekend in June.

Asheville Regional Airport (AVL)

Airport is located 9 miles south of town.

☞ *Airport Information:*

Location: Atlanta sectional N35.26.17 W82.32.51
Airspace: Class C service 1130-0400Z*
Other times Class G
Attended: Continuously
Elevation: 2165 feet
Fuel: 100LL, Jet A
TPA: 3000 feet msl lgt acft
3400 feet msl hvy acft
Runway: 16-34: 8001 x 150 asph
FBO: Asheville Jet Center
828/684-6832

☞ *Communication:*
CTAF: 121.1
Unicom: 122.95
App/Dep: 125.8 (340-159º), 124.65 (160-339º), 1130-0400Z*
Atlanta Center 132.625 (0400-1130Z*)
Tower: 121.1 (1130-0400Z*)
Ground: 121.9
ATIS: 120.2 (1130-0400Z*)

☞ *Transportation:*
Taxi: 828/681-0051
Car Rental: Avis 828/684-7144; Budget 828/684-2272

NC

☞ *Lodging:*
Asheville: **Fairfield Inn** 828/684-1144; **Holiday Inn** 828/684-1213;
Days Inn Airport 828/684-2281; **Cedar Crest B & B** 828/252-1389;
Howard Johnson-Biltmore 828/274-2300. **Quality Inn Biltmore**
828/274-1800 is located besides Biltmore Estate.

☞ *Restaurants:*
Asheville: Various upscale or gourmet eateries are located on
Biltmore Estate 800/543-2961. Try the vegetarian food at the
Laughing Seed Cafe 828/252-3445. **Salsas** 828/252-9805 is a busy
Mexican place.

BILTMORE ESTATE
(largest "home" in America approximately 12 miles from airport)
One North Pack Square, Asheville, NC 28801; Tel: 800/543-2961;
Internet: www.biltmore.com
Admission is $29.95 with prices varying for special events.
Open daily except Thanksgiving and Christmas.

Built in the 1890s as the home of George Vanderbilt, Biltmore Estate
was the embodiment of this era and quickly became a vibrant center
of society, entertainment, and the arts. Start with a self-guided tour
of this 250-room French Renaissance-style chateau filled with
priceless antiques and art. Then visit the gardens, landscaped by
Frederick Law Olmsted, designer of New York's Central Park. The
seven gardens, esplanades, and terraces on over 70 acres include a
shrub garden, formal walled garden, an Italian garden's pools, a
conservatory, and a 2,000-bush rose garden. The azalea garden is
home to the world's most complete collection of native azaleas. The
winery, which has been in existence only for twelve years, is open for
year-round tastings and behind-the-scenes tours. George
Vanderbuilt didn't build Biltmore Estate to spend his wealth; he built it
for a place to spend his time and watch the kaleidoscopic turning of
the seasons, which are a joy to admire to this day. Seasonal events
are held throughout the year.

NC

PACK PLACE EDUCATION, ARTS & SCIENCE CENTER
(approximately 9 miles from airport)
2 S. Pack Square, Asheville, NC 28801; Tel: 828/257-4500
Admission charged.

This is the site of five attractions in one complex. The Asheville Art
Museum houses 20th-century art by American artists, contemporary

crafts, and art related to the Southeast region. Gems and minerals are on display at the Colburn Gem & Mineral Museum. Other options are Health Adventure, the Diana Wortham Theatre, or the Y.M.I. Cultural Center.

WHILE YOU'RE THERE: Admire a 10-acre garden of plants native to the Appalachian Region at the **Botanical Gardens** 828/252-5190. Admission is free. The popular **Mountain Dance and Folk Festival** 828/258-6101 or 800/257-1300 in August features bluegrass and traditional dancing.

Charlotte
Douglas Int'l Airport (CLT)
Airport is located 4 miles west of town.

☞ *Airport Information:*

Location: Charlotte sectional N35.12.84 W80.56.59
Airspace: Class B
Attended: Continuously
Elevation: 749 feet
Fuel: 100LL, Jet A
TPA: 2300 feet msl
Runway: 18R-36L: 10000 x 150 asph
18L-36R: 8676 x 150 asph
05-23: 7501 x 150 asph
FBO: Signature Flight Support
704/359-8670

☞ *Communication:*

Unicom: 122.95
App: Charlotte 126.15 (360-179⁰ above 8000')
125.35 (180-359⁰ above 8000')
Dep: Charlotte 124.0 (360-179⁰ above 8000')
120.5 (180-359⁰ above 8000')
App/Dep: Charlotte 120.05 (360-179⁰ 8000' and below)
134.75 (180-359⁰ 8000' and below)
Tower: 118.1 (Rwys 18L-36R, 05-23), 126.4 (Rwy 18R-36L)

Ground: 121.9 (360-179°), 121.8 (180-359°)
Clnc Del: 127.15
ATIS: Arrival 121.15, departure 132.1

☞ *Transportation:*
Taxi: 704/333-1111; 704/332-8001
Car Rental: Alamo 704/359-9985; Dollar 704/359-4700
        Avis 704/359-4580

☞ *Lodging:*
Charlotte: **Sheraton Airport Plaza** 704/392-1200. The **Days Inn Central** 704/333-4733 and **Doubletree Hotel** 704/347-0070 have downtown locations.
Fort Mill, SC: **Comfort Inn** 803/548-5200, **Holiday Inn Express** 803/548-0100; both hotels are near the theme park.

☞ *Restaurants:*
Charlotte: Waiters that sing will serve you at the upscale **Bravo** 704/372-5440 inside the Adams Mark Hotel. The **Southend Brewery & Smokehouse** 704/358-HOPS serves the usual pub fare.

CAROLINAS AVIATION MUSEUM
(adjacent to airport)
4108 Airport Drive, Charlotte, NC 28208; Tel: 704/359-8442; Internet: www.webserve.net/cam. Open daily.

Aviation history comes alive with a variety of aircraft, military and aviation-oriented memorabilia. On display is a replica of the Wright Glider, the Wright Brothers' early attempt at achieving flight. See helicopters from the Vietnam War era, the world's largest single engine biplane, and a 1944 Link Trainer used by the military to train its pilots in WW II. Aircraft engines of various sizes are on exhibit as well as a "hands on" jet flight simulator. The museum is also an aircraft restoration facility.

NC

CAROWINDS
(water and theme park approximately 8 miles from airport)
P.O. Box 410289, Charlotte, NC 28241; Tel: 800/888-4FUN or 704/588-2600; Internet: www.carowinds.com
Open mid-March through October. Water Works is open from end of April through September. Call for operating days.
Admission, including Water Works, is $31.99 for adults, $19.99 for children under 48" tall.

Paramount's Carowinds has more than 50 thrilling rides, including six extreme roller coasters that will test your adrenaline output. There is also action-packed adventure in the motion simulator theater, a Paramount Theatre, nine football fields worth of water fun, and various shows and attractions.

WHILE YOU'RE THERE: An Omnimax theater, indoor rainforest, hands-on science museum, and other fun things can be experienced by visiting **Discovery Place** 800/935-0553 or 704/372-6261. Kids especially will enjoy this place.

Hatteras
Billy Mitchell Airport (HSE)

Airport is located 4 miles east of town.
Caution: Watch for airport closure at night.

☞ *Airport Information:*
Location: Charlotte sectional N35.13.97 W75.37.07
Attended: Unattended
Elevation: 17 feet
Fuel: Unavailable
TPA: 800 feet msl
Runway: 07-25: 3000 x 75 asph

☞ *Communication:*
CTAF: 122.9
App/Dep: Washington Center 135.5
ASOS: 118.375

☞ *Transportation:*
Taxi: 252/995-6047

☞ *Lodging:*
Buxton: Within walking distance of the beach, the **Comfort Inn - Hatteras Island** 919/995-6100 is a pretty, gray shingled building. The **Cape Hatteras Motel** 919/995-5611 offers apartments and efficiencies and due to its location is a favorite with windsurfers. **Cape Hatteras B & B** 919/995-6004 or 800/252-3316 is an 8-room inn located 500 feet from the ocean.
Hatteras: **Holiday Inn** 252/986-1110

☞ *Restaurants:*
Buxton: Naturally, fresh fish and seafood are the specialty at **Billy's Fish House** 919/995-5151. **Smokin' Chicken** 919/995-5502
Hatteras: Seafood platters, hush-puppies and crab imperial are famous at the **Channel Bass Restaurant** 919/986-2250. **Rocco's Pizza Inc.** 919/986-2150 has all sorts of Italian food. A nightly seafood buffet is available at **Sonny's Waterfront Restaurant** 919/986-2922.

FOX WATER SPORTS
(water sport rentals approximately 5 miles from airport)
Highway 12, Buxton, NC 27920; Tel: 919/995-4102

The Cape Hatteras Lighthouse in Buxton is one of the favorite places in the Outer Banks for surfing and fishing. Rent surfboards and other water sports equipment from Fox Water Sports. Windsurfing is famous at the Canadian Hole, on the Pamlico Sound side of Hatteras Island. Or just enjoy bird-watching, shelling, and sunbathing on the beautiful and endless beaches.

HATTERAS HARBOR MARINA
(approximately 5 miles from airport)
P.O. Box 537, Hatteras, NC 27943; Tel: 800/676-4939

Hatteras Village is perhaps best known for having the only charter fishing fleet on Hatteras Island. Take a boat to the nearby Gulf Stream waters for exciting deep sea fishing for the famous blue and white marlin, dolphin, sailfish, wahoo, tuna, and others. Fall and spring are the best times for surf and pier fishing, while off-shore fishing is best in summer.

WHILE YOU'RE THERE: Whether riding on the beach or in the maritime forest, it is always a treat. Contact **Buxton Stables** at 919/995-4659. **Cape Hatteras Lighthouse** 919/995-4474, at 208 feet, is the tallest in America. Climb the stairs for a view over the Atlantic Ocean. A **visitor center** 919/473-4474 displays the island's maritime history. The **Graveyard of the Atlantic Museum** 919/986-2995 is dedicated to maritime history and shipwrecks of the Outer Banks, with emphasis on the periods from 1524 to 1945.

Hendersonville Airport

(0A7)
Airport is located 2 miles east of town.

☞ *Airport Information:*
Location: Atlanta sectional N35.18.46 W82.25.99
Attended: 1330-2230Z*
Elevation: 2084 feet
Fuel: 100LL
TPA: 3000 feet msl
Runway: 14-32: 3075 x 40 asph
FBO: Aerolina 828/693-1897

☞ *Communication:*
CTAF: 123.0
Unicom: 123.0

☞ *Transportation:*
Taxi: 828/693-3221
Car Rental: U-Save 828/696-2200

☞ *Lodging:*
Hendersonville: **Weeping Creek Cottages** 828/693-0496 or
800/988-4585 rents cottages. Bikes and a pool are available. The
Westhaven B & B 828/693-8791 has 4 rooms to rent. **Comfort Inn**
828/693-8800

NC

WESTERN NORTH CAROLINA AIR MUSEUM

(located adjacent to airport)
1340 Gilbert Street, Hendersonville, NC 28792; Tel: 828/698-2482
Open Sat, Sun and Wed.
Admission is free.

This is the first air museum in the state. Featured are its vintage,
replica, and antique airplanes. Some fly regularly from the grass field
at the museum.

WHILE YOU'RE THERE: Historic Johnson Farm 828/891-
6585, a late 19th-century tobacco farm, is operated year-round as a
heritage education center and farm museum.

Kill Devil Hills
First Flight Airport (FFA)

Airport is located 1 mile west of town.
Caution: Watch for airport closure during night time.

☞ *Airport Information:*
Location: Charlotte sectional N36.01.09 W75.40.28
Attended: Unattended
Elevation: 13 feet
Fuel: Unavailable
TPA: 813 feet msl
Runway: 02-20: 3000 x 60 asph

☞ *Communication:*
CTAF: 122.9

☞ *Transportation:*
Taxi: 252/261-3133
Car Rental: Outer Banks Chrysler 252/441-1146
B & R 252/473-2141

☞ *Lodging:*
__Kill Devil Hills:__ The **Comfort Inn** 919/480-2600 has an oceanfront
location. **First Flight Inn** 252/441-5007; **Days Inn Mariner** 252/441-
2021; **Days Inn** 252/441-7211; **Ramada Inn** 252/441-2151
__Nags Head:__ A nostalgic, 1932-built B & B is the **First Colony Inn**
252/441-9234 or 800/368-9390. The **Quality Inn** 252/441-7191
features a private gazebo on the 450-foot beach.

NC

☞ *Restaurants:*
__Kill Devil Hills:__ **Dare Devil's Pizzeria** 252/441-6330 has subs and
stromboli as well as pizzas. Steak lovers, stop by the **Western
Sizzlin Restaurant** 252/441-4594.
__Nags Head:__ For delicious steamers visit **Lance's Seafood Bar &
Market** 252/441-7501. For casual waterfront dining visit the
Windmill Point Restaurant 252/441-1535. Homemade BBQ ribs
and chicken are a favorite at **Jockey's Ribs** 252/441-1141. Hungry
souls should visit the **Surf and Turf Buffet at Soundside Pavillion**
252/441-0535, the largest Outer Banks buffet.

KITTY HAWK KITES AND OUTER BANK OUTDOORS
(hang gliding and outdoor recreational activities approximately 6 miles from airport)
P.O. Box 1839, Nags Head, NC 27959; Tel: 252/441-4124 or 800/334-4777; Internet: www.kittyhawk.com

Jockey Ridge State Park is a mecca for hang gliders with its windswept sand dunes reaching from 110 to 140 feet. It is also the location of the main store and flight center for Kitty Hawk Kites. Activities offered include hang and paragliding lessons and rentals, as well as kayak eco-tours in serene waters or sailing their trimaran. Try out wall climbing or rent bikes and in-line skates for exploring the many Outer Bank trails. Kite-making workshops and demonstrations are exciting for kite lovers. Events, tours, workshops, or clinics—you are sure not to be bored at this place if you like the outdoors.

NAGS HEAD GOLF LINKS
(approximately 8 miles from airport)
5615 S. Sea Chase Drive, Nags Head, NC 27959; Tel: 252/441-8073

A tough but picturesque 18-hole course is located on Nags Head. Designed by Bob Moore, it is a windswept, Scottish-links-style course among rolling dunes and pot bunkers.

WRIGHT BROTHERS NATIONAL MEMORIAL

NC

(approximately 2 miles from airport)
U.S. 158 Bypass, Kill Devil Hills, NC, Tel: 252/441-7430; Internet: www.nps.gov/wrbr/wright/htm
Open daily except Christmas.
Admission is $4 per car.

Kill Devil Hills was the site of the first powered flight, on December 17, 1903, by Wilbur and Orville Wright. Pay attention to the boulder on the left-hand side of the visitor center. It marks the area where the first aircraft "returned to earth." A replica of the Flyer is shown inside the center. Experiments with kites and gliders are on display. Orville recorded that historic moment of first flight as lasting about 12 seconds! Yet it ended up changing the world. It is suggested that you stop first at the visitor center, where the story of the Wright Brothers is told through exhibits and full-scale reproductions of the 1902 glider and 1903 flying machine.

WHILE YOU'RE THERE: Surfers can rent boards from **Whalebone Surf Shop** 252/261-8737. Size and difficulty of waves vary almost hourly according to tides and weather conditions. In May keep an eye out for the **Hang Gliding Spectacular** or in June for the **Rogallo Kite Festival** 252/441-4124. **Jockey Ridge State Park** 252/441-7132 contains the tallest sand dune in the Eastern USA and has a 1.5-mile self-guided nature trail. Bring your camera and binoculars or watch the gorgeous sunset! **Atlantic Ocean Rentals** 252/441-7823 in Nags Head rents bikes. Contact the **Charter Boat "Gannet"** 252/441-6292, a 53-foot custom-built sportfisherman, to spend a day on the water and catch a prize.

Manteo (MQI)
Dare Co. Reg. Airport

Airport is located 1 mile northwest of town.

☞ *Airport Information:*

Location: Charlotte sectional N35.55.14 W75.41.73
Attended: 1300-0000Z*
Elevation: 14 feet
Fuel: 100LL, Jet A
TPA: 1000 feet msl
Runway: 05-23: 4300 x 100 asph
17-35: 3303 x 75 asph
FBO: Airport Authority
252/473-2600

☞ *Communication:*

CTAF: 122.8
Unicom: 122.8
App/Dep: Washington Center 124.725
AWOS: 128.275

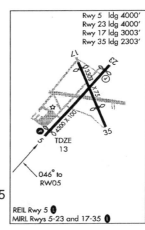

Rwy 5 ldg 4000'
Rwy 23 ldg 4000'
Rwy 17 ldg 3003'
Rwy 35 ldg 2303'

TDZE
13

046° to
RW05

REIL Rwy 5 ●
MIRL Rwys 5-23 and 17-35 ●

NC

☞ *Transportation:*

Taxi: 252/473-0200; 252/441-2500
Car Rental: B & R 252/473-2600

193

☞ *Lodging:*

__Manteo:__ The **Tranquil House Inn/1587** 252/473-1587 or 800/458-7069 is a country inn overlooking Shallowbag Bay. Furnished with antiques is **The Scarborough Inn** 252/473-3979. Wide porches invite lounging. About 100 rooms and an indoor/outdoor pool are available at the **Elizabethan Inn** 252/473-2101 or 800/346-2466.

☞ *Restaurants:*

__Manteo:__ **Anna Livia's Restaurant** 252/473-3753 has the usual seafood, chicken, and pasta menu but is located on the way to the play featured below. Indulge in fresh seafood at **Clara's Seafood Grill & Steam Bar** 252/473-1727 on Manteo's waterfront. German atmosphere, with polka music and waiters in lederhosen, prevails at the **Weeping Radish Brewery & Bavarian Restaurant** 252/473-1157. The food consists of typical pot roast, bratwurst, and potato salad fare.

THE LOST COLONY

(outdoor drama approximately 2 miles from airport)
1409 Highway 64/264, Manteo, NC 27954; Tel: 919/473-3414 or 800/488-5012; Internet: www.outerbanks-nc.com/lostcolony
Mid-June through August only.
Tickets are $16 for adults, $8 for children 12 years and under. Sundays are discounted.

NC

An outdoor historical drama tells the story of the first English settlement in the New World on Roanoke Island in 1587, which later mysteriously disappeared. Be entertained by a unique blend of drama, energetic dance, music, and dazzling costumes.

WHILE YOU'RE THERE: Call **Capt. JP Boat Cruises** 252/473-9491 or 800/495-5835 to join a dinner or dinner/dance cruise. Follow a map purchased at **Manteo Booksellers** 252/473-1221 for a self-guided walking tour of Manteo. A 54-foot custom sportfisher charter boat for Gulf Stream fishing is available by calling **Capt. Jim Horning** at 252/473-5319. Take a tour to watch dolphins and other coastal wildlife with **Nags Head Dolphin Watch** 252/480-2236. Gardeners may enjoy a stroll through **Elizabethan Gardens** 252/473-3234. It is a living memorial to the first English colonists and designed with elements of the Elizabethan period.

Ocean Isle Beach
Ocean Isle Airport (60J)

Airport is located 1 mile north of town.

☞ *Airport Information:*
Location: Charlotte sectional N33.54.51 W78.26.20
Attended: Unattended
Elevation: 32 feet
Fuel: Unavailable
TPA: 800 feet msl
Runway: 06-24: 4000 x 75 asph

☞ *Communication:*
CTAF: 122.9

☞ *Transportation:*
Taxi: 910/287-3197

☞ *Lodging:*
Ocean Isle: **Clarion Inn** 910/579-9001; **Sea Trail Plantation and Golf Resort** 800/624-6601 see below.

☞ *Restaurants:*
Ocean Isle: **Italian Fisherman Restaurant** 910/579-2929

SEA TRAIL PLANTATION AND GOLF RESORT
NC

(approximately 7 miles from airport)
211 Clubhouse Road, Sunset Beach, NC 28468; Tel: 800/624-6601;
Internet: www.seatrailresort.com

Sea Trail has three distinctly different courses. The Rees Jones course is a straightforward course, bounding along wide fairways, large mounds, swales, and water on 11 holes. Built around several man-made lakes, the Willard Byrd course demands strategically placed tee shots. The 18th hole is a picturesque and scenic finish between two beautiful ponds. Rolling hills, woods and large waste areas characterize the Dan Maples course. It is unique in its use of waste bunkers. One extends the length of No. 15 for 400 yards, making it a challenge for most everybody. Keep a lookout for ospreys along the holes next to Calabash Creek. Instruction is available through the Golf Learning Center. Should you tire of Sea Trail's courses, there are more than 30 other courses within a short driving distance. Shore birds and coastal wildlife abound on Bird Island. Located south of Sunset Beach, it is an undeveloped barrier island that can only be reached by boat or on foot at low tide. Sunset Beach is a nesting ground for sea turtles. Local turtle watchers fence off the nests and patrol nightly during the season to keep predators away.

You can also arrange for canoeing, kayaking, sailing, horseback riding, fishing, and adventure cruises.

WHILE YOU'RE THERE: The **Museum of Coastal Carolina** 910/579-1016 focuses on the natural history of the coastal region. You can admire a shell collection, native American artifacts, tide and solar exhibits, and antique fishing equipment.

Pinehurst/Southern Pines
Moore Co. Airport (SOP)

Airport is located 3 miles north of town.

☞ *Airport Information:*

Location:	Charlotte N35.14.21 W79.23.49
Attended:	1100-0400Z*
Elevation:	461 feet
Fuel:	100LL, Jet A
TPA:	1500 feet msl
Runway:	05-23: 5503 x 150 asph
	14-32: 2100 x 100 turf
FBO:	910/692-3212

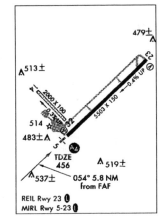

☞ *Communication:*

CTAF:	123.05
Unicom:	123.05
App/Dep:	Fayetteville 127.8
Clnc Del:	127.0
AWOS:	127.575

☞ *Transportation:*

Taxi:	910/692-2011
Car Rental:	National 910/692-4449

☞ *Lodging:*
Pinehurst: See **Pinehurst Resort and Countryclub** 800/487-4653
listing below.

PINEHURST RESORT AND COUNTRYCLUB
(golf resort approximately 5 miles from airport)
P.O. Box 4000, Pinehurst, NC 28374; Tel: 800/487-4653; Internet:
www.pinehurst.com
Be aware that day visitors who wish to play golf may not make
reservations for tee times in advance.

Pinehurst Resort and Countryclub is a golf players' Mecca. Envision
the mild climate, a resort that opened in 1900 and no less than
seven 18-hole championship golf courses. And in between rounds
there is the PGA/World Golf Hall of Fame to visit. (Open only March
through November.) Follow in the footsteps of Roosevelt,
Rockefeller, and Du Pont and relax at the resort or take advantage
of 10,000 acres of grounds laid out by the firm of Frederick Law
Olmsted, who designed New York's Central Park. The gun club has
nine shooting ranges for skeet and trap. Sail on the private lake or
play a game of tennis on one of the many courts. Jogging, biking,
and horseback riding amidst swaying pines are on offer as well. Yet
golf remains the main attraction and is synonymous with Pinehurst.
Pinehurst No. 2 is the most celebrated one. Featuring small, sloping
greens, it was designed by Donald Ross and opened in 1907. But
don't forget the other six championship courses, which are also
memorable. If you wish to improve your game you can choose from
a variety of lessons at the Golf Advantage School.

NC

WHILE YOU'RE THERE: Another resort nearby is the **Mid
Pines Resort** 800/323-2114 or 910/692-2114. Features are a
Donald Ross–designed 18-hole golf course, tennis courts, and pool.
A visit to **Sandhills Horticultural Gardens** 910/695-3882 is free.
See a formal English and specialized conifer gardens.

Wilmington Int'l Airport

(ILM)

Airport is located 3 miles northeast of town.

☞ *Airport Information:*

Location: Charlotte sectional N34.16.24 W77.54.15

Airspace: Class D service 1100-0400Z*
Other times class E
Terminal radar service area

Attended: Continuously

Elevation: 33 feet

Fuel: 100LL, Jet A

TPA: 800 feet msl non-turbine acft
1200 feet msl turbine acft

Runway: 06-24: 8015 x 200 asph-conc
17-35: 7003 x 150 asph

FBO: Air Wilminton 910/763-0146
Aeronautics 910/763-4691

☞ *Communication:*

CTAF: 119.9

Unicom: 122.95

App/Dep: 135.75 (344-163°), 118.25 (164-343°)
121.4 (east) (1100-0500Z*)
Washington Center 135.5 (0500-1100Z*)

Tower: 119.9 (1100-0500Z*)

Ground: 121.9

Clnc Del: 121.9

ATIS: 121.1

☞ *Transportation:*

Taxi: 910/762-4464

Car Rental: Budget 910/762-9247; Hertz 910/762-1010

☞ *Lodging:*

Wrightsville Beach: The **Blockade Runner Resort Hotel** 910/256-2251 or 800/541-1161 is located on the oceanfront. The **Silver Gull** 910/256-3738 is a motel next to the pier.

Wilmington: A historic district location is the feature at the **Inn at St. Thomas Court** 910/343-1800 or 800/525-0909. The **Inn on Orange** 910/815-0035 is a B & B with garden and pool. The **Wilmington Hilton** 910/763-9881 overlooks the Cape Fear River, and is a short stroll from historic and cultural attractions. **Ramada Inn** 910/799-1730

☞ *Restaurants:*
Wilmington: **Bojangles Famous Chicken** 910/452-3998

WATER WAYS SAILING SCHOOL
(approximately 7 miles from airport)
P.O. Box 872, Wrightsville Beach, NC 28480; Tel: 910/256-4282 or 800/562-SAIL

A variety of courses is available to suit your requirements at this sailing school. Choose from basic sailing to bare-boat charter, coastal navigation, advanced coastal cruising, and celestial navigation. Advance study is required so you can get the most out of your course. With never more than four students on a boat, you are assured a high level of attention and hands-on time. Water Ways fleet boat size ranges from 30 to 45 feet, and their safety equipment exceeds Coast Guard requirements. For lodging you may choose from live-aboard or shoreside accommodations.

WHILE YOU'RE THERE: Take a self-guided tour to the **USS North Carolina Battleship Memorial** 910/251-5797, an authentically restored WWII battleship. Summer only! Civil War buffs may enjoy a visit to the **Fort Fisher State Historic Site** 910/458-5538, a large Confederate earthwork fortification. With more than 600 shipwrecks to choose from, scuba divers with a liking for wreck diving may contact **Aquatic Safaris** 910/392-4386. **Historic Wilmington Carriage Tours** 910/253-4894 has carriage tours narrated by a costumed driver through the historic district.

NC

Akron
Canton Reg. Airport (CAK)

Airport is located 10 miles southeast of town.

☞ *Airport Information:*

Location: Detroit sectional N40.54.98 W81.26.55
Airspace: Class C 1100-0500Z*
Other times Class D
Attended: Continuously
Elevation: 1228 feet
Fuel: 100LL, Jet A
TPA: 2000 feet msl
Runway: 05-23: 7598 x 150 asph
01-19: 6397 x 150 asph
14-32: 5600 x 150 asph
FBO: Air Camis 330/896-3765
McKinley Air 800/225-6446

☞ *Communication:*

Unicom: 122.95
App/Dep: 125.5 (007º-186º), 118.6 (187º-006º)
126.4 (1100-0500Z*)
Cleveland Center 134.9 (0500-1100Z*)
Clnc Del: 132.05
Tower: 118.3
Ground: 121.7
ATIS: 121.05

OH

☞ *Transportation:*

Taxi: 330/494-5800
Car Rental: Budget 330/253-3540; Hertz 330/896-1331

☞ *Lodging:*

Canton: **Sheraton Inn** 330/494-6494; **Best Western** 330/497-8799;
Residence Inn by Marriott 330/493-0004

☞ *Restaurant:*
Akron: **Lou & Hy's Deli** 330/836-9159 serves delicious sandwiches and cheesecake.

INVENTOR PLACE AND NATIONAL INVENTORS HALL OF FAME
(approximately 10 miles from airport)
221 S. Broadway, Akron, OH 44308; Tel: 330/762-4463 or 800/968-4332
Open daily, except major holidays.
Admission is $7.50; $6 for ages 3 to 17 and seniors.

Visit the place where American ingenuity takes center stage and stretch your own imagination at the Inventors Workshop and Hands-on Exhibits. All ages are encouraged to follow their own curiosity and creativity. For inspiration, take a look at the sheer genius displayed by more than 100 creative thinkers at the Inventors Hall of Fame.

PRO FOOTBALL HALL OF FAME
(approximately 4 miles from airport)
2121 George Halas Drive, N.W., Canton, OH 44708; Tel: 330/456-8207
Open daily.
Admission is $10 for adults; $5 for ages 6 to 14 years old.

Pigskin prevails at the Pro Football Hall of Fame, in the mother city of the National Football League. Exhibits pay tribute to more than 100 years of passes, punts, kicks, downs, rushes and goals. A state-of-the-art turntable theater features NFL action in Cinemascope. Displays in the enshrinement room honor those who have received football's highest honor.

OH

Batavia
Clermont Co. Airport (I69)
Airport is located 2 miles west of town.

☞ *Airport Information:*
Location: Cincinnati sectional N39.04.70 W84.12.62
Attended: Mon-Fri 1400Z* to dusk
                Sat 1400-2200Z*, Sun 1600Z* to dusk

Elevation:	848 feet
Fuel:	100LL, Jet A
TPA:	1848 feet msl
Runway:	04-22: 3705 x 75 asph
FBO:	Eastern Cincinnati Aviation 513/735-9500

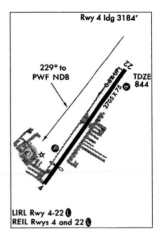

Rwy 4 ldg 3184'

229° to PWF NDB

TDZE 844

LIRL Rwy 4-22
REIL Rwys 4 and 22

☞ *Communication:*

CTAF:	122.7
Unicom:	122.7
App/Dep:	Cincinnati 121.0
Clnc Del:	124.9

☞ *Transportation:*

| Taxi: | 513/251-7733 |

Car Rental: Budget 513/752-2009; Enterprise 513/752-3338

☞ *Lodging:*

Cincinnati: **Holiday Inn** 513/752-4400; **Red Roof Inn** 513/528-2741

THE VINEYARD GOLF COURSE
(approximately 2 miles from airport)
600 Nordyke Road, Cincinnati, OH 45255; Tel: 513/474-3007

Located on the site of an old vineyard, this course was selected as runner-up for Best New Public Course of 1987 by *Golf Digest.* The Vineyard is a demanding but fair test of golf, with rolling hills and narrow fairways surrounded by trees.

OH

WHILE YOU'RE THERE: Visit **Sporty's Pilot Shop** 513/543-8633 or 513/735-9000 on the field.

Chillicothe
Ross Co. Airport (RZT)
Airport is located 6 miles northwest of town.

☞ *Airport Information:*

| Location: | Cincinnati sectional N39.26.48 W83.01.35 |
| Attended: | 1300Z* to dusk |

Elevation:	725 feet
Fuel:	100LL, Jet A
TPA:	1700 feet msl lgt acft
	2300 feet msl turbine acft
Runway:	05-23: 5400 x 100 asph
	12-30: 3130 x 125 turf -
	CLOSED INDEFINITELY
FBO:	TRM Aviation 740/773-4788

Rwy 12 ldg 2800'
227° to ICURI
TDZE 716
3130 X 125
5400 X 100

REIL Rwys 5 and 23
MIRL Rwy 5-23

☞ *Communication:*
CTAF: 122.8
Unicom: 122.8
App/Dep: Columbus 132.3

☞ *Transportation:*
Taxi: 740/775-5966
Car Rental: Enterprise 740/773-0875

☞ *Lodging:*
***Chillocothe*: Comfort Inn** 740/775-3500. **Holiday Inn Express**
740/779-2424 is Chillicothe's newest hotel. **The Greenhouse B & B**
740/775-5313 is an 1894 Queen Anne Victorian home listed in the
National Register of Historic Places.

☞ *Restaurants:*
***Chillicothe:* Cardo's Pizza** 740/775-2564. **Casa Del Taco** 740/773-
7650 serves Mexican fare. **Harvester Restaurant and Cellar**
740/773-4663

TECUMSEH!

OH

(Outdoor drama approximately 8 miles from airport)
P.O. Box 73, Chillicothe, OH 45601; Tel: 740/702-7677 (no calls
accepted before March).
Performances mid-June to September. Tickets are $13 and $15 for
adults, $6 for children.

Tecumseh! is a professional outdoor drama recounting the life of
the legendary Shawnee leader. A spectacle of unbelievable
proportions involving a cast and crew of 80 people, a dozen horses,
and 13 stages. The seating is in comfortable stadium seats under a
canopy of stars, encircled by forests. Backstage tours and buffet
dinner available on site. Rainchecks are issued in the event of
cancellation due to inclement weather.

Cincinnati
Blue Ash Airport (ISZ)

Airport is located 6 miles northeast of town.

☞ *Airport Information:*

Location: Cincinnati sectional N39.14.80 W84.23.34
Attended: Apr-Nov 1130Z* to 1 hour after dusk
Dec-Mar 1230Z* to 1 hour after dusk
Elevation: 856 feet
Fuel: 100LL, Jet A
TPA: 1700 feet msl single engine
1900 feet msl multi engine
Runway: 06-24: 3500 x 75 asph
FBO: Co-op Aircraft Service
513/791-8500
Exec Aviation 513/984-3881

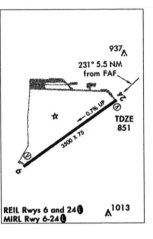

☞ *Communication:*

CTAF: 123.0
Unicom: 123.0
App/Dep: 121.0
Clnc Del: 124.9
AWOS: 118.475

☞ *Transportation:*

Taxi: 513/821-2066; 513/984-5264
Car Rental: Contact FBO

OH

☞ *Lodging:*

Cincinnati: **Holiday Inn Downtown** 513/241-8660. Check into the sightseeing packages of the **Regal Cincinnati Hotel** 513/352-2100. The **Omni Netherland Plaza** 513/421-9100 is downtown's grand art deco hotel.

☞ *Restaurant:*

Cincinnati: Expect exquisite French food at the formal **Maisonette** 513/721-2260. At the water's edge is the **Montgomery Inn at the Boathouse** 513/721-7427 famous for its barbecued ribs. For live jazz on weekends go to the **Main Street Brewery** 513/665-4677.

BLUE ASH GOLF COURSE
(approximately 3 miles from airport)
4040 Cooper Road, Cincinnati, OH 45241; Tel: 513/745-8577

Test your skills on this fine public course with 18 holes at par 72. The layout features four lakes around seven holes and a creek that comes into play on nine holes. Sixty sand traps round out Blue Ash's traditional style. Low green fees add to the enjoyment of this well groomed course.

PARAMOUNT'S KINGS ISLAND
(amusement and water park approximately 10 miles from airport)
6300 Kings Island Drive, Kings Mills, OH 45034; Tel: 800/288-0808
Open weekends from mid-April to Labor Day.
Admission is $34.99 for adults and $19.99 for children 3 to 6 years.

"Kids of all ages" will enjoy the rides at this park, with its eight theme areas. Try the longest wooden roller coaster, The Beast, winding its 7,400 feet through 35 rugged, densely wooded acres. Or King Cobra, a stand-up coaster! A total of eight roller coasters are sure to give you plenty of thrills. Cool off at Water Work's 16 aquatic attractions or relax with live stage entertainment.

WHILE YOU'RE THERE: If you are into works by Rembrandt, Turner, Goya, and Gainsborough pay the **Taft Museum** 513/241-0343 a visit. A good selection of European and American paintings is on view at the **Cincinnati Art Museum** 513/721-5204.

Cleveland (BKL)
Burke Lakefront Airport

OH

Airport is located 1 mile north of town.

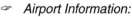 *Airport Information:*
Location: Detroit sectional N41.31.05 W81.41.01
Airspace: Class D service Mon 1200*Z to Sat 0400Z*
Sat 1200-0400Z*, Sun 1300-0500Z*
Attended: Continuously
Elevation: 584 feet
Fuel: 100LL, Jet A
TPA: 1500 feet msl

Runway:	06L-24R: 6198 x 150 asph
	06R-24L: 5200 x 100 asph
FBO:	Business Aircraft Center
	216/781-1200, Million Air
	216/861-2030

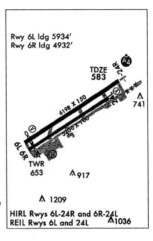

Rwy 6L ldg 5934'
Rwy 6R ldg 4932'
TDZE 583
6198 X 150
741
TWR 653
A 917
A 1209
HIRL Rwys 6L-24R and 6R-24L
REIL Rwys 6L and 24L
A 1036

☞ *Communication:*

CTAF:	124.3
Unicom:	122.95
App/Dep:	Cleveland 125.35
Clnc Del:	121.9 when tower closed
Tower:	Lakefront 124.3
	(Mon to Sat 1200- 0400Z*,
	Sat 1200-0400Z*,
	Sun 1300-0500Z*)
Ground:	121.9
ATIS:	125.25 during tower hours

☞ *Transportation:*

Taxi: 216/861-7433 or 800/413-2527; 216/623-1500
Car Rental: National 216/781-1200; Thrifty 216/861-2030

☞ *Lodging:*

Cleveland: The **Embassy Suites Hotel** 216/523-8000 is located downtown. **Omni International Hotel** 216/791-1900

☞ *Restaurants:*

Cleveland: **Hornblower's** 216/363-1151 has good views of Lake Erie as well as being close to the Rock and Roll Hall of Fame. Expect seafood, pastas and sandwiches. Located in Little Italy is **La Dolce Vita** 216/721-8155 with typical Italian fare.

OH

ROCK AND ROLL HALL OF FAME
(approximately 1/2 mile from airport)
1 Key Plaza, Cleveland, OH 44114; Tel: 216/781-7625; Internet: www.rockhall.com
Open daily.
Admission is $14.95 for ages 12 and over.

The idea for a rock museum was to honor all those that have made an exceptional contribution to modern music. Annually selected by an international panel of rock "experts," the inductees must have released a record 25 years prior to their nomination. I.M. Pei, the architect, wanted the building to "echo the energy of rock and roll" and designed an impressive looking tinted-glass pyramid right on the shore of Lake Erie. Dynamic interactive exhibits, original films and videos, the actual analog Sun recording studio where Elvis Presley made his first record, stage costumes — the world's most extensive rock and roll collection is featured here. Collectors will enjoy the souvenir and record store on the ground floor. Worthwhile seminars and workshops that feature Hall of Fame inductees and leading rock writers are held throughout the year.

WHILE YOU'RE THERE: The Great Lakes Science Center 216/694-2000 focuses on the Great Lakes' environment and technology with dozens of hands-on exhibits and an Omnimax Theater.

Columbus (CMH)
Port Columbus Int. Airport
Airport is located 6 miles east of town.

☞ *Airport Information:*

Location: Cincinnati sectional N39.59.88 W82.53.50
Airspace: Class C
Attended: Continuously
Elevation: 815 feet
Fuel: 80, 100, Jet A
TPA: 1800 feet msl
Runway: 10R-28L: 10250 x 150 asph
10L-28R: 8000 x 150 asph
FBO: Airnet Systems
614/237-9777
Lane Aviation 614/237-7290

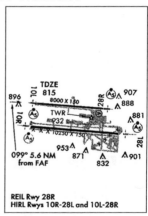

REIL Rwy 28R
HIRL Rwys 10R-28L and 10L-28R

OH

☞ *Communication:*

Unicom: 122.95
App/Dep: Columbus 119.15
132.3 (100-279°); 125.95(280-099°); 118.2; 119.65
Tower: Columbus 132.7
Ground: 121.9
Clnc Del: 126.3
ATIS: 124.6

☞ *Transportation:*
Taxi: 614/224-4141; 614/299-1191
Car Rental: Avis 800/331-1212; Thrifty 800/367-2277

☞ *Lodging:*
Columbus: **Airport Radisson Hotel** 614/475-7551; **Quality Inn** 614/861-0084; **German Village Inn** 614/443-6506

☞ *Restaurants:*
Columbus: Stop by **Lindey's** 614/228-4343 or **Katzinger's Deli** 614/228-3354 while touring the German Village.

OHIO HISTORY OF FLIGHT MUSEUM
(located on field)
4275 Sawyer Road, Port Columbus Int'l Airport, Columbus, OH 43219; Tel: 614/231-1300
Open daily.
Admission is $2 for adults, $1.50 for children.

The Ohio History of Flight Museum has vintage aircraft on display at their new facility at the Port Columbus Int'l Airport. Aviation-related video tapes can be viewed upon request.

WHILE YOU'RE THERE: Start at the **German Village Meeting House** 614/221-8888 for walking tours to explore the German Village, a neighborhood of brick homes built by immigrants in the 19th century. Contemporary art is housed at the **Wexner Center for the Arts** 614/292-0330 at the Ohio State University Campus.

Dayton
James Cox Dayton Int'l
Airport (DAY)

Airport is located 9 miles north of town.

☞ *Airport Information:*
Location: Cincinnati sectional N39.54.14 W84.13.16
Airspace: Class C
Attended: Continuously

Elevation:	1010 feet
Fuel:	100, Jet A
TPA:	1800 feet msl lgt acft
	2500 feet msl hvy acft
Runway:	06L-24R: 10901 x 150 asph
	18-36: 8500 x 150 asph
	06R-24L: 7000 x 150 asph
FBO:	Stevens Aviation
	937/454-3400
	Wright Bros Aero
	937/890-8900

☞ *Communication:*

Unicom:	122.95
App/Dep:	Dayton 118.85 (091-180º)
	127.65 (000-090º)
	134.45 (181-359º); 118.0; 126.5
Tower:	Dayton 119.9
Ground:	121.9
Clnc Del:	121.75
ATIS:	125.8

☞ *Transportation:*

Taxi:	937/228-1155
Car Rental:	Avis 937/898-8357; Dollar 937/454-8430
	National 937/890-0100

☞ *Lodging:*
Dayton: **Dayton Airport Inn** 800/543-7577

UNITED STATES AIR FORCE MUSEUM
(approximately 10 miles from Dayton Int'l Cox airport)
Wright-Patterson AFB, OH 45433; Tel: 513/255-3286
Open daily, except major holidays.
Admission is free.

Over 200 aircraft and missiles and interesting aeronautical displays can be viewed at the oldest and largest military aviation museum in the world. Over one and a half million visitors from around the world come here each year to tour this facility telling aviation history from the days of the Wright Brothers at Kitty Hawk to the Space Age. Documentary films are shown on weekends and holidays. A shuttle bus takes you to a museum annex holding approximately 25 aircraft, including a collection of presidential aircraft. Films are shown on a large screen at the IMAX theater, putting you at the center of the action as no ordinary movie can.

WHILE YOU'RE THERE: To see where Dayton natives Orville and Wilbur Wright first practiced flying, visit the **Dayton Aviation Heritage National Historic Park** 937/225-7705.

Galion Munic. Airport (GQQ)

Airport is located 3 miles northeast of town.

☞ *Airport Information:*

Location: Detroit sectional N40.45.20 W82.43.43
Attended: Mon-Fri 1300-2100Z*
Elevation: 1225 feet
Fuel: 80, 100LL
TPA: 2000 feet msl
Runway: 05-23: 3504 x 75 asph
FBO: 419/468-8487

☞ *Communication:*

CTAF: 122.8
Unicom: 122.8
App/Dep: Mansfield 124.2
(1100-0400Z*)
Cleveland Center 134.9
(0400-1100Z*)
Clnc Del: 126.8

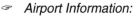

Rwy 5 ldg 3317'

3505 x 75

TDZE
1225

050° to
MAP WPT

MIRL Rwy 5-23 ●
REIL Rwys 5 and 23 ●

OH

☞ *Lodging:*

Galion: **Hometown Inn** 419/468-9906

THE MID-OHIO SCHOOL

(driving school approximately 8 miles from airport)
94 North High Street, Suite 50, Dublin, OH 43017; Tel: 614/793-4615; Internet: www.midohio.com/school.htm

If you either own a high-performance vehicle or want to learn the techniques of high-performance driving, this is the place for you. Or enroll in the Car Control Clinic to experience emergency situations that occur daily on the roadways in a safe environment. Most courses are 1-day courses. Based at the Mid-Ohio Sports Car Course, it is a 2.4 mile, 15-turn competitive road course. Although courses are primarily targeted towards the everyday driver, they also offer programs for racing competitors.

✈ ✈ ✈

Kent State University Airport (1G3)

Airport is located 3 miles west of town.

☞ *Airport Information:*

Location: Detroit sectional N41.09.11 W81.25.00
Attended: Mon-Fri 1130Z*-dusk
Sat-Sun 1300Z*-dusk
Elevation: 1150 feet
Fuel: 100LL, Jet A
TPA: 2000 feet msl
Runway: 01-19: 4000 x 60 asph
FBO: Commercial Aviation Corp.
330/686-1234

☞ *Communication:*

CTAF: 122.7
Unicom: 122.7
App/Dep: Akron/Canton 118.6
(1100-0500Z*)
Cleveland Center 120.775 (0500-1100Z*)
Clnc Del: 125.65

OH

☞ *Transportation:*

Taxi: 330/929-3121
Car Rental: Beckwith Leasing 330/686-1234

☞ *Lodging:*

Kent: **Inn of Kent** 330/673-3411

☞ *Restaurants:*

Kent: Full dining services are available at the **Blossom Music Center** 216/231-1111 or 800/686-1141.

BLOSSOM MUSIC CENTER

(outdoor shows/concerts approximately 10 miles from airport)
11001 Euclid Avenue, Cleveland, OH 44106; For tickets call tel:
216/231-1111 or 800/686-1141.

Bring your picnic to an evening filled with music. The Blossom Music
Center is the summer home of the Cleveland Orchestra, with
concerts from July to September. Or choose from their repertoire of
special events, which have included Rod Stewart, Pearl Jam,
Metallica, Jimmy Buffet and the Spice Girls. Seating is available
under the cover of the pavilion or on the lawn. The Blossom Music
Center is located in Cuyahoga Falls, adjacent to the Cuyahoga
Valley National Recreation Area. There are two entrances, the Main
Gate on Steels Corners Road and the Valley Gate off of
Northhampton Road.

Mansfield
Lahm Munic. Airport (MFD)

Airport is located 3 miles north of town.

☞ *Airport Information:*

Location: Detroit sectional N40.49.29 W82.31.00
Airspace: Class D 1100-0400Z*
Attended: 1200-0300Z*
Elevation: 1297 feet
Fuel: 100LL, Jet A
TPA: 2300 feet msl
Runway: 14-32: 9000 x 150 asph
                05-23: 6795 x 150 asph
FBO: Richland Aviation
                419/524-4261

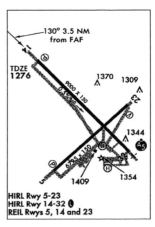

☞ *Communication:*

CTAF: 119.8
Unicom: 122.95
App/Dep: 124.2; 127.35
                  (1100-0400Z*)
                Cleveland Center 134.9 (0400-1100Z*)
Tower: 119.8 (1100-0400Z*)
Ground: 121.8

ATIS: 125.3

☞ *Transportation:*
Taxi: 419/524-7111
Car Rental: Hertz 419/524-3513; U-Save 419/524-4261

☞ *Lodging:*
Mansfield: **Econo Lodge** 419/589-3333; **Travelodge** 419/756-7600

SNOW TRAILS SKI AREA
(approximately 10 miles from airport)
3100 Possum Run Road, Mansfield, OH 44903; Tel: 800/644-6754 office, 800/332-2000 ski conditions

The rolling hills of Mansfield provide a perfect setting for the Snow Trails Ski Resort. Take lessons at the ski school or just hit the slopes, which stay open seven days and nights a week during the season. Snow Trails hosts the Ohio Winter Ski Carnival every February.

Middletown
Hook Munic. Airport (MWO)

Airport is located 2 miles north of town.

☞ *Airport Information:*
Location: Cincinnati sectional N39.31.86 W84.23.72
Attended: Sep-Apr 1200-0200Z*
 May-Aug 1200-0300Z*
Elevation: 651 feet
Fuel: 100LL, Jet A
TPA: 1500 feet msl
Runway: 05-23: 6100 x 100 asph
 08-26: 2984 x 300 turf
FBO: Miami Valley Aviation
 513/423-5757

☞ *Communication:*
CTAF: 123.0
Unicom: 123.0

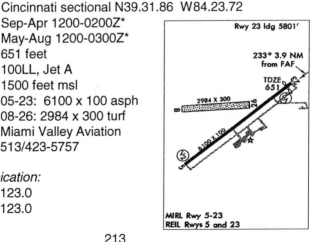

Rwy 23 ldg 5801'

233° 3.9 NM from FAF

TDZE 651

2984 X 300

6100 X 100

MIRL Rwy 5-23
REIL Rwys 5 and 23

App: Dayton 118.85
Dep: Dayton 126.5
Clnc Del: Dayton 119.4

☞ *Transportation:*
Taxi: 513/425-9999
Car Rental: Enterprise 513/423-3000

☞ *Lodging:*
Middletown: **Holiday Inn** 513/727-8440

WEATHERWAX GOLF COURSE
(approximately 3 miles from airport)
5401 Mosiman Road, Middletown, OH 45042; Tel: 513/425-7886

Featuring 4 different courses with 9 holes each, this course lets you play a variety of combinations. The Highland Course is tight. The Woodside Course is long, and the Valley View and Meadows Courses are the most open. Hosting many tournaments, Weatherwax was designed by Arthur Hills.

Millersburg
Holmes Co. Airport (10G)

Airport is located 2 miles southwest of town.

OH

☞ *Airport Information:*
Location: Detroit sectional N40.32.23 W81.57.26
Attended: Mon-Sat 1300-2300Z*
              Sun 1700-2300Z*
Elevation: 1218 feet
Fuel: 100LL, Jet A
TPA: 2000 feet msl
Runway: 09-27: 3498 x 65 asph
FBO: Holmes County Aviation
         330/674-2686

☞ *Communication:*
CTAF: 123.0
Unicom: 123.0

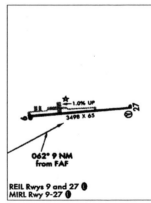

App/Dep: Indianapolis Center 124.45

☞ *Transportation:*
Taxi: Contact FBO
Car Rental: Contact FBO or 330/893-2308

☞ *Lodging:*
Millersburg: Amish Country Inn 330/893-3000; **Comfort Inn** 330/674-7400

☞ *Restaurants:*
Millersburg: Dutch Harvest Restaurant 330/893-3333

AMISH FARM
(approximately 8 miles from airport)
4363 State Route 39, Berlin, OH 44610; Tel: 330/893-3232
Open April to October.
Admission is $6 for adults, $4 for ages 3 to 12 years old.

Ohio has the largest Amish population in the world. They are much less tourist-oriented than the highly publicized Pennsylvania Dutch. Find out about the Amish lifestyle through slide presentations, demonstrations, and tours, and enjoy a buggy ride.

New Philadelphia
Clever Airport (PHD)

Airport is located 3 miles southeast of town.

OH

☞ *Airport Information:*
Location: Detroit sectional N40.28.26 W81.25.19
Attended: Apr-Sep 1300-0100Z*; Oct-Mar 1300-2200Z*
Elevation: 895 feet
Fuel: 80, 100LL, Jet A
TPA: 1890 feet msl lgt acft
                2390 feet msl hvy acft
Runway: 14-32: 3950 x 100 asph
                11-29: 2050 x 100 turf
FBO: Haines Aviation 330/339-6078

☞ *Communication:*
CTAF: 122.8
Unicom: 122.8
App/Dep: Akron-Canton 125.5
(1100-0500Z*)
Cleveland Center 134.9
(0500-1100Z*)
ASOS: 119.275

☞ *Transportation:*
Taxi: 330/343-1563
Car Rental: Enterprise 330/343-5948

☞ *Lodging:*

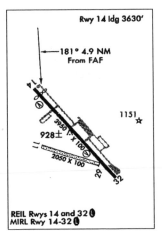

New Philadelphia: Days Inn 330/339-6644; **Holiday Inn** 330/339-7731; **Schoenbrunn Inn** 330/339-4334

TRUMPET IN THE LAND
(outdoor drama approximately 1 mile from airport)
P.O. Box 450, New Philadelphia, OH 44663; Tel: 330/339-1132
Performances mid-June to mid-August. Nightly, except Sundays.
Admission $13 for adults, $6 for children.

Trumpet in the Land is one of three outdoor dramas presented at the Schoenbrunn Amphitheater. The play tells the story of the first settlement in Ohio during the turbulent American Revolution. It is filled with Indian raids, horses, soldiers, music, dance and spectacular theatrical effects. The other two plays are *The White Savage* and *Cinderella.* No refunds for cancellations but rainchecks are handed out for any future performances of the same show.

OH

✹ ✹ ✹

Put-In-Bay Airport (OH30)
Airport is located 1 mile southwest of town.

☞ *Airport Information:*
Location: Detroit sectional N41.35.21 W82.49.70
Attended: May-Sep 1300-0100Z*
Oct-Apr 1230-2230Z*
Elevation: 595 feet
Fuel: Not available
TPA: 1600 feet msl

Runway: 03-21: 2870 x 75 asph
FBO: 419/285-3371

☞ *Communication:*
CTAF: 122.8
Unicom: 122.8

☞ *Transportation:*
Taxi: 419/285-6161

☞ *Lodging:*
Put-in-Bay: The **Park Hotel** 419/285-3581 is a restored Victorian hotel built in the 1870s with a downtown location. Clean and grill your catch at the facilities provided at the **Bird's Nest Motel** 419/285-6119, a family-oriented accommodation. The **Bay House B & B** 419/285-2822 is a historical home in a quiet setting with 8 guest rooms.

☞ *Restaurants:*
Put-in-Bay: Live entertainment, fresh seafood, pizzas, burgers, and tacos — all can be tasted at **The Boardwalk** 419/285-7281 on the waterfront. The **Beer Barrel Saloon** 419/285-7281 supposedly has the world's longest bar with 160 stools; 56 beers are on tap.

HARDWATER CHARTERS
(fishing and boat charters approximately 1 mile from airport)
P.O. Box 386, Put-in-Bay, OH 43456; Tel: 419/285-3106

South Bass Island is the largest of the Bass Islands and the name says it all. Avid anglers and weekend fisherman alike have discovered what islanders have known for years: the fishing is very good in the waters surrounding the island. From early April to late May perch, crappie, rock bass, and smallmouth can be taken from the shoreline. Schools of walleye scatter along the reefs surrounding the island. Catfish are plentiful in June. Take a licensed fishing guide with you or just charter a boat for your excursion. Winter ice fishing becomes luxurious with the rental of heated ice fishing shanties.

OH

ISLAND BIKE RENTAL
(approximately 1 mile from airport)
P.O. Box 419, Put-in-Bay, OH 43456; Tel: 419/285-2016; Internet: www.put-in-bay-trans.com

Outdoor enthusiasts that are drawn to the island welcome the large selection of bikes available. How about trying out a tandem bike? All-electric mini cars run all day and hold from 2 to 6 passengers.

STONEHENGE ESTATE TOUR
(approximately 1 mile from airport)
808 Langram Road, P.O. Box 599, Put-In-Bay, OH 43456; Tel: 419/285-2585; Internet: www.stonehenge-put-in-bay.com
Admission is $3.50 for adults, $1.50 for children 6 to 12 years old.

One reason why Put-in-Bay is the most visited of the American Lake Erie Islands. Take a self-guided cassette tour of this beautifully restored stone farmhouse and wine press cottage. Both buildings date back to the 1800s and contain antiques and island memorabilia.

THE ALASKAN BIRDHOUSE WILDLIFE MUSEUM
(approximately 1/2 mile from airport)
P.O. Box 489, Meechen Road, Put-in-Bay, OH 43456; Tel: 419/285-2141
Admission is $3 for adults and $1.50 for children 6 to 12 years old.

On display are over 100 different animals in their natural habitats. Guided tours are informative and include a discussion about bears, moose, ducks, geese, fish, and whales.

THE TOUR TRAIN
(approximately 1 mile from airport)
Box 190, Put-in-Bay, OH 43456; Tel: 419/285-4855; Internet: www.put-in-bay-trans.com
Tickets are $8 for adults, and $1.50 for children 6 to11 years old.

OH

This narrated tour is one of the best ways to see the island. It lasts one hour and stops at several island attractions along its route. Among them is Perry's Victory and International Peace Memorial. The third tallest memorial in the USA, it commemorates Commodore Oliver Hazard Perry's victory over the British fleet during the War of 1812.

WHILE YOU'RE THERE: Put-in-Bay Parasailing 419/285-3703 operates from May through September from downtown at the boardwalk. **Ted's Tackle Shop** 419/285-3172 sells live bait, fishing licenses, and marine supplies at a downtown location.

Sandusky (SKY)

Griffing-Sandusky Airport

Airport is located 3 miles southeast of town.

☞ *Airport Information:*

Location: Detroit sectional N41.26.00 W82.39.14
Attended: 1300Z* to dusk
Closed Christmas day
Elevation: 580 feet
Fuel: 100LL, Jet A
TPA: 1380 feet msl lgt acft
1970 feet msl hvy acft
Runway: 09-27: 3559 x 60 asph
Runway: 18-36: 2593 x 40 asph
FBO: Griffing Flying Service
419/626-5161

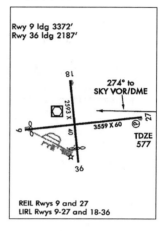

Rwy 9 ldg 3372'
Rwy 36 ldg 2187'

8 l

274° to
SKY VOR/DME

2593 X 40

3559 X 60

TDZE
577

36

REIL Rwys 9 and 27
LIRL Rwys 9-27 and 18-36

☞ *Communication:*

CTAF: 123.0
Unicom: 123.0
App/Dep: Cleveland Center 127.9

☞ *Transportation:*

Taxi: 419/626-1361
Car Rental: Enterprise 419/621-8181; Kaspar 419/625-8035

☞ *Lodging:*

Sandusky: Cedar Point Resorts 888/775-4242, within walking distance of all the fun and excitement, has three properties, the only accommodations on the Cedar Point Peninsula. **Howard Johnsons** 419/625-1333. **Clarion Sandusky** 419/625-6280. **Park Inn International** 419/626-4436 is near the Causeway Drive leading to Cedar Point. **Wagner's 1844 Inn** 419/626-1726 is a block from downtown and has three guest rooms.

☞ *Restaurants:*

Sandusky: Meals with a view of Sandusky can be had at the **Breakwater Cafe** 419/726-0866. The area's fresh seafood is prepared at the **Bay Harbor Inn** 419/625-6373 and the **Boathouse** 419/285-5665 has barbecued ribs and chicken.
Huron: **Sawmill Creek Lodge** 419/433-3800

OH

CEDAR POINT AMUSEMENT PARK
(approximately 5 miles from airport)
P.O. Box 5006, Sandusky, OH 44871; Tel: 419/626-0830; Internet: www.cedarpoint.com
Open mid-May to early September, with weekends only through mid-October.
Admission schedule runs from $6.95 to $32.95. Pricing is higher for 2-day tickets including admittance to Soak City.

Listed in the Guinness Book of Records for the most roller coasters in the world, Cedar Point Amusement Park is just a fun place to be. Overlooking Lake Erie, the 128-year-old park offers 12 of the nation's highest-rated coasters. A decade after it was built, Magnum, the grand dame, the first steel coaster to break the 200-foot barrier, still towers above the others. With everything from the world's highest and fastest inverted coasters to "training coasters" for kids, Cedar Point offers rides for everybody. Power Tower, new in '98, blasts you 24 stories into the sky and rockets you towards earth from 240 feet up!! Keep that adrenaline in check — if you can! A total of 60 rides, family attractions, special children's areas, live entertainment, and a mile-long sandy beach provide something for all ages. The Cedar Point Guide (call 800/BEST-FUN) contains discount coupons.

SAWMILL CREEK GOLF & RACKET CLUB
(approximately 4 miles from airport)
2401 Cleveland Road W., Huron, OH 44839; Tel: 419/433-3789

OH

A Tom Fazio course among the scenic wetlands along the shores of Lake Erie, it is not as easy a course as it looks. Water, marshland, and a stiff breeze off the lake will challenge the average golfer. Eighteen holes at par 71. The Sawmill Creek Lodge is on the same premises.

WHILE YOU'RE THERE: Celebrate summer at **Soak City** 419/627-2350 and refresh yourself in their wave pool, winding and dark slides, water playground, and wild river raft trip through canyons and rocking waves. Soak City is located next to the amusement park, and combination tickets are available. Rent boats of all sorts or take sailing lessons from **Adventure Plus Yacht Charters and Sailing** 419/625-5000 at the Sandusky Harbor Marina.

Youngstown
Warren Reg. Airport (YNG)

Airport is located 10 miles north of town.

☞ *Airport Information:*

Location: Detroit sectional N41.15.60 W80.40.63
Airspace: Terminal Radar Service Area
Attended: Continuously
Elevation: 1196 feet
Fuel: 100LL, Jet A
TPA: 2200 feet msl
Runway: 14-32: 9000 x 150 asph
05-23: 4987 x 150 asph
01-19: 3742 x 100 asph
FBO: Winner Aviat. 330/856-5000

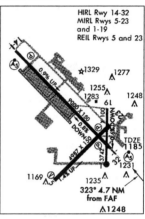

☞ *Communication:*

Unicom: 122.95
App/Dep: 133.95 (NE); 128.25 (SW)
127.15 (1100-0500Z*)
Cleveland Center 120.7(0500-1100Z*)
Clnc Del: 118.25
Ground: 121.9
Tower: 119.5
ATIS: 123.75

☞ *Transportation:*
Taxi: 330/545-5419
Car Rental: Avis 330/539-5130; Hertz 330/743-1577

OH

☞ *Lodging:*
Warren: Many of the 144 rooms of the **Avalon Inn** 330/856-1900
overlook a flat, green expanse of Midwestern country.

AVALON LAKES GOLF COURSE
(approximately 4 miles from airport)
9519 E. Market Street, Warren, OH 44484; Tel: 330/856-8898

Pete Dye teamed up with William Newcomb to design the par 71
challenge. It is a nice flat course that makes you use every club.
Anyway you slice it, the pro shop does not expect you to return the
half dozen complimentary balls. The Avalon Inn is on the premises.

PENNSYLVANIA

Canadensis (8N4)
Flying Dollar Airport
Airport is located 2 miles north of town.

☞ *Airport Information:*
Location: New York sectional N41.13.01 W75.14.98
Attended: Continuously
Elevation: 1400 feet
Fuel: Unavailable
TPA: 2400 feet msl
Runway: 02-20: 2405 x 100 turf
FBO: 717/595-3465

☞ *Communication:*
CTAF: 122.9

☞ *Transportation:*
Taxi: 717/264-4452
Car Rental: Enterprise 717/267-0674

☞ *Lodging:*
Skytop: **Skytop Lodge** 800/345-7759 (see next entry); **Daniels Hill Top Lodge** 717/595-7531

☞ *Restaurants:*
Skytop: **Overlook Inn & Restaurant** 717/595-7519

SKYTOP LODGE
(four-season resort approximately 2 miles from airport)
One Skytop, Skytop, PA 18357; Tel: 800/345-7759; Internet: www.
skytop.com

Whether you are after a romantic getaway or outdoor activities, Skytop Lodge is most likely to satisfy your needs. Fishing, skiing, golfing, mountain biking, hiking, bird-watching, miniature golf, archery, tennis, rowboats, ice-skating, sledding, snowshoeing . . . it's all possible. Health club, sauna, and spa facilities round out the choices. Theme weekends such as ballroom dancing, wildlife, and Edgar Allan Poe weekends are held throughout the year. The spectacular scenery of the Pocono Mountains is the perfect background for your leisure escape.

Centre Hall (N74)
Penn's Cave Airport
Airport is located 4 miles northeast of town.

☞ *Airport Information:*

Location: Detroit sectional N40.53.42 W77.36.15
Attended: Daylight hours
Elevation: 1260 feet
Fuel: 100LL, Jet A
TPA: 2500 feet msl
Runway: 07-25: 2500 x 40 asph
FBO: Air Atlantic Airlines 814/364-1477

☞ *Communication:*

CTAF: 122.8
Unicom: 122.8

PENN'S CAVE
(cave approximately 1 mile from airport)
Route 192 East, Centre Hall, PA 16828; Tel: 814/364-1664
Open February through November.
Admission is $8.50

PA

Penn's Cave touts itself as America's only all-water navigable cavern. It is rich in history, geology, and natural beauty. Take a one-mile boat tour floating past stalactites and stalagmites, or try your luck at gemstone panning. Take a nature walk to the cave or use the courtesy phone to call for pickup.

Chambersburg Munic. Airport (N68)

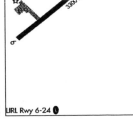

Airport is located 3 miles north of town.

☞ *Airport Information:*

Location: Washington sectional N39.58.38 W77.38.60
Attended: Unattended
Elevation: 697 feet
Fuel: None available
TPA: 1497 feet msl
Runway: 06-24: 3300 x 75 asph
FBO: Not available

☞ *Communication:*

CTAF: 122.8
Unicom: 122.8
App/Dep: Harrisburg 124.1

☞ *Lodging:*

Chambersburg: **Days Inn** 717/263-1288; **Hampton Inn** 717/261-9185

ADVANCED AERO SPORT
(skydiving located at airport)
3506 Airport Road, Chambersburg, PA 17201; Tel: 800/526-3497
Appointment necessary.

Looking for the thrill of your life? Here it is! Choose from the Accelerated Freefall Program, where you are accompanied by two instructors guiding you through your first skydive, or do a Tandem Skydive. This option has you securely attached to a professionally certified tandem master, after less than an hour of training. And to top it all off, you can have it all recorded on videotape! Weight limitation of 225 pounds applies to both of the above-mentioned options.

Easton Airport (N43)

Airport is located 3 miles north of town.

☞ *Airport Information:*

Location: New York sectional N40.44.48 W75.14.58
Attended: Daylight hours, unattended at Christmas
Elevation: 399 feet msl
Fuel: 100LL
TPA: 1200 feet msl
Runway: 18-36: 1953 x 50 asph
09-27: 1835 x 100 turf
FBO: Moyer Aviation
610/258-0473

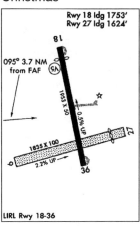

Rwy 18 ldg 1753'
Rwy 27 ldg 1624'
095° 3.7 NM from FAF (SN)
1953 X 50
0.5% UP
1835 X 100
2.2% UP
27
36
LIRL Rwy 18-36

☞ *Communication:*

CTAF: 123.0
Unicom: 123.0
App/Dep: Allentown 124.45
(above 3000' from S)
119.65 (above 3000' from N)
118.2 (3000' and below)

☞ *Transportation:*

Taxi: 610/258-2888
Car Rental: Enterprise 610/253-7599; Dollar 610/258-2384

☞ *Lodging:*

Easton: **Days Inn** 610/253-0546

BERTIL ROOS INDY-STYLE RACING SCHOOL

(racecar driving courses approximately 5 miles from airport)
P.O. Box 221, Blakeslee, PA 18610; Tel: 800/722-3669; Internet:
www.racenow.com

PA

The Nazareth Speedway is, according to the racing school, the world's fastest one-mile oval. There are just three corners, you stay in top gear all around, and you need to brake only once per lap. You get to drive "a real racecar" on a wide, open racetrack on their half-day or one-day racing program. Be aware that programs cannot be run on a wet track and must be rescheduled. No refunds. Driving suits and helmets are provided.

East Stroudsburg
Stroudsburg - Pocono
Airport (N53)

Airport is located 3 miles north of town.

☞ *Airport Information:*

Location: New York sectional N41.02.15 W75.09.64
Attended: 1300Z* to dusk
Elevation: 480 feet
Fuel: 80, 100LL, Jet A
TPA: 1280 feet msl
Runway: 08-26: 3087 x 30 asph
FBO: Nelson Aviation 717/421-8900

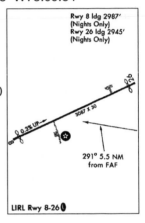

☞ *Communication:*

CTAF: 123.0
Unicom: 123.0
App/Dep: Allentown 119.65 (above
                    3000')
                  118.2 (below 3000')

☞ *Transportation:*

Taxi: 717/421-6068
Car Rental: Save U 717/421-6913

☞ *Lodging:*

Delaware Water Gap: **Glenwood Hotel & Resort** 800/833-3050;
Best Western 570/421-2200.

East Stroudsburg: For private chalets, fireplaces, jacuzzis and
sports facilities, make your reservation at **Birchwood Resort**
570/629-0222.

☞ *Restaurants:*

Delaware Water Gap: A 24-hour spot, the **Delaware Water Gap
Diner** 570/476-0132 serves inexpensive but good food. Next to the
Shawnee Inn is **Mimi's Streamside Cafe** 570/424-6455. **Trails' End
Cafe** 570/421-1928 gets its name from being one block from the
Appalachian Trail. They serve bistro-style food.

PA

CAMELBACK SKI AREA
(approximately 10 miles from airport)
Exit 45 on Route I-80; P.O. Box 168, Tannersville, PA 18372;
Tel: 570/629-1661; Snow report: 800/233-8100; Internet: www.
skicamelback.com

Camelback has 100% snowmaking capabilities and nighttime skiing.
Mountain elevation of 2,050 feet gives a vertical drop of 800 feet to
let your skis run on. Plenty of lifts take you to about 30 slopes and
trails, the longest one approximately 1 mile long. Snowboarding and
tubing are possible. As with most ski resorts, try to avoid the
crowded weekends or holidays.

PACK SHACK ADVENTURES
(climbing and other outdoor activities approximately 6 miles from the
airport)
88 Broad Street, Delaware Water Gap, PA 18327; Tel: 570/424-8533
or 800/424-0955

Climbing Mt. Tammany in the Delaware Water Gap National
Recreation Area has become a popular sport and Pack Shack
Adventures has been offering instruction since 1974. Private (one-
on-one) and semi-private (two persons per instructor) lessons insure
high-quality instruction. Basic, intermediate and advanced levels are
offered along with all necessary equipment. Ice climbing is available
during winter as weather permits. They also offer canoeing, rafting,
kayaking, tubing, hiking, cross-country skiing, and snowshoeing trips
and tours. Spring is the best time for rafting the Delaware, when
water flow is the swiftest. The river is calm in summer and best for
canoeing and tubing.

SHAWNEE INN & GOLF RESORT
(approximately 3 miles from airport)
One River Road, Shawnee on Delaware, PA 18356; Tel: 570/424-
4000 ext. 1413 or 800/SHAWNEE ext. 1413; Internet: www.
shwaneeinn.com

PA

Built in 1912, this restored historic resort overlooks the Delaware
River at the Delaware Water Gap. Recreational opportunities abound
all seasons. During spring, summer, and fall, Shawnee offers golf on
its legendary Tillinghast–designed 27-hole course. Twenty-four of the
27 holes are on an island in the Delaware River with fantastic
scenery. The links at Shawnee hosted the 1938 PGA
Championships where Sam Snead lost famously to Paul Runyon and

later, the 1967 NCAA Championships were won by the great Hale Irwin. Canoeing, rafting, swimming, biking, hiking, riding and tennis—it's all there. During winter you can take advantage of close-by Shawnee Mountain with its ski school, rental shop, and 23 trails. Cross-country, sledding, and ice skating are all a possibility. Fall is the time for the annual Hot-air Balloon Festival.

WHILE YOU'RE THERE: The Delaware Water Gap National Recreation Area is a perfect spot to spend some time outdoors. Horseback riding enthusiasts contact **Shawnee Stables** 570/421-9763. Rent bikes or skis from **Shawnee Mountain** 570/421-7231. Please note that mountain bikes are allowed only on ungated roads inside the Delaware Water Gap National Recreation Area. For canoeing, rafting, or tubing call **Shawnee Canoe Trips** 570/421-1500 or 800/742-SHAWNEE.

American shad, smallmouth bass, walleye, eel, and catfish can be caught in the Delaware River. Rainbow, brook, and brown trout are found in most streams. Just don't forget to get your fishing license. The **Alpine Slide at Camelback** 570/629-1661 is open spring through fall with bumperboats, a pool, waterslide, and kids' rides.

Gettysburg
Doersom Airport (W05)

Airport is located 2 miles west of town.

☞ *Airport Information:*
Location: Washington sectional N39.50.46 N77.16.45
Attended: Dawn to dusk
Elevation: 590 feet
Fuel: 80, 100LL
TPA: 1500 feet msl
Runway: 06-24: 3096 x 40 asph

☞ *Communication:*
CTAF: 122.8
Unicom: 122.8

☞ *Transportation:*
Car Rental: Enterprise 717/337-9000

PA

☞ *Lodging:*
Gettysburg: Walk to Battlefield restaurants, museums and shops from the **Quality Inn** 717/334-1103. The **Best Western Gettysburg Hotel 1797** 717/337-2000 is a historic landmark. **Comfort Inn of Gettysburg** 717/337-2400; **Econo Lodge** 717/334-6715; **Hampton Inn** 717/338-9121; **The Old Appleford Inn** 800/275-3373 or 717/337-1711 is an 1867 Victorian mansion in the heart of the historic district. Expect costumed staff and history demonstrations with muskets, cannon, or cavalry at the **Battlefield B & B Inn** 717/334-8804 located 5 minutes from town.

☞ *Restaurants:*
Gettysburg: For casual dining on steaks and pasta, **Krackerjack's Cafe** 717/334-5648 is the right choice. Ghost stories and bullet holes will be on your mind while dining at **Farnsworth House 1863** 717/334-8838. The really hungry should patronize **General Pickett's All-U-Can-Eat Buffet Restaurant** 717/334-7580.

GETTYSBURG NATIONAL MILITARY PARK
97 Taneytown Road, Gettysburg, PA17325; Tel: 717/334-1124;
Open daily, except major holidays.

During three days in July 1863, 50,000 men died here in the Civil War battle. At Gettysburg, more men fought and died than in any other battle before or since on North American soil. Although the Battle of Gettysburg did not end the war or attain any major war aim for the North or South, it remains the great battle of the war. Four months later Abraham Lincoln delivered his Gettysburg Address at the dedication of the National Cemetery.
Gettysburg Battlefields Bus Tours 717/334-6296 offers 23-mile narrated bus tours of the battlegrounds and monuments. Auto tour maps can be picked up at the visitor center (address and telephone number mentioned above). A steam-train ride is available through Gettysburg Railroad Steam Train 717/334-6932. Bikes can be rented on the battleground on 610 Taneytown Road 717/334-1258. National Riding Stables 717/334-1288 has 2-hour rides with a licensed guide or audiotape.

PA

Lehighton
Arner Memorial
Airport (22N)

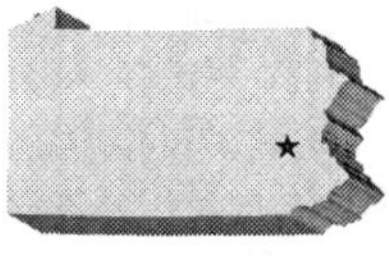

Airport is located 3 miles southwest of town.

☞ *Airport Information:*
Location: New York sectional N40.48.57 W75.45.69
Attended: 1300Z* to dusk
Elevation: 534 feet
Fuel: 100LL, Jet A
TPA: 1700 feet msl
Runway: 08-26: 3000 x 50 asph
FBO: Arner Flying Service
717/386-2330

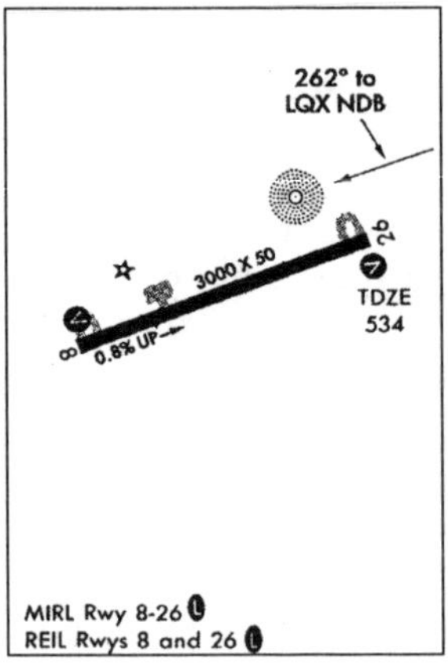

☞ *Communication:*
CTAF: 123.05
Unicom: 123.05
App/Dep: Allentown 119.65
(above 3000')
118.2 (3000' and below)

☞ *Transportation:*
Car Rental: A & A Auto 717/386-3064

☞ *Lodging:*
Jim Thorpe: Choose from guest rooms or suites with whirlpools
(good for soaking after that bike ride!) and fireplaces at **The Inn of
Jim Thorpe** 800/329-2599.

☞ *Restaurants:*
Jim Thorpe: Continental Irish American cuisine is served at the
Emerald Restaurant 717/325-8995.

POCONO WHITEWATER ADVENTURES
(approximately 5 miles from airport)
HC-2 Box 2245, Route 903, Jim Thorpe, PA 18229; Tel: 800/
WHITEWATER, Internet: www.whitewaterrafting.com

During the spring, it's whitewater rafting on the Lehigh River.
Summer float trips start July and last through the calmer water

months. Yet check with them for weekends when the Army Corps of Engineers opens the dam during the summer if you are looking for whitewater. Though Pocono Whitewater Adventures is primarily a rafting company, they also run guided mountain bike tours through the area. They know the trails and lead you to whatever you fancy — flat novice cruising territory with gorgeous river scenery, a steep jaunt up the mountain, or through the quaint Victorian tourist village of Jim Thorpe! The Lehigh Gorge ride is their most popular biking day trip. Guided hikes through the Gorge are always an experience as well.

WHILE YOU'RE THERE: The **Blue Mountain Ski Area** 610/826-7700 has a vertical drop of 1,080 feet with 20 slopes and trails and 7 lifts. Call for the snow report at 800/235-2226.

Palmyra
Reigle Field (58N)
Airport is located 2 miles south of town.

☞ *Airport Information:*
Location: New York sectional   N40.17.26   W76.34.65
Attended: 1230-2230Z*
Elevation: 489 feet
Fuel: 80, 100LL
TPA: 1500 feet msl
Runway: 13-31: 1950 x 40 asph
FBO: Reigle Aviation 717/8385519

☞ *Communication:*
CTAF: 122.8
Unicom: 122.8

PA

☞ *Transportation:*
Taxi: 717/939-7805
Car Rental: Hess Ford 717/533-9115; Enterprise 717/274-9771

☞ *Lodging:*
Hershey: **The Hershey Lodge** 800/533-3131 is a resort with in-, outdoor pool, miniature golf, and three restaurants. A classic Mediterranean design is reflected at award-winning **Hotel Hershey**

717/533-2171 or 800/533-3131. Close by the attractions is the **Chocolatetown Motel** 717/533-2330. **Best Western Inn** 717/533-5665; **Days Inn** 717/534-2162; **Holiday Inn Express** 717/583-0500

☞ *Restaurants:*
Hershey: The Hershey Lodge and **Hotel Hershey** 800/533-3131 have fine family dining. Italian is on the menu at **Lucy's Cafe** 717/534-1045. **Spinner's Restaurant** 717/533-9050 serves a wide variety of food.

HERSHEY'S CHOCOLATE WORLD
(simulated chocolate factory 6 miles from airport)
100 West Hersheypark Drive, Hershey, PA 17033; Tel: 800/HERSHEY, Internet:www.800hershey.com
Open daily.
Admission is free.

Travel like a cocoa bean from a tropical jungle through the "factory" in a simulated tour that lets you experience how chocolate is made. Free sample given at the end of tour, but a big gift and souvenir shop can satisfy that chocolate craving.

HERSHEYPARK
(theme park 6 miles from airport)
100 West Hersheypark Drive, Hershey, PA 17033; Tel: 800/HERSHEY; Internet: www.800hershey.com
Open from May to September.
Admission is $29.95 for adults, $16.95 for children ages 3 to 8 years.

It all started out as a picnic ground for Hershey factory workers back in 1907. Now it is a big amusement park with six roller coasters and more than 55 rides, including six drenching water rides and 20 kiddy rides. Their newest ride is Great Bear, an inverted looping steel roller coaster allowing you to plummet from 120 feet high—twisting, turning and corkscrewing your way through loops and spirals. The Sweetest Parade on Earth features a marching band and 14 life-sized Hershey's-Product Characters. Unless you have a total aversion to theme parks, it's hard not to like this clean and pretty one on 110 acres. Hersheypark grounds are the site of the annual hot-air balloon fest, end of October.

WHILE YOU'RE THERE: Seventy-two holes of golf are yours to choose from in Hershey. Visit the botanical and rose gardens with the newly added butterfly house. Contact **800/Hershey** for info.

PA

Reading
Spaatz Field (RDG)
Airport is located 3 miles northwest of town.

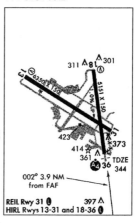

☞ *Airport Information:*

Location: New York sectional N40.22.71 W75.57.92
Airspace: Class D service 1100-0500Z*
Attended: 1000-0500Z
Elevation: 344 feet
Fuel: 100LL, Jet A
TPA: 1400 feet msl
Runway: 13-31: 6350 x 150 asph
18-36: 5151 x 150 asph
FBO: Aerodynamics 610/373-3000
AVITAT-Reading 610/372-4728

☞ *Communication:*

CTAF: 119.9
Unicom: 122.95
App/Dep: Reading 125.15 (1100-0500Z*)
Harrisburg 124.1 (0500-1100Z*)
Tower: 119.9 (1100-0500Z*)
Ground: 121.9
ATIS: 127.1

☞ *Transportation:*

Taxi: 610/374-5111; 610/478-1111
Car Rental: Avis 610/372-6636; Hertz 610/374-1448

☞ *Lodging:*

Reading: **Holiday Inn** 610/929-4741; **Sheraton Berkshire Inn**
610/376-3811

MID-ATLANTIC AIR MUSEUM
(located on field)
Road #9, Box 9381, Reading, PA 19605; Tel: 610/372-7333
Open daily, except major holidays.
Admission is $3 for adults and $2 for children.

The Mid-Atlantic Air Museum was established in 1980 for the
purpose of collecting and preserving vintage aircraft of civil and
military origin. So take a step back in time and enter the "Golden Age

of Flight." Surround yourself with aircraft whose history is not only part of the development of aviation but is also closely intertwined with the growth and defense of our nation. Aircraft, from single-engine trainers to multi-engine transports and bombers, have been restored to flying condition and actually participate in airshows. You may also tour work areas to view the restoration process.

Smoketown Airport

(37PA)
Airport is located adjacent to town.

☞ *Airport Information:*
Location: New York sectional N40.02.47 W76.12.08
Attended: 1300-2200Z*
Elevation: 370 feet
Fuel: 80, 100LL
TPA: 1200 feet msl
Runway: 10-28: 2400 x 50 asph
FBO: Glick Aviation 717/394-6476

☞ *Communication:*
CTAF: 123.05
Unicom: 123.05

☞ *Transportation:*
Taxi: 717/392-7327; 717/397-8108
Car Rental: Hertz 717/569-4345

PA

☞ *Lodging:*
Paradise: Stay at the **Verdant View Farm** 717/687-7353 with a family that opens their farmhouse to visitors to observe day-to-day farm life. A simple but comfortable accommodation.
Bird-in-Hand: The Victorian style *Village Inn of Bird-in-Hand* 717/293-8369 has 11 guest rooms with modern amenities.
Strasburg: The newly renovated **Historic Strasburg Inn** 717/687-7691 or 800/872-0201 is situated on 58 acres overlooking Amish farms, still carefully tilled as they were over a century ago.
Lancaster: **Best Western Eden Resort** 717/569-6444

☞ *Restaurants:*
Bird-in-Hand: Expect hearty Pennsylvania Dutch home cooking at

the **Bird-in-Hand Family Restaurant** 717/768-8266 as well as at **The Amish Barn Restaurant** 717/768-8886.
Strasburg: Local fare, a weekday lunch buffet, and a selection of French/American cuisine at dinnertime are served at the formal **Strasburg Inn** 717/687-7691.

AMISH COUNTRY TOURS
(approximately 2 miles from airport)
Plain and Fancy Farm, Route 340 between Bird-in-Hand and Intercourse; Tel: 717/768-3600
Daily tours during the summer. Weekends only during winter.
Tours are $17.95 for adults and $10.95 for children.

Tourists come to Pennsylvania Dutch Country mainly to observe the Old Order Amish, who cling to a centuries-old way of life. Descendants of German and Swiss immigrants came to the area to escape religious persecution. It's a crowded place in summertime but you'll discover much charm along backroad lanes dotted with farms and fields worked by mules. Kerosene or gas lamps are being used in lieu of electricity and transportation is by horse-drawn buggy. Take a 2 ½-hour van tour to see one-room schools, Amish farmland and cottage industries. Be aware that many restaurants, shops, and farmer's markets may be closed on Sunday. If you are staying overnight, check if the hotel offers packages that already include a tour.

ED'S BUGGY RIDES
(approximately 5 miles from the airport)
Route 896, Strasburg, PA 17572; Tel: 717/687-0360
Rides are $7 for adults and $3.50 for children.

Travel the scenic back roads of the Amish farmlands in an authentic buggy. Watch bearded farmers and their horses working in the field or just enjoy the beautiful scenery for about a 3-mile stretch.

PA

WHILE YOU'RE THERE: The **visitor center** 717/397-3531 in Lancaster has maps for self-guided tours and organizes guided tours. To really get a feel for the place, rent a bike at **Strasburg Bike Rental** 717/687-8222. If you like trains, the **Strasburg Railroad** 717/687-7522 gives 45-minute rides in original steam trains. Experience the daily life of a self-sufficient community that has remained virtually unchanged for more than 250 years at **The Amish Village** 717/687-8511. A huge indoor **Farmers Market** 717/393-9674 is located in Bird-in-Hand. The **Great Adventure Balloon Club** 717/397-3623 offers a bird's-eye view of Lancaster.

State College
University Park
Airport (UNV)

Airport is located 3 miles north of town.

☞ *Airport Information:*

Location: Detroit sectional N40.50.96 W77.50.92
Attended: 1100-0430Z*
Elevation: 1239 feet
Fuel: 100LL, Jet A
TPA: 2039 feet msl lgt acft
2239 feet msl hvy acft
Runway: 06-24: 6700 x 100 asph
16-34: 2350 x 50 asph
FBO: 814/865-5511

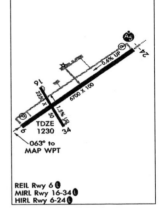

☞ *Communication:*

CTAF: 122.8
Unicom: 122.8
App/Dep: New York Center 134.8
Clnc Del: 118.55
AWOS: 127.65 (04030-1030Z*)

☞ *Transportation:*

Taxi: 814/353-6001
Car Rental: Avis 814/237-9750; National 814/237-1771
Hertz 814/237-1728

☞ *Lodging:*

State College: See **Toftrees Resort** 814/234-8000 below;
Courtyard by Marriott 814/238-1881; **The Nittany Lion Inn**
814/865-8500 is a colonial-style inn with 237 rooms.

☞ *Restaurants:*

State College: Patronize **Le Papillon** 814/234-8000 at Toftrees
Resort for formal dinners.

TOFTREES RESORT
(golf approximately 5 miles from airport)
One Country Club Lane, State College, PA 16803; Tel: 814/234-
8000 or 800/458-3602

Toftrees has been rated as the top public and resort course in the state by *Golf Digest* and has hosted the Pennsylvania PGA Championship for 10 of the past 11 years; 18 holes at par 72 are challenging but the scenery is magnificent. Rolling hills, woods, water, and constant changes of the elevation require a strategic approach—especially hole 9, which requires a 220-yard carry over water. The resort itself is surrounded by the golf course and offers beautiful views of the rolling hills of Happy Valley. Facilities include a heated outdoor pool, tennis courts, boat rentals, and croquet. Toftrees does not have its own health club but offers access to one nearby.

Toughkenamon (N57)
New Garden Airport

Airport is located 1 mile west of town.

☞ *Airport Information:*

Location: Washington sectional N39.49.83 W75.46.19
Attended: Daylight hours
Elevation: 436 feet
Fuel: 80, 100LL
TPA: 1500 feet msl
Runway: 06-24: 3695 x 50 asph
FBO: New Garden Aviation
610/268-2048

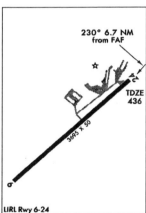

☞ *Communication:*

CTAF: 122.8
Unicom: 122.8
App/Dep: Philadelphia 124.35
Clnc Del: 125.6

PA

☞ *Transportation:*
Car Rental: Enterprise 610/444-9454

☞ *Lodging:*
Kennett Square: **Longwood Motor Inn** 610/444-3515

LONGWOOD GARDENS
(approximately 4 miles from airport)
Route 1, P.O. Box 501, Kennett Square, PA 19348; Tel: 610/388-1000; Internet: www.longwoodgardens.org
Open daily.
Admission is $12 for adults ($8 on Tuesdays).

Longwood Garden is sure to delight anyone who loves exquisite flowers, majestic trees, and opulent architecture. Starting out as a working farm back in 1700, Longwood Gardens has been turned into a horticultural showplace. Twenty outdoor gardens and 20 indoor gardens with four acres of greenhouses display a variety of themes such as the Idea Garden, Topiary Garden, Rose Arbor, Italian Water, and so on. The blending of fountains, canals, moats, woodland streams, and formal Italian pools with their respective displays is one of the most striking features. Events are held throughout the year—flower shows, gardening demonstrations, performing arts events, and seasonal festivals. The Christmas display at the Conservatory and outdoor Christmas lighting are sure to get you into the right spirit. Books, gifts, and plants are for sale in the Garden Shop. A restaurant is on site.
Longwood Gardens is also an ideal spot to watch birds, some of them termed rare or very rare.

Wellsboro
Grand Canyon State Airport (N38)

Airport is located 4 miles southwest of town.

☞ *Airport Information:*

Location:	Detroit sectional N41.43.67 W77.23.79
Attended:	Daylight hours
Elevation:	1899 feet
Fuel:	80, 100LL
TPA:	2700 feet msl
Runway:	10-28: 3600 x 60 asph
FBO:	717/724-4851

☞ *Communication:*
CTAF: 122.8
Unicom: 122.8
App/Dep: Elmira 119.45 (1100-0500Z*)
New York Center 133.35
(0500-1100Z*)

☞ *Transportation:*
Car Rental: Jim West 717/724-1066

☞ *Lodging:*
Wellsboro: The **Grand Canyon Motel
and Resort** 717/724-4774 is located 1
mile east of Harrison State Park.
Pennwells Hotel-Lodge 717/724-2111;
The **Four Winds B & B** 800/368-7963 is an 1870s country Victorian
with pool.

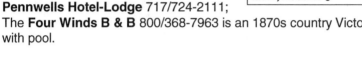

TDZE
1899
3600 X 60

MIRL Rwy 10-28 ⓞ
REIL Rwys 10 and 28 ⓞ

MOUNTAIN TRAIL HORSE CENTER
(approximately 10 miles from airport)
R.D. 2, P.O. Box 53, Wellsboro, PA 16901; Tel: 717/376-5561

The Grand Canyon Country location for these outfitters' trail-riding
trips is in some of Pennsylvania's most beautiful and rugged terrain,
with pristine tracts of forest land. For overnight trips, camp will be
prepared for you in the forest by experienced guides or you may end
up at a cabin with wildlife teeming around you. Look for deer, black
bears, and eagles. Day trips include a hearty lunch and range from
four to six hours. Your outing will be a wilderness experience, riding
over all sorts of terrain. If you are not keen on riding a horse or have
smaller children with you, travel the old railroad bed through Pine
Creek Gorge in a covered horse-drawn wagon. Morning, afternoon,
or evening wagon rides available. Be sure to get advance
reservations. Prices for trail rides depend on the number of people in
your group and whether you choose a basic or deluxe trip.

PA

Block Island State Airport

(BID)
Airport is located 1 mile west of town.

☞ *Airport Information:*

Location: New York sectional N41.10.09 W71.34.67
Attended: Nov-Apr 1400-2200Z*
May-Oct 1300-0300Z*
Elevation: 109 feet
Fuel: Not available
TPA: 1000 feet msl
Runway: 10-28: 2502 x 100 asph
FBO: Hawthorne Aviation
401/466-5511

☞ *Communication:*

CTAF: 123.0
Unicom: 123.0
App/Dep: Providence 125.75
(1100-0500Z*)
Boston Center (0500-1100Z*)
Clnc Del: 120.1
AWOS: 134.775

☞ *Transportation:*

Taxi: 401/466-2882
Car Rental: 401/466-2028; 401/466-2029

RI

☞ *Lodging:*

Block Island: **The 1661 Inn & Hotel Manisses** 401/466-2421 or 800/MANISSE is named for the year that Block Island was settled. It offers 18 guest rooms at the Inn, each of which is named after one of the original settlers from Massachusetts Bay. To escape religious oppression, they purchased the island and settled on it. The hotel has each of its rooms named after a famous ship wrecked before 1870. The charm of this pretty building comes mostly from the beauty of its site, perched above the village harbor on a meadow.

Guests can watch the sun rising over the Atlantic. Set amidst magnificent gardens and grounds is **The Atlantic Inn** 401/466-5883 or 800/224-7422, a Victorian inn and restaurant.

☞ *Restaurants:*
Block Island: "Impressive for both originality and variety" and "unexpectedly sophisticated" is how *Gourmet* magazine described the menu at **The Hotel Manisses** 401/466-2421 or 800-MANISSE. Fresh seafood is the specialty. **Finn's Seafood Restaurant** 401/466-2473 specializes in lobster and seafood prepared fresh from their fish market. Use the take-out window if you prefer picnics. **Block Island Burrito** 401/466-2973; **Capizzano's Pizza** 401/466-2829

BLOCK ISLAND PARA-SAIL
Box 216, Block Island, RI 02807; Tel: 401/466-2474

Experience is not necessary to try out para-sailing. You will be up to 600 feet above the ocean. Flying side-by-side is possible with the new tandem bar.

OCEANS & PONDS
(fishing charters and various rentals approximately 2 miles from airport)
Ocean & Connecticut Avenue, Box 136, Block Island, RI 02807; Tel: 401/466-5131 or 800/ORVIS-01

Onshore, inshore, and deep sea fishing trips are available through this outfitter. Right around midsummer the bluefish start running! The freshwater ponds have bass, perch, and pickerel, but don't forget to get a license. The Orvis shop also rents kayaks, canoes, and rods for fishing. Guides are available.

THE MOPED MAN
435 Water Street, Block Island, RI 02807; Tel: 410/466-5444

RI

Over one-fourth of Block Island is preservation land harboring rare birds and the natural beauty of breathtaking scenery. Its freshwater ponds are a haven for migrating birds — up to 150 species may visit. Rent a bike to explore the miles of seaside roads, to reach the gorgeous lighthouses, or just to enjoy the views while getting a workout on the many hills of this beautiful island. A full range of bicycles, from 6-speed cruisers to 21-speed mountain bikes to kid's bikes, is offered. If you want to see the island with more comfort and speed, a single- or double-seater moped is the way to go. Call ahead during the summer months to reserve your choice.

WHILE YOU'RE THERE: Guided trail rides on the beach and pony rides for children are available year round from **Rustic Rides Farm** 401/466-5060. **Old Harbor Bike Shop** 401/466-2029 rents bikes, mopeds, cars, vans and jeeps. Use the Greenway, a network of trails that wind through park, and private lands all the way from the center of the island to the southern shore.

Newport State Airport (UUU)
Airport is located 2 miles northeast of town.

☞ *Airport Information:*

Location: New York sectional N41.31.95 W71.16.89
Attended: Nov-Apr 1300-2300Z*; May-Oct 1200-0200Z*
Elevation: 172 feet
Fuel: 100LL
TPA: 1200 feet msl
Runway: 04-22: 2999 x 75 asph
16-34: 2623 x 75 asph
FBO: Aquidneck Aviation
401/848-7080

☞ *Communication:*
CTAF: 122.8
Unicom: 122.8
App/Dep: Providence 128.7
(1100-0500Z*)
Boston Center (0500-1100Z*)
Clnc Del: 127.25
AWOS: 132.075

☞ *Transportation:*
Taxi: 401/849-5454
Car Rental: Rent-a-Car 401/846-3250; Thrifty 401/846-3200

☞ *Lodging:*
Newport: On the water's edge on a 32-acre site sits the **Inn at Castle Hill** 401/849-3800. It's a three-story Victorian mansion built in 1874. **The Francis Malbone House** 401/846-0392 has 18 rooms

and is furnished with period reproductions. Very basic but clean is the **Harbour Base Pineapple Inn** 401/847-2600.

☞ *Restaurants:*
Newport: **Flo's Clam Shack** 401/847-8141 has choice mollusks. **Black Pearl** 401/846-5264 is a sailor's hangout on the waterfront. Make sure you have reservations. Watch the freshest of seafood being prepared at **Scales & Shells** 401/848-9378.

ADVENTURE SPORTS RENTALS
(approximately 5 miles from airport)
The Inn at Long Wharf, America's Cup Avenue, Newport, RI 02840; Tel: 401/849-4820

Surrounded on three sides by water, Newport is one of the great sailing spots of the world. It hosted the America's Cup for 35 years. A 25-year wait for a slip at the marina attests to its popularity. Adventure Sports Rentals provides sailboats, kayaks, canoes, and waverunners.

HAMMERSMITH FARM
(museum approximately 5 miles from airport)
Ocean Drive, Newport, RI; Tel: 401/846-7346
Open from April to mid-November and Christmas.

Hammersmith Farm was the site of the wedding of Jacqueline Bouvier and John F. Kennedy. As the childhood summer home of Jacqueline, it has lots of memorabilia. Guided tours.

NEWPORT MUSIC FESTIVAL
(approximately 4 miles from airport)
P.O. Box 3300, Newport, RI 02840; Tel: 401/846-1133; Box Office Phone: 401/849-0700; Internet: www.newportmusic.org

1998 was the 30th season of the Newport Music Festival presenting unique chamber music programs, American debuts of international artists, world-class artists, and special events in the grand "summer cottages" of Newport. Three, four, and even five concerts a day are held during a 2-week period in July. Special events include a children's concert and concert cruises.

R I

THE PRESERVATION SOCIETY OF NEWPORT CTY.
(historic properties for public viewing approx. 5 miles from airport)
424 Bellevue Avenue, Newport, RI 02840; Tel: 401/847-1000;

Internet: www.newportmansions.org
Admission charged for either individual properties or combination tickets.
Only during the summer are all properties open daily.

Newport was a summer playground for America's wealthiest families in the 19th century. A myriad of mansions are open to the public. Nine extravagant historic properties can be toured with the Preservation Society of Newport County. One of the most sumptuous of Newport's "cottages" is the Marble House. It contains "tons" of marble and rooms covered entirely in gold. It was built in 1892 for William K. Vanderbilt and has original furnishings. Resembling a 16th-century northern Italian palace, The Breakers is a National Historic Landmark and was built for Cornelius Vanderbilt. The grounds overlook the Atlantic Ocean and Cliff Walk. Chateau-Sur-Mer is one of the finest examples of lavish Victorian architecture in America. It was built in 1852 for William S. Wetmore, who made his fortune in the China trade. The Green Animals Topiary Garden in Portsmouth has 21 shrubs sculpted as animals. There are 80 sculpted trees, shrubs, fruit and vegetable gardens, and formal flower beds. Avoid long lines during the summer by going early or viewing less popular mansions!

WANTON-LYMAN-HAZARD HOUSE
(approximately 4 miles from airport)
17 Broadway, Newport, RI 02840; Tel: 401/846-0813 (Newport Historical Society)
Admission charged.
Open June 15 to September 1, Thursday to Sunday.

Built in 1675, it is Newport's oldest surviving residence. It is furnished with authentic period furniture and has a two-room plan typical of the time.

R I

WHILE YOU'RE THERE: The **Museum of Yachting** 401/847-1018 has lots of pictures of America's Cup Racing, yachts and mansions. Daily and weekly crewed yacht charters and harbor tours are offered by **Old Port Marine Services** 401/847-9109. Spring and fall are the best times for watching scores of songbirds at the **Norman Bird Sanctuary** 401/846-2577 and the **Sachuest Point National Wildlife Refuge** 401/847-5511. Snowy owls and red-tailed hawks may be seen in fall and winter.

✈ SOUTH CAROLINA ✈

Charleston AFB - Int'l Airport (CHS)

Airport is located 9 miles northwest of town.

☞ *Airport Information:*
Location: Charlotte sectional N32.53.92 W80.02.43
Airspace: Class C
Attended: Continuously
Elevation: 46 feet
Fuel: 100, Jet A
TPA: 1100 feet msl lgt acft
1600 feet msl hvy acft
Runway: 15-33: 9001 x 200 conc
03-21: 7000 x 150 conc
Check for runway closures!
FBO: New Charleston Aviation
843/744-2581

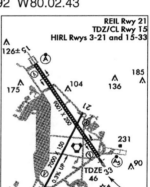

☞ *Communication:*
Unicom: 122.95
App: 120.7 (151-330º); 135.8 (331-150º); 119.3
Dep: 120.7 (151-330º); 135.8 (331-150º)
Tower: 126.0
Ground: 121.9
Clnc Del: 118.0
ATIS: 124.75

☞ *Transportation:*
Taxi: 843/767-7117
Car Rental: Avis 843/767-7030; Hertz 843/767-4552
National 843/767-3078

SC

☞ *Lodging:*
Charleston: Both the **Holiday Inn** 803/744-1621 and the **Radisson Inn** 803-744-2501 are near the airport. See under Charleston

Executive Airport below for additional listings.

☞ *Restaurants:*
Charleston: See listing under Charleston Executive Airport below.

MAGNOLIA PLANTATION AND GARDENS
(approximately 3 miles from airport)
Route 61, Charleston, SC 29414; Tel: 843/556-1012
Open daily.
Admission to grounds $9; house tours $5; tram tours $4; swamp tours $4.

One of several plantations in the area, Magnolia Plantation has been in the Drayton family since 1671. It includes the country's oldest garden, which is world famous for its abundance of colors and scents. Azaleas, dogwoods, and daffodils are show stoppers in spring. The camellia (900 varieties) and azalea (250 varieties) collection is considered the largest in North America. The garden also features the Barbados Tropical Garden (Thomas Drayton arrived from Barbados), a nature Train Tour, a petting zoo, wildlife observation tower, nature trails, wildlife art gallery, rental bikes, herb garden, topiary garden, and horticultural maze. Bird-watchers, bring your binoculars, as you will not be disappointed.

WHILE YOU'RE THERE: Rent a canoe to paddle through the 125-acre Waterfowl Refuge or the **Audubon Swamp Garden** 843/556-1012 or 800/367-3517. This preserved swamp, complete with moss-draped blackwater cypress and alligators, is traversed by bridges, boardwalks, and dikes.

Charleston Executive Airport (JZI)

Airport is located 6 miles southwest of town.

☞ *Airport Information:*
Location: Charlotte sectional N32.42.05 W80.00.18
Attended: 1200-0300Z*
Elevation: 20 feet
Fuel: 100LL, Jet A
Runway: 09-27: 5000 x 150 conc

Runway: 04-22: 4311 x 150 conc
FBO: Charleston Executive Aviation
843/559-2401

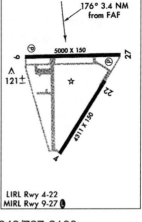

☞ *Communication:*
CTAF: 122.8
Unicom: 122.8
App/Dep: 120.7
Clnc Del: 127.5

☞ *Transportation:*
Taxi: 843/723-2383; 843/577-6565
Car Rental: Enterprise 803/723-6215

☞ *Lodging:*
Charleston: The **Battery Carriage House** 843/727-3100 or 800/775-5575 is a renovated mansion furnished with period antiques. The **Victoria House Inn** 843/720-2944 or 800/933-5464 has 18 guest rooms. If you want to stay at Charleston's prime hotel, book with the **Charleston Place Hotel** 843/722-4900.

☞ *Restaurants:*
Charleston: Local fare in an 1800s warehouse setting is served at **Magnolias** 843/577-7771. An unusual and large variety of fish, even for a seafood restaurant, is on the menu at **Hyman's Seafood Company** 843/723-6000. **BJ's at the Farm** 843/722-8904 serves good burgers. For a special evening out with dining and dancing on a luxury yacht, visit the **Spirit of Charleston** 843/722-2628.
Kiawah Island: **Kiawah Island Resort** 843/768-2121 or 800/654-2924 offers seven dining options from casual to upscale.

KIAWAH ISLAND GOLF & TENNIS RESORT
(approximately 10 miles from airport)
12 Kiawah Beach Drive, Kiawah Island, SC 29455; Tel: 803/768-2121 or 800/654-2924

Many consider Kiawah Island to have one of the finest collections of golf courses in the country. A semitropical barrier island with pleasant weather year-round does not invite just golfers, though. Ten miles of secluded, white, sandy beaches entice shell collectors, sunbathers, bikers, bird-watchers, joggers—you choose your favorite activity—and all this with breathtaking scenery. Golfers can sample five courses. The Pete Dye–designed Ocean Course is famous for hosting the dramatic 1991 Ryder Cup and the 1997 World Cup of

SC

Golf. With every hole offering dramatic views of rolling dunes and Atlantic surf, it has earned its place among the world's greatest. The Tom Fazio course, Osprey Point, is well protected by sand and built on a series of islands. You will cross ten wooden bridges during a round. Jack Nicklaus's Turtle Point Course is highlighted by three ocean holes and was the spot for the 1990 PGA Cup Matches. Water is the key hazard on Cougar Point, a course laid out by Gary Player. Kiawah's latest addition, Oak Point, is a Scottish-American-style course designed by Clyde Johnston.

If tennis is what you prefer to play, you will be pleased to know that the resort is ranked number 3 on *Tennis Magazine's* prestigious "Top 10 Greatest U.S. Tennis Resorts" and hosted the 1998 Fed Cup.

LOW COUNTRY CARRIAGE CO.
(horse and carriage tours approximately 8 miles from airport)
14 Hayne Street, Charleston, SC 29401; Tel: 843/577-0042

Charleston, a port city steeped in history, lends itself to leisurely and lively carriage tours. Block after block of old buildings have been restored. Elegant porticos and piazzas of magnificent homes, which once belonged to barons and earls who presided over the great coastal plantations, line cobblestone streets catching the breezes. Charleston still resembles an 18th-century picture come to life with its charm and beauty. Tours leave from Market/Church Street, where you can find everything from antiques to produce.

WHILE YOU'RE THERE: Try a different kind of tour — **Ghosts of Charleston Tours** 843/723-1670 offers ghost tours of some of Charleston's most prominent haunted dwellings! Pick up details from the well-equipped **visitor center** 843/853-8000 for walking tours and homes that are open for viewing. A view of the city from the harbor is possible by taking a two-hour cruise with **Schooner Pride** 843/559-9686.

Columbia
Owens Downtown
Airport (CUB)

Airport is located 2 miles south of town.

☞ *Airport Information:*

Location: Charlotte sectional N33.58.23 W80.59.71
Attended: 1100-0300Z*
Elevation: 194 feet
Fuel: 100LL, Jet A
TPA: 982 feet msl
Runway: 13-31: 4999 x 75 asph
FBO: Midlands Aviation
803/771-7915

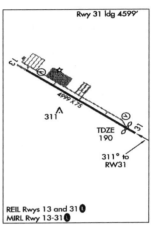

Rwy 31 ldg 4599'

311°

TDZE
190

311° to
RW31

REIL Rwys 13 and 31 ●
MIRL Rwy 13-31 ●

☞ *Communication:*

CTAF: 122.8
Unicom: 122.8
App/Dep: Columbia 133.4
Clnc Del: 124.4
ASOS: 119.675

☞ *Transportation:*

Taxi: 803/799-3311
Car Rental: Budget 803/779-1212

☞ *Lodging:*

Columbia: **Holiday Inn** 803/799-7800; **Adams Mark** 803/771-7000
or 800/444-2326

☞ *Restaurants:*

Columbia: Craving for barbecue? **Maurice Gourmet Barbecue -
Piggie Park** 803/796-0220 won't disappoint you.

SC

RIVERBANKS ZOO AND GARDEN
(approximately 6 miles from the airport)
Greystone Blvd., Columbia, SC 29202; Tel: 803/779-8717
Open daily.
Admission is $6.25 for adults and $3.75 for children 3 to12 years old.

Riverbanks Zoo is ranked among the top ten in the nation. Over

2,000 animals roam in open habitats and endangered species have reproduced here. Pass through a rainforest, a desert, an undersea kingdom, and a Southern farm and keep your eyes open for demonstrations and feedings of some animals. The Botanical Garden consists of formal gardens and woodland trails.

WHILE YOU'RE THERE: Guided canoe and kayak trips are offered by the **River Runner Outdoor Center** 803/771-0353.

Florence Reg. Airport (FLO)
Airport is located 3 miles east of town.

☞ *Airport Information:*
Location:	Charlotte sectional N34.11.12 W79.43.43
Airspace:	Class D service 1130-0300Z*
Attended:	1130-0300Z*
Elevation:	148 feet
Fuel:	100LL, Jet A
TPA:	1000 feet msl
Runway:	09-27: 6500 x 150 asph
	01-19: 6001 x 150 asph
FBO:	Carolina Air Service
	843/667-9627

☞ *Communication:*
CTAF:	125.1
Unicom:	122.95
App/Dep:	Florence 118.6 (256-074º),
	135.25 (075-255º), (1130-0300Z*)
	JAX Center 133.45 (0300-1130Z*)
Tower:	125.1 (1130-0300Z*)
Ground:	121.9
ATIS:	123.625 (1130-0300Z*)

☞ *Transportation:*
Car Rental: Avis 843/669-7695; National 843/662-9077

☞ *Lodging:*
Florence: **Heritage Inn** 803/662-0461; **Best Western** 803/678-9292

FLORENCE AIR & MISSILE MUSEUM

(located on field)
P.O. Box 1326, Florence, SC 29503; Tel: 803/665-5118
Open daily. Admission is $5 for adults and $3 for children.

A self-guided tour will lead you by a variety of military aircraft from 1940 to 1970. Also on display are aviation, space, and military artifacts.

Hilton Head Island
Hilton Head Airport (HXD)

Airport is located 3 miles east of town.

☞ *Airport Information:*

Location:	Charlotte sectional N32.13.45 W80.41.86
Attended:	1130-0400Z*
Elevation:	20 feet
Fuel:	100LL, Jet A
TPA:	1200 feet msl lgt acft
	1500 feet msl hvy acft
Runway:	03-21: 4300 x 75 asph
FBO:	Hilton Head Air Service
	843/681-6386
	Carolina Air Center
	843/689-3200

```
Rwy 3 ldg 4000'
Rwy 21 ldg 4000'
                        120± △
             TDZE
              19
                            4300 X 75
                                    ☆78
                                   66
111±△
    3  △87±
REIL Rwys 3 and 21◐
MIRL Rwy 3-21◐
```

☞ *Communication:*

CTAF:	123.0
Unicom:	123.0
App/Dep:	Savannah 125.3
	(1100-0400Z*), Jax Center 120.85 (0400-1100Z*)
Clnc Del:	121.1

☞ *Transportation:*

Taxi:	843/681-6666; 843/681-5883
Car Rental:	Budget 843/689-4242

SC

☞ *Lodging:*
Hilton Head Island: **Hampton Inn** 843/681-7900; **Comfort Inn** 843/842-6662; **Motel 6** 843/785-2700; **Holiday Inn** 843/785-5126;

Palmetto Dunes Resort 843/785-1199 see below; **Sea Pines Resort** 800/SEA-PINES see below.

PALMETTO DUNES RESORT
(tennis and golfing approximately 5 miles from the airport)
P.O. Box 4798, Hilton Head Island, SC 29938; Tel: 843/785-1199;
Internet: www.palmettodunesresort.com

Palmetto Dunes Resort is a four-diamond resort featuring five excellent golf courses, two hotels (Hyatt Regency Hilton Head and Hilton Resort Hotel), the award-winning Palmetto Dunes Tennis Center, the largest deep-water marina on the island and, of course, miles of beautiful beach. Kayaks are ready to be used for exploration of scenic creeks. Boating, sailing, in-shore fishing, windsurfing, biking, crabbing, and nature tours are the activities one can choose from. In addition there are daily tennis clinics and Round Robins taking place on 25 courts of the tennis center.
Each of Palmetto's five golf courses is named after its renowned designer. Featuring a unique lagoon system and generous landing areas, the Robert Trent Jones Course is the oldest of the five. Tree-lined fairways and a distance of almost 6,900 yards are the characteristics of the George Fazio Course. Two courses are named after Arthur Hills. One is located at Palmetto Dunes and has hosted the Palmetto Dunes/Golf World Collegiate. The other Arthur Hills course and the course by Bob Cupp are located at Palmetto Hall Plantation and have successfully passed the scrutiny of critics. Facilities are open to the public, but reservations are recommended. Vacation villas come from one to four bedrooms and have full kitchens and living rooms.

SEA PINES RESORT
(golf and tennis resort approximately 6 miles from the airport)
32 Greenwood Drive, Hilton Head Island, SC 29928; Tel: 800/SEA-PINES, Internet: www.seapines.com

There is a tranquil beauty to vast tidal marshes, pristine forests and miles of sand. Enjoy it at Sea Pines while playing golf, tennis, horseback riding, biking, swimming, or just relaxing. For a round of golf choose from three 18-hole courses, with Harbour Town Golf Links being ranked very high by many PGA Tour Professionals. Home of the Heritage Classic, it features early examples of architect Pete Dye's trademarks of railroad ties. Well-placed tee shots and approaches are essential to good scoring, and the well-protected greens are among the smallest of any tournament course in the

SC

country. Although Harbour Town gets most of the attention, Ocean Course and Sea Marsh Course can hold their own. Ocean Course was the first golf course on Hilton Head Island and re-opened in 1995 after a major reconstruction led by Mark McCumber & Associates. Lagoons, bunkers, and contouring were used to create a contemporary course that appeals to golfers of all levels. Many of Sea Marsh's holes traverse lagoons and marshes that make it both beautiful and challenging. Pines, palmettos, and moss-draped oaks line broad fairways. Daily clinics and private instruction are available. Sea Pines Raquet Club at Harbour Town, home of The Family Circle Cup, has been the site of more nationally televised events than any other location. There are 28 courts and a full schedule of services and programs. Vacation accommodations range from homes to villas with one to six bedrooms. It should be noted that registered guests of Sea Pines receive special rates for using the golf courses and tennis courts.

VAN DER MEER TENNIS UNIVERSITY
(approximately 5 miles from airport)
Shipyard Plantation, P.O. Box 5902, Hilton Head Island, SC 29938; Tel: 800/438-0793 or 843/686-8804

Van Der Meer Tennis University offers programs for all skill levels and all ages. Choose from weekend to week-long clinics to fine-tune your game. Adult programs feature video analysis, competitive drilling, supervised match play, and strategy sessions. A total of 48 courts, seven of them covered, are at your disposal. Some clinics are personally conducted by Dennis Van der Meer, a once top-rated player in his native South Africa and now known as the "pro who teaches the pros."

WHILE YOU'RE THERE: Contact the **Hilton Head Chamber of Commerce** 843/785-3673 for a schedule of free outdoor concerts at Harbour Town and Shelter Cove. They also can provide you with the details on the ever-so-popular fishing tournaments in the area.

SC

Manning
Santee-Cooper Regional
Airport (MNI)

Airport is located 7 miles south of town.

☞ *Airport Information:*
Location: Charlotte sectional N33.35.23 W80.12.52
Attended: Mon-Fri 1300-2200Z*
Elevation: 104 feet
Fuel: 100LL
TPA: 900 feet msl
Runway: 02-20: 3601 x 75 asph
FBO: Precision Air 803/478-2211

☞ *Communication:*
CTAF: 122.8
Unicom: 122.8
App/Dep: Shaw 118.85 (100-0300Z*)
　　　　　Jax Center 127.95
　　　　　　(0330-1100Z*)

☞ *Transportation:*
Car Rental: Prothro 803/435-2387

☞ *Lodging:*
Manning: **Economy Inn** 803/473-4021; **Comfort Inn** 803/473-7550

REEL WILD CHARTERS
(fishing approximately 10 miles from airport)
RR 4, Manning, SC 29102; Tel: 803/478-7321

Historically, Santee-Cooper area streams have teemed with fish, and the marshes and fields with game birds. Then the Santee-Cooper hydroelectric project created two lakes, Marion and Moultrie, connected by a canal. Because they were not fully cleared of stumps and timber before the flooding, the lakes offer a haven for such species as striped bass, crappie, bream, white bass, and largemouth bass. Several world records have been set here, among them an Arkansas blue catfish that weighed 109.4 pounds and a 58-pound channel cat. Capt. Bret Betler of Reel Wild Charters is a resource for fishermen who need guidance, service, and equipment. He has

SC

appeared on outdoor television shows, including the *In-Fisherman, Young America Outdoors* and *Carolina Outdoors*, as well as being a Pro-Tec School of Bassin's Pro Team instructor. He specializes in giant catfish, stripers, and largemouth bass.

WHILE YOU'RE THERE: Of the numerous other guide services in the area, **Randy's Guide Service** 803/478-8184 also offers deer hunting parties in addition to the usual fishing trips. **Cooper's Landing Fishing Guide Service** 888/PRO-GUIDE offers guide services as well as boat rentals, bait, tackle, fishing licenses — whatever you need! If you prefer, fish with 1 to 6 people for 8 hours a day on a 30-foot fully equipped pontoon boat, with rods and reels furnished. Contact **800/ASK-FISH** for up-to-date fishing reports, as well as fishing regulations.

Mount Pleasant
East Cooper Airport (8S5)

Airport is located 9 miles northeast of town.

☞ *Airport Information:*
Location:　Charlotte sectional N32.53.88 W79.46.97
Attended:　1300-0100Z*
Elevation:　13 feet
Fuel:　100LL, Jet A
TPA:　800 feet msl
Runway:　17-35: 3700 x 75 asph
FBO:　Aero-East 843/884-8837

☞ *Communication:*
CTAF:　122.7
Unicom:　122.7
App/Dep:　Charleston 135.8

☞ *Transportation:*
Taxi:　843/577-6565
Car Rental:　Enterprise 843/881-2489

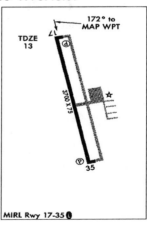

☞ *Lodging:*
Mount Pleasant: **Comfort Inn East** 843/884-5853; **Days Inn Mt. Pleasant** 843/881-1800

PATRIOTS POINT NAVAL AND MARITIME MUSEUM
(approximately 7 miles from airport)
U.S. 17, Mount Pleasant, SC 29464; Tel: 843/884-2727
Open daily.
Admission is $10 for adults, $5 for children.

The aircraft carrier *Yorktown*, which replaces the original lost during WWII, is berthed here. See how 3,000 crewmen worked and lived on this "small city." The length of three football fields, it houses exhibits of bomber and fighter planes on the hangar bay and showcases letters and mementos of the crew. Also open for tours are the submarine *Clamagore*, the Coast Guard cutter *Ingham*, the destroyer *Laffey*, a re-creation of a Vietnam naval support base, and the Medal of Honor Museum. The Navy Flight Simulator lets visitors experience a five-minute air war over Iraq.

WHILE YOU'RE THERE: Guided kayak and canoe tours of local rivers and swamps are offered by **Coastal Expeditions** 843/884-7684 on Sullivan's Island.

Myrtle Beach
Int'l Airport (MYR)

Airport is located 3 miles southwest of town.

☞ *Airport Information:*

Location:	Charlotte sectional N33.40.79 W78.55.70
Airspace:	Class C service 1100-0400Z*
Attended:	1100-0300Z*
Elevation:	26 feet
Fuel:	100LL, Jet A
TPA:	1000 feet msl lgt acft
	1500 feet msl hvy acft
Runway:	17-35: 9502 x 150 asph-conc
FBO:	Myrtle Beach Aviation 843/477-1860

☞ *Communication:*

CTAF:	128.45
Unicom:	122.95

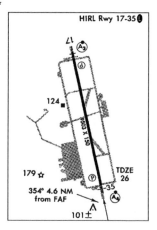

App/Dep:	127.4 (171-321°); 119.2 (322-170°); (1100-0400Z*)
	Jax Center 128.7 (0400-1100Z*)
Tower:	128.45 (1100-0400Z*)
Ground:	120.3
AWOS:	124.5
ATIS:	123.925

☞ *Transportation:*
Taxi: 843/448-5555
Car Rental: Budget 843-448-1586; National 843/626-3687

☞ *Lodging:*
Myrtle Beach: Myrtle Beach is lined with mega hotels. Some of them are the **Sands Resorts** 800/845-6701; **Surf Rider** 800/334-7873; **Bar Harbor Motel** 800/334-2464; **Landmark Resort** 800/845-0658.
Murrells Inlet: Both the **Brookwood** 843/651-2550 and the **Ocean View Motel** 843/651-2500 are smaller establishments with less than 40 units each.

CAPT. DICK'S EXPLORER ADVENTURES
(cruises approximately 10 miles from airport)
P.O. Box 306, Murrells Inlet, SC 29576; Tel: 843/651-3676 or 800/344-3474; Internet: www.captdick.com

Murrells Inlet is a picturesque fishing port and famous for its many excellent seafood restaurants. Contact Capt. Dick's Explorer Adventures for fishing excursions to troll mackerel, dolphin, tuna, wahoo, marlin, and sailfish. Bottom fishing is for snapper, grouper, and triggerfish. Helpful deckhands offer free fishing instruction and assistance with equipment or fish handling if needed. Parasailing, jet skiing, and boat rentals available. Discover saltwater marsh on the Explorer Adventure. On this trip specimens will be retrieved from the marsh and put into touch-tanks where they may be observed. All living specimens are returned to the water.

DOWNWIND SAILS

SC

(watersport rentals approximately 5 miles from airport)
Ocean Blvd. at 29th Ave.S., Myrtle Beach, SC 29577; Tel: 843/448-7245

Natural beauty, a climate with distinct but mild and pleasant seasons, and a variety of activities have made the "Grand Strand" a choice vacation and retirement spot for generations of Carolinians and tourists alike. The fine white sand and dunes of the beaches make for good swimming, sunbathing, strolling, and shelling. More active people can rent surfboards, jet skis, windsurfers, Hobie Cats, and sailboats from Downwind Sails.

THE LEGENDS
(golf complex approximately 7 miles from airport)
P.O. Box 2038, Myrtle Beach, SC 29578; Tel: 800/552-2660

Tom Doak designed Legend's Heathland Course, a course with a different look due to its absence of trees. It's the best of the Legend's three courses with huge putting surfaces and plenty of mounds and contours. Supposed to be "fun" when windy, which it almost always is. The Moorland Course, a P.B. Dye design, is tougher to play. Last but not least, the Parkland is surrounded by marsh and features a nice layout with long distances between holes.

WHILE YOU'RE THERE: For an abundance of drenching rides, visit **Wild Water and Wheels** 843/238-9453 or **Myrtle Waves Water Park** 843/448-1026. Contact **Myrtle Beach Golf Holiday** 843/448-5942 or 800/845-4653 for golf package plans.

North Myrtle Beach
Grand Strand Airport (CRE)

Airport is located 1 mile northwest of town.

☞ *Airport Information:*

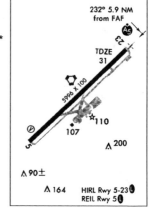

Location:	Charlotte sectional
	N33.48.71 W78.43.44
Airspace:	Class D service 1200-0200Z*
Attended:	1130-0300Z*
Elevation:	33 feet
Fuel:	100LL, Jet A
TPA:	800 feet msl lgt acft
	1540 feet msl hvy acft
Runway:	05-23: 5996 x 100 asph
FBO:	Ramp 66 843/272-5337

☞ *Communication:*

CTAF: 124.6

Unicom:	122.95
App/Dep:	Myrtle Beach 119.2 (1100-0400Z)
	Jax Center 128.7 (0400-1100Z)
Tower:	124.6 (1200-0200Z)
Ground:	121.8

☞ *Transportation:*
Taxi: 843/448-3181; 843/448-3360
Car Rental: Ramp 66 803/272-5337

☞ *Lodging:*
North Myrtle Beach: One of the smaller inns, the **St. Charles Inn** 843/272-6748 has only 9 units. The **Fanta Sea Inn** 843/249-1058, **Ocean Mist** 843/249-8745 or 800/750-4413, **Sea Horse** 843/249-1332, and the **Blue Parrot Inn** 843/272-7727 or 800/742-6243 are smaller establishments as well. **Best Western Inn & Suites** 843/280-4555; **Economy Inn** 843/272-6196; **Super 8** 843/249-7339; **Holiday Inn** 843/272-6153

TIDEWATER GOLF CLUB
(approximately 9 miles from the airport)
4901 Little River Neck Road, North Myrtle Beach, SC 29582; Tel: 843/249-3829 or 800/446-5363

With all the golf courses in this area, the Tidewater Course stands out with its nomination as best new public course in 1990 by both the *Golf Digest* and *Golf Magazine*. Ken Tomlinson designed this course, with U.S. champion Hale Irwin acting as consultant. The result is an inspiring course winding along the Intracoastal Waterway and Cherry Grove Beach Inlet with some holes in wooded areas. Great care was taken not to disturb the original flow of the land while providing peaceful views of the water.

WIND N BEACH
(kayak and canoe tours approximately 10 miles from the airport)
6104 Frontage Road, North Myrtle Beach, SC 29577; Tel: 843/272-4420

SC

At low tide, North Myrtle Beach has the widest beaches in the area— the perfect place for sun-seekers and "water rats." With the help of guided kayak or canoe tours by Wind N Beach, it is a treat to explore the coastal marshes, barrier island, and coastal rivers in the area. Be ready to watch a playful porpoise, sunning alligator, or rising egret.

TENNESSEE

Chattanooga
Lovell Field (CHA)

Airport is located 5 miles east of town.

☞ *Airport Information:*

Location: Atlanta sectional N35.02.12 W85.12.23
Airspace: Class C service 1100-0450Z*; Other times Class E
Attended: Continuously
Elevation: 682 feet
Fuel: 100LL, Jet A
TPA: 1500 feet msl lgt acft
2200 feet msl hvy acft
Runway: 02-20: 7401 x 150 asph
15-33: 5000 x 150 asph
FBO: Krystal Aviation 423/490-4600

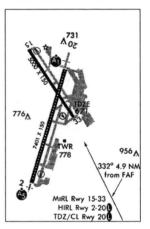

☞ *Communication:*

CTAF: 118.3
Unicom: 122.95
App: Chattanooga 125.1
(021-199º); 119.2 (200-020º)
126.5 (1100-0450Z*)
Dep: Chattanooga 125.1 (021-199º); 119.2 (200-020º);
(1100-0450Z*)
App/Dep: Atlanta Center 132.05 (0450-1100Z*)
Tower: 118.3 (1100-0450Z*)
Ground: 121.7
Clnc Del: 120.95
ATIS: 119.85

TN

☞ *Transportation:*
Taxi: 423/624-1410
Car Rental: Dollar 423/855-2277

☞ *Lodging:*

Chattanooga: The lobby of the **Chattanooga Choo Choo Holiday Inn** 423/266-5000 or 800/TRACK-29, once a 1909 Beaux Arts style Southern Railroad terminal, is now a 30-acre vacation complex. You can sleep aboard an authentic restored railcar acting as a suite. Free downtown shuttle gets you to area attractions. (Be aware that this hotel is about 19 miles from town!!) The **Bluff View Inn** 423/265-5033 is a B & B overlooking the Tennessee River in three restored homes downtown. The **Radisson Read House Hotel** 423/266-4121 or 800/333-3333 is considered the grand dame of the hotels and dates from the 1920s. Its thirteen floors of museum-quality art memorialize the Civil War. **Chattanooga Marriott** 423/756-0002; **Days Inn** 423/267-9761; **Comfort Suites** 423/265-0008; The **Sky Harbor Bavarian Inn** 423/821-8619 offers a spectacular view overlooking the Tennessee River and city skyline from its Lookout Mountain location.

☞ *Restaurants:*

Chattanooga: Don't miss dining at the **Choo Choo Complex** 423/266-5000, where you can dine in a railroad car in the Diner. The Bluff View Art District is host to **The Loft** 423/266-3061 serving a fine selection of beef, chicken, and seafood. The **Big River Grille and Brewing Works** 423/267-2739 with its spectacular setting has tantalizing food and brews, and the **Back Inn Cafe** 423/265-5033, a bistro in a turn-of-the-century mansion, serves upscale Italian cuisine. For barbecue, head to the **Rib & Loin** 423/499-6465.

CHICKAMAUGA/CHATTANOOGA NATIONAL MILITARY PARK

(approximately 7 miles from airport)
110 E. Brow Road, Lookout Mountain, TN 30750; Tel: 423/821-7786
Open daily.
Admission is free.

This is America's first and largest National Military Park, dedicated to the memory of Civil War soldiers from both the North and South. Participate in a guided tour during the summer or take a self-guided tour. The visitor center offers an audiovisual presentation.

TN

LAKE WINNEPESAUKAH AMUSEMENT PARK

(approximately 8 miles from airport)
P.O. Box 490, Rossville, GA 30741; Tel: 706/866-5681
Open April through September.
Admission charged.

Fun and excitement for all ages, with over 30 rides, games, an arcade, and the usual amusement park trappings. Ride the Cannon Ball roller coaster, tour the park on the C.P. Huntington train, or paddle a paddleboat.

LOOKOUT MOUNTAIN INCLINE RAILWAY
(approximately 6 miles from airport)
827 East Brow Road, Lookout Mountain, TN 37350; Tel: 423/821-4224
Open daily except Christmas.
Tickets are $8 for adults and $4 for children.

Chattanooga comes from a Creek word meaning "rock rising to a point." A breathtaking grade of 72.7 degrees near the top gives the Incline the unique distinction of being the world's steepest passenger railway. On a clear day the panorama reveals seven states.

TENNESSEE AQUARIUM
(approximately 4 miles from airport)
One Broad Street, Chattanooga, TN 37401; Tel: 800/262-0695; Internet: www.tennis.org
Open daily except Christmas and Thanksgiving.
Admission is $10.95 for adults, $5.95 for children 3 to 12 years old. Combination tickets with IMAX theater are $14.95 and $8.95, respectively.

The world's largest freshwater aquarium on Ross's Landing, the town's original name, houses the largest turtle collection and another 7,000 creatures, including fish, mammals, birds, reptiles and amphibians in a five-story building. Journey through a spectacular 60-foot canyon and two living forests. Giant IMAX movies are shown on a six-story screen in 3-D. Ross's Landing Park and Plaza surrounding the aquarium commemorates Chattanooga's Civil War history.

WHILE YOU'RE THERE: A special treat for children is the **Creative Discovery Museum** 423/756-2738, where hands-on fun encourages one to explore the artist, inventor, scientist, and musician in oneself. A short riverwalk pathway from the aquarium leads you to the Bluff View Art District, starring the **Hunter Museum of American Art** 423/267-0968 exhibiting the most complete and important collection of American Art in the Southeast. The **River Gallery** 423/267-7353 contains an eclectic collection of fine art. Visit during mid-June and you will find the riverfront bustling with 4 stages

TN

for live music and the South's largest block party — the **Riverbend Festival** 423/265-4112. The **Southern Belle** 800/766-2784 or 423/266-4488 cruises the Tennessee River and departs from Chestnut Street in downtown.

Rock City Garden 706/820-2531 atop Lookout Mountain is technically located in Georgia and provides a self-guided tour through nice scenery. Deep inside Lookout Mountain is **Ruby Falls** 423/821-2544 — a thundering 145-foot waterfall and cavern. Authentic steam trains of the **Tennessee Valley Railroad** 423/894-8028 offer rides across the river and through tunnels for six miles.

Crossville Memorial - Whitson Field (CSV)

Airport is located 3 miles west of town.

☞ *Airport Information:*
Location: Atlanta sectional N35.57.08 W85.05.10
Attended: 1400Z* to dark
Elevation: 1881 feet
Fuel: 100LL, Jet A
TPA: 2700 feet msl
Runway: 08-26: 5418 x 100 asph
FBO: Crossville Flying Service
                931/484-5016

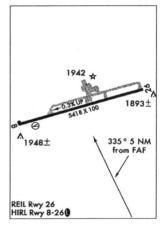

☞ *Communication:*
CTAF: 122.7
Unicom: 122.7
App/Dep: Atlanta Center 133.6

☞ *Transportation:*
Car Rental: U-Save 931/484-5016

☞ *Lodging:*
Crossville: **Fairfield Glade Resort** 931/484-7521 see following entry; **Best Western Leisure Inn** 931/484-1551; **Ramada Inn** 931/484-7581

☞ *Restaurants:*
Crossville: **Long John Silver** 931/484-7415

FAIRFIELD GLADE RESORT
(golf approximately 10 miles from airport)
101 Peavine Road, P.O. Box 1849, Fairfield Glade, TN 38557; Tel:
931/484-7521 or 800/251-6778

Stonehenge Course at the Fairfield Glade Resort has hosted the
Tennessee State Open for eight years and was designed by Joe
Lee. It is the only course in the state with bentgrass tees, fairways,
and greens. The 18-hole course features rock outcroppings on a
mountainous layout with lakes and streams. Check for possible
closure of the course during January and February. Fairfield Glade
Resort does not just offer good golf. It is a complete resort with three
pools, tennis courts, marina, and miniature golf. You do not have to
be a resort guest to play golf. For non-golfers there are facilities for
horseback riding and bike riding. Located on 12,000 acres on the
Cumberland plateau, it is a place to relax and wind down.

Greeneville
Green Co. Munic.
Airport (GCY)
Airport is located 2 miles north of town.

☞ *Airport Information:*

Location:	Cincinnati sectional N36.11.58 W82.48.91
Attended:	1230-0000Z*
Elevation:	1608 feet
Fuel:	100LL, Jet A
TPA:	2400 feet msl
Runway:	05-23: 6302 x 100 asph
FBO:	Greeneville Aviation Service
	423/639-6275

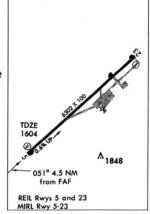

☞ *Communication:*

CTAF:	122.7
Unicom:	122.7
App/Dep:	Tri City 119.25
	(1100-0500Z*)
	Atlanta Center 127.85
	(0500-1100Z*)

TN

AWOS: 128.425

☞ *Transportation:*
Taxi: 423/636-0123; 423/638-5252
Car Rental: Enterprise 423/638-1644; U-Save 423/638-1755

☞ *Lodging:*
Greeneville: **General Morgan Inn & Conference Center** 423/787-1000 or 800/223-2679. The **Hilltop House B & B Inn** 423/639-8202 dates back to the 1920s and has good mountain views.

GRAYSBURG HILLS GOLF COURSE
(approximately 10 miles from airport)
Route 1, Box 1415, Chuckey, TN 37641; Tel: 423/234-8061

Situated in a valley with three lakes in the center, this family-run 18-hole course has some great holes. Designed by Rees Jones, it is nicely landscaped and has over fifty sandtraps. The course rambles through rolling hills and 9 holes are being added.

Memphis Int'l Airport
(MEM)
Airport is located 3 miles south of town.

☞ *Airport Information:*

Location:	Memphis sectional N35.02.61 W89.58.61
Airspace:	Class B
Attended:	Continuously
Elevation:	335 feet
Fuel:	100LL, Jet A
TPA:	1800 feet msl lgt acft
	2300 feet msl hvy acft
Runway:	18R-36L: 9319 x 150 conc
	18L-36R: 9000 x 150 conc
	09-27: 8936 x 150 asph
	18C-36C: 8400 x 150 conc
	Watch for runway closure!
FBO:	Wilson Air Center 901/345-2992 or 800/464-2992

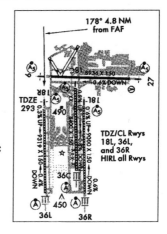

TN

☞ *Communication:*

Unicom: 122.95
App: 119.1 (176-355º); 125.8 (356-175º)
Dep: 124.65 (176-355º); 124.15 (356-175º)
Tower: 118.3 (Rwy 09-27)
119.7 (Rwy 18L-C, 36R-C)
128.425 (Rwy 18R-36L)
Ground: 121.9; 121.65
Clnc Del: 125.2
ATIS: 127.75

☞ *Transportation:*

Taxi: 901/324-4202; 901/577-7777; 901/323-3333
Car Rental: Alamo 901/332-8412; Avis 901/345-3514

☞ *Lodging:*

__Memphis:__ Elegance and charm of a bygone era are evident at the downtown landmark, **The Peabody** 901/529-4000 or 800/PEABODY. Take a look up in the lobby, to see the original stained glass skylights while you are there. Located downtown, just a 3-minute walk to Beale Street, is the **Radisson Hotel** 901/528-1800. Elvis fans will enjoy 24-hour Elvis videos at the **Elvis Presley Hotel** 901/332-1000. The **Holiday Inn Mt. Moriah** 901/362-8010 is minutes from the airport. **Days Inn Downtown** 901/527-4100; **Comfort Inn Downtown** 901/526-0583

☞ *Restaurants:*

__Memphis:__ Barbecue, a local passion, is served at **Jim Neely's Interstate BBQ** 901/775-2304, and **The Rendezvous** 901/523-2746. "Diner" food is served at the **Buntyn** 901/458-8776.

GRACELAND

(estate once owned by Elvis Presley approximately 2 miles from airport)
3717 Elvis Presley Blvd., Memphis, TN 38116; Tel: 800/238-2000 or 901/332-3322; Internet:www.elvis-presley.com
Admission for combined ticket to all attractions is $19.50 for adults. Reservations recommended during summer.

TN

Tour the property Elvis bought in 1957, when he was just 22 years old, for $100,000. A guided tour will lead you through the TV Room holding three screens, a Trophy Room full of the King's platinum, gold, and silver records, stage outfits, and gun collection, as well as the Jungle Room with its waterfalls, where he recorded Moody Blue. Walk by the burial site strewn with flowers by fans. Check out Elvis's personal airplanes and Lisa Marie's washroom outfitted with 24-carat gold and the blue suede bathroom!! The Automobile Museum's pink Cadillac and Harley Davidson golf cart are more spoils of stardom.

SUN STUDIO
(recording studio approximately 6 miles from airport)
706 Union Ave., Memphis, TN 38103; Tel: 901/521-0664
Daily tours.
Admission is $8.50.

When you step into the Sun Records studio, still just like it was in the 1950s, you step into the room that helped launch the sound that would change American music forever. Among the legends that recorded here were Elvis Presley, Johnny Cash, B.B. King, Roy Orbinson,and Jerry Lee Lewis. Take a look at Elvis's original mike stand and a drum kit.

WHILE YOU'RE THERE: Don't miss the famous World War II B-17 bomber *Memphis Belle* at the **Mississippi River Museum** 800/507-6507 on Mud Island. The **Memphis Music Hall of Fame** 901/525-4007 honors musicians of Memphis, showing rare photographs, instruments, film footage, and memorabilia.

Nashville Int'l Airport
(BNA)
Airport is located 5 miles southeast of town.

☞ *Airport Information:*

Location:	Atlanta sectional N36.07.47 W86.40.69
Airspace:	Class C
Attended:	Continuously
Elevation:	599 feet
Fuel:	100LL, Jet A
TPA:	1500 feet msl lgt acft; 2000 feet msl hvy acft
Runway:	13-31: 11030 x 150 asph, conc
	02R-20L: 8000 x 150 conc
	02C-20C: 8000 x 150 conc
Runway:	02L-20R: 7702 x 150 asph
FBO:	Signature Flight Support 615/361-3000

TN

Communication:
Unicom: 122.95
App: 127.175 (019-199°)
120.6 (200-018°)
Dep: 119.35 (200-018°)
118.4 (019-199°)
Tower: 128.15 (Rwy 02R-20L)
118.6 (Rwys 02L-20R,
02C-20C, 13-31)
Ground: 121.9 (west); 132.95 (east)
Clnc Del: 126.05
ATIS: Arrival 135.1
Departure 135.675

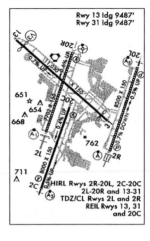

☞ *Transportation:*
Taxi: 615/254-5031; 615/242-7070; 615/256-0101
Car Rental: Avis 615/361-1212; Budget 615/366-0822
Hertz 615/361-3131; Thrifty 615/361-6050

☞ *Lodging:*
Nashville: The **Opryland Hotel** 615/889-1000 is a huge place with interior gardens and a lake. It is near the Grand Ole Opry and General Jackson Showboat. A new property downtown is the **Courtyard by Marriott Downtown** 800/321-2211. The **Comfort Inn Hermitage** 615/889-5060 is near the attraction with the same name. A restored historic landmark, **The Hermitage Suite Hotel** 615/244-3121 is within walking distance of downtown attractions. Nestled on 23 acres of rolling hillside, just minutes from the airport, is the **Sheraton Music City Hotel** 615/885-2200. **Days Inn Downtown** 615/242-4311; **Days Inn Airport** 615/361-7666

☞ *Restaurants:*
Nashville: The **Big River Grille & Brewing Works** 615/251-4677 is a brew pub serving seven house brews and the food to go with them. Work up an appetite taking dance lessons at the **Wildhorse Saloon** 615/251-1000. Fondue lovers visit **The Melting Pot** 615/742-4970. Italian is served at **Antonio's of Nashville** 615/646-9166 and **Amerigo Italian Restaurant** 615/320-1740.

TN

BELLE MEADE PLANTATION
(approximately 10 miles from airport)
5025 Harding Road, Nashville, TN 37205; Tel: 615/356-0501;
Internet: www.citysearch.com/nas/plantation;
Open daily, except Thanksgiving, Christmas and New Years.
Admission is $8 adults, $3 children 6 to 12 years old.

Meet the Old South at the "Queen of Tennessee Plantations." A
century of history and architecture are represented by a log cabin,
smokehouse, Greek Revival mansion, creamery and carriage house
and stables. Also features one of the largest antique carriage
collections in the South. The mansion is furnished with antiques and
decorative arts of the period. The 1853 plantation was the first
thoroughbred breeding farm and host to eight U.S. presidents.

COUNTRY MUSIC HALL OF FAME AND MUSEUM
(approximately 6 miles from airport)
4 Music Square East, Nashville, TN 37203; Tel: 615/256-1630 or
800/816-7652
Open daily, except Thanksgiving, Christmas and New Years.
Admission is $10.75 for adults, $4.75 children 6 to 11 years old.

Tennessee's capital, famous for its country music dating back to the
twenties, is rightly home to the Country Music Hall of Fame and
Museum. Exhibits include Elvis's solid gold Cadillac, Gram Parsons's
acoustic guitar, Boxcar Willie's hobo hat, and a myriad of costumes,
guitars, manuscripts, and personal treasures of the stars. Admission
includes a trolley tour of Music Row and a visit to historic RCA Studio
B, where you may have the opportunity to view recording sessions in
the oldest remaining studio in Nashville. Elvis Presley and Dolly
Parton recorded hits there from 1957 to 1977, as did the Monkees,
Everly Brothers, Jim Reeves, and Willie Nelson. Music Row is
surrounded by office blocks occupied by Sony, Warner, Mercury,
and other recording industry companies.

GRAND OLE OPRY
(country music approximately 5 miles from airport)
2804 Opryland Drive, Nashville, TN 37214; Tel: 615/889-6611
Performances Friday and Saturday night as well as matinees on
various days during peak tourist season.
Evening performances are $22.

TN

The Grand Ole Opry is America's longest-running radio show and
still broadcasting live every Friday and Saturday night. It is the place

to hear country music. Superstars, "Hall of Famers," and legends perform on stage of the Grand Ole Opry House, a 4,400-seat broadcast studio. Best to have advance reservations.

YOU'RE THE STAR RECORDING STUDIO
(public recording studio approximately 5 miles from airport)
172 Second Avenue N., Suite 110, Nashville, TN 37201; Tel: 615/742-9942
Open daily, except major holidays.

Ever dreamed of being a famous singer? You're the Star makes it possible. Record your own single or video from a choice of more than 500 backing tracks. Audio recording is $16.95 and video recording costs $24.95. Costumes, fake instruments, lyrics, and two practices are provided.

WHILE YOU'RE THERE: Board the **General Jackson Showboat** 615/889-6611 for a cruise on the Cumberland River with live entertainment. The **Parthenon** 615/862-8431, a full-scale reproduction of the famous Greek temple, was originally built for the Tennessee Centennial Exposition in 1897 and now holds art galleries. Visit the home of President Andrew Jackson, **The Hermitage** 615/889-2941, a magnificent old plantation home turned museum.

Sevierville
Gatlinburg - Pigeon Forge Airport (GKT)

Airport is located 2 miles southeast of town.

☞ *Airport Information:*

Location: Atlanta sectional N35.51.47 W83.31.72
Attended: Daylight hours
Elevation: 1014 feet
Fuel: 100LL, Jet A
TPA: 1800 feet msl lgt acft; 2000 feet msl hvy acft
Runway: 10-28: 5506 x 75 asph
FBO: Gatlinburg Pigeon Forge; Aviation Center 423/453-8393

TN

270

☞ *Communication:*
CTAF: 123.0
Unicom: 123.0
App/Dep: Knoxville 132.8
AWOS: 126.875

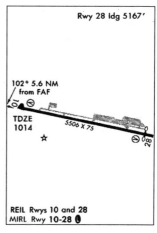

☞ *Transportation:*
Taxi: 423/429-3531
Car Rental: 423/453-8918

☞ *Lodging:*
Gatlinburg: The **Homestead House**
423/436-6166 is in downtown Gatlinburg
and has a heated pool and tennis court.
Each unit at the **Smokey Mountain**
Chalet Rental 423/436-5926 or 800/883-7134 has a wood burning
fireplace. Chalets can accommodate two to eight people. Rooms at
the **Rocky Waters Motor Inn** 423/436-7861 or 800/824-1111 have
private balconies overlooking a stream and the Great Smokies. At
the **Highlands Condominium Rentals** 800/352-8589 you will enjoy
a good view due to its elevation above Gatlinburg. The **Eight Gables**
Inn 800/279-5716 is a B & B with a four-diamond award by AAA.
Another B & B, the **Olde English Tudor Inn** 423/436-7760 or
800/541-3798 has seven guest rooms near downtown. **Hampton Inn**
423/436-4878

☞ *Restaurants:*
Gatlinburg: Aviation memorabilia decorate the interiors at **Waldo**
Pepper's 423/436-7003. Twelve different trout recipes are on the
menu of the **Smoky Mountain Trout House** 423/436-5416. For a
taste of southwestern food give **Cactus Jack's** 423/430-2105 a try.

GREAT SMOKY MOUNTAINS NATIONAL PARK
(visitor center is approximately 10 miles from airport)
Gatlinburg, TN 37738; Tel: 423/436-1200

The Great Smoky Mountains National Park is the largest wilderness
area in the eastern U.S., encompassing a half-million acres of
Appalachian peaks. The name Smoky comes from the smoke-like
haze enveloping the mountains. The park boasts unspoiled forests
but there is heavy visitor traffic. Wildflowers and migrating birds
abound in late April and early May. Summer is the time for blooming
rhododendrons, and autumn shows its best colors usually during
mid-October. Roads offer an introduction to the park, but serious

TN

hikers find 850 miles of trails. Stop by the visitor center just south of Gatlinburg for useful information and maps (and do read the info available in case of bear encounters). Bird-watchers can search for more than 200 species in the park, with 20 different kinds of warblers using it for breeding grounds. Rainbow and brown trout as well as smallmouth and rock bass can be caught in many park streams. Trout stamps are not needed, but a fishing license is required. Be aware that the possession of brook trout is prohibited. **Old Smoky Outfitters** 423/430-1936 offers guided fishing and fly-fishing instruction. Bikes can be rented at the **Cades Cove general store** 423/448-9034 which is across the Cades Cove Ranger Station. Cades Cove is ideal for level-to-rolling biking terrain. Explore the forest along streams and through forests on horseback, making use of numerous riding trails. Contact **Smoky Mountain Stables** 423/436-5634 for horses.

WHILE YOU'RE THERE: Winter visitors can take advantage of the **Ober Gatlinburg Ski Resort** 423/436-5423 or 800/251-9202 to ski eight slopes and trails. At **Dollywood** 800/365-5996, Dolly Parton's theme park, you can expect live show performances, craft showcases, and rides and attractions. Photography workshops are offered by **Beneath the Smoke** 423/436-3460 and store personnel can point you to the best spots to take your sunrise/sunset pictures.

NOTES:

VERMONT

Burlington Int'l Airport
(BTV)
Airport is located 3 miles east of town.

☞ *Airport Information:*
Location: Montreal sectional N44.28.38 W73.09.02
Airspace: Class C
Attended: 1100-0500Z*
Elevation: 334 feet
Fuel: 100LL, Jet A
TPA: 1335 feet msl non-turbine acft
1835 feet msl turbine acft
Runway: 15-33: 8320 x 150 asph
01-19: 3611 x 75 asph
FBO: Valet Air Services
802/863-3626

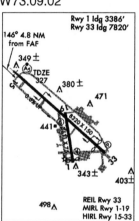

☞ *Communication:*
Unicom: 122.95
App/Dep: 121.1
Tower: 118.3
Ground: 121.9
ATIS: 123.8

☞ *Transportation:*
Taxi: 802/863-1889
Car Rental: Avis 802/864-0411; Budget 802/658-1211
National 802/864-7441

☞ *Lodging:*
Burlington: Sheraton-Burlington Hotel 802/862-6576
Shelburne: The Inn at Shelburne Farms 802/985-8498 has
beautiful lake and mountain views and offers turn-of-the-century
elegance. It is located on the same property as the working farm
mentioned below. It has 24 rooms and is open mid-May to mid-
October.

VT

☞ *Restaurants:*
Burlington: Your cravings for Italian food can be satisfied at **Sweet Tomatoes** 802/660-9533. Pizzas are done in their wood-fired oven. The **Dog Team Tavern** 802/388-7651 is an antique-filled place with good food.
Shelburne: "Serving You Steak, Seafood & Smiles" is the motto at the **Sirloin Saloon** 802/985-2200.

SHELBURNE MUSEUM
(approximately 9 miles from airport)
P.O. Box 10, U.S. Route 7, Shelburne, VT 05482; Tel: 802/985-3346
Open late May to late October.
Admission is $17.50 for adults and tickets are valid for 2 days.

Shelburne Museum is one of the world's great museums of American folk art, artifacts, and architecture. Thirty-seven exhibit buildings include three galleries of American paintings, seven furnished historic homes, and Vermont community buildings such as a school and general store. Depending on the season, you can enjoy one of the finest lilac gardens in New England, herb and perennial gardens, or typical Vermont fall foliage.

SHELBURNE FARMS
(approximately 8 miles from the airport)
Bay & Harbour Road, Shelburne, VT 05482; Tel: 802/985-8686
Open late May through mid October.
Admission is $5 for adults and $3 for children.

Visit a 1,400-acre working farm. See cheddar cheese being made, gather eggs, or try milking a cow! For the not so adventurous, the walking trails through meadows and woodlands offer for a stroll along a stretch of Lake Champlain's waterfront.The original landscaping was designed by the creator of New York's Central Park. Guided tours are available.

WHILE YOU'RE THERE: Sailboards, boat rentals, and lessons can be had from the **Burlington Community Boathouse** 802/865-3377 at the Burlington Harbour. Windsurfing on Lake Champlain is very popular. Due to the vastness of the lake, 121 miles long and 12 miles across, you can always count on some big air! Guided kayak and canoe tours are offered by **Paddleways** 802/660-8606.

VT

Lyndonville
Caledonia Co. Airport (6B8)

Airport is located 3 miles north of town.

☞ *Airport Information:*

Location: Montreal sectional N44.34.15 W72.01.08
Attended: Tue-Fri 1400-2000Z*; Sat-Sun 1400-2200Z*
Elevation: 1188 feet
Fuel: 100LL
TPA: 2199 feet msl
Runway: 02-20: 3300 x 60 asph
FBO: 802/626-3353

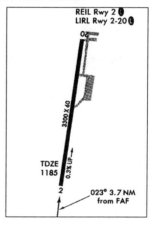

☞ *Communication:*

CTAF: 122.8
Unicom: 122.8
App/Dep: Boston Center 135.7

☞ *Transportation:*
Taxi: 802/626-8402
Car Rental: Quality Motor 802/748-2209

☞ *Lodging:*
Burke: For fully furnished townhouses and condos located on the mountain call **Burke Mountain** 802/626-3305. Adjacent to the ski resort is **The Old Cutter Inn** 802/626-5152. It is a small country inn with fine dining and 9 rooms.

☞ *Restaurants:*
Burke: Swiss chef Fritz Walther will prepare your food at **The Old Cutter Inn** 802/626-5152. **Darling's Restaurant** 802/626-9924 offers good food and wines at the Inn at Mountain View Creamery. A 10-minute drive will take you there from the alpine ski resort. Enjoy their hot cider by the fireplace.

BURKE MOUNTAIN SKI RESORT
(approximately 7 miles from airport)
Burke Mountain, East Burke, VT 05832; Tel: 802/626-3305; Cross-country skiing information 802/626-8338.

Still a quiet, unspoiled section of the Green Mountain State, it is an up-and-coming ski area. It offers value and trails with character.

Burke's peak rises to 3,267 feet and has trails for the advanced as well as the beginning skier. The alpine area features a vertical rise of 2,000 feet and a total of 4 lifts to take you to 31 trails. Snowboarding, ski school, and rentals are there for your convenience. The cross-country area has a total of 50 miles of trails, 40 miles of which are machine tracked. Instruction, rental, and repair services are available.

Morrisville
Stowe State Airport (MVL)

Airport is located 2 miles southwest of town.

☞ *Airport Information:*

Location: Montreal sectional N44.32.08 W72.36.84
Attended: 1200-2300Z*
Elevation: 732 feet
Fuel: 100LL, Jet A
TPA: 1700 feet msl
Runway: 01-19: 3701 x 75 asph
FBO: Whitcomb Aviation
802/888-7845

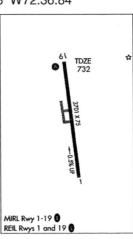

☞ *Communication:*

CTAF: 122.8
Unicom: 122.8
App/Dep: Boston Center 135.7
ASOS: 135.625

☞ *Transportation:*

Taxi: 802/888-4052
Car Rental: 802/253-7608

☞ *Lodging:*

Stowe: The Trapp Family Lodge 802/253-8511 see below; **Topnotch at Stowe** 800/451-8686 see below. Laura Ashley decor, four-poster beds, and fireplaces await you at **Ye Olde England Inne** 802/253-7558. **The Gables Inn** 800/GABLES-1 is a smoke-free classic Vermont country inn. Contact **All Season Rentals** 800/54-STOWE for houses, condos, apartments, or chalets. **Craftsbury Outdoor Center** 800/729-7751 see below.

VT

Stowe: An authentic team of Italian chefs will prepare your food at the **Trattoria La Festa Restaurant** 802/253-9776. Seafood is the specialty at **The Partridge Inn Seafood Restaurant** 802/253-8000.

BEAVER LAKE TROUT CLUB
(approximately 3 miles from airport)
Box 5270, RFD #1, Morrisville, VT 05661; Tel: 802/888-3746

Fish their 14-acre lake stocked with 14,000 trout, 14" to 28". Boat rentals are available and equipment is included. The lake is limited to 30 anglers per day for either catch and release or catch and keep. Reservations are recommended.

CRAFTSBURY OUTDOOR CENTER
(approximately 9 miles from airport)
P.O. Box 31, Craftsbury Common, VT 05827; Tel: 800/729-7751; Internet: www.craftsbury.com

The Craftsbury Outdoor Center, a great place to visit year-round, is located by a beautiful lake on 140 private acres. White clapboard villages and hillside farms define the landscape. Just tell the mountain biking guides what type of ride you like and they direct you to the perfect trail. Thorough maps and bikes are provided. Or choose to take a guide with you. Other summer sports include world-class sculling, canoeing, hiking, and running camps. Cross-country skiing and snowshoeing are available during winter as well as pond skating, weather permitting. The Craftsbury area is known for its spectacular fall foliage as well as being a good place to enjoy birding and spring wildflowers. Simple but comfortable lodging is available on site, yet day visitors are very welcome.

THE TRAPP FAMILY LODGE
(cross-country ski center approximately 10 miles from airport)
42 Trapp Hill Road, Stowe, VT 05672; Tel: 802/253-8511; Internet: www.trappfamily.com

Owned by the family that inspired the movie *Sound of Music*, it is the oldest cross-country ski center and one of the finest. Over 60 miles of cross-country trails, snowshoeing trails, old-fashioned horse-drawn sleigh rides, and guided nature hikes will keep you busy. Six full-time instructors have been trained by Nordic director Charlie Yerrick. Austrian cuisine, nightly entertainment, and nice mountain views promise a wonderful stay. Free shuttle to alpine skiing at

VT

Stowe is available. Indoor pool and fitness center. During the months of June through August, classical concerts are held in the meadows on Sunday evenings.

TOPNOTCH AT STOWE RESORT AND SPA
(approximately 10 miles from airport)
On the Mountain Road, Route 18, Stowe, VT 05672; Tel: 800/451-8686; Internet: www.topnotch-resort.com/spa

Relax at this top-rated spa, one of the state's poshest, with floor-to-ceiling windows and a circular stone fireplace in the lobby. Treat yourself to a full-body massage or herbal wrap or simply luxuriate under the hydromassage waterfall. No matter what time of year you visit, there are plenty of diversions. Sleighrides, cross-country trails and four indoor tennis courts reward winter visits. Mountain bike rentals or horseback riding entice for visits during the summer. Or just relax and enjoy the view of Mt. Mansfield from this 4-star/5-diamond rated resort.

WHILE YOU'RE THERE: Rent bikes, in-line skates, cross-country skis or snowshoes at the **Mountain Bike Center** 802/253-7919 to take advantage of the asphalt recreation path that runs parallel to Mountain Road. Fly-fisherfolk should head to the **Fly Rod Shop** 802/253-7346 three miles south of Stowe. The owner can show you how to tie a fly or take advantage of the free fly-fishing class on the shop's pond. Fishing licenses are available as well. Fancy snowmobiling — contact **Nichols Snowmobile Rentals** 802/253-7239. For trail rides, hay rides, and riding lessons, contact **Edson Hill Riding Stables** 802/253-8954.

West Dover
Mount Snow (4V8)
Airport is located 1 mile southwest of town.

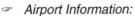

☞ *Airport Information:*
Location: New York sectional N42.55.63 W72.51.94
Attended: Unattended
Elevation: 1953 feet
Fuel: 100LL
TPA: 2800 feet msl

VT

Runway: 01-19: 2650 x 75 asph
FBO: North Air 802/464-8481

☞ *Communication:*
CTAF: 122.8
Unicom: 122.8
App/Dep: Boston Center 123.75

☞ *Transportation:*
Taxi: 802/464-2076
Car Rental: Contact FBO

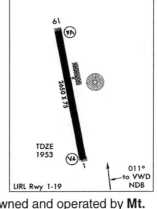

☞ *Lodging:*
Mt. Snow: There is a large choice of accommodation from rooms to condos owned and operated by **Mt. Snow** 800/451-4211 right on the mountain. The 14-room **Inn at Mount Snow** 802/464-3300 is located at the base of Mt. Snow within walking distance to the lifts. A very special place is the **Inn at Saw Mill Farm** 802/464-8131 just down the road from alpine skiing. This place demonstrates that the huge open spaces of abandoned barns can be turned into special inns with great success. Elegance, attention to detail, and delicious-tasting food have earned it more awards than we like to mention here! No matter when you visit, summer or winter, make sure you reserve well in advance.

☞ *Restaurants:*
Mt. Snow: The **Inn at Saw Mill Farm** 802/464-8131 is the recipient of the only Gold Rating in Vermont from the National Restaurant Association. Romantic dining with candlelight is provided at the **Mountaineer Inn** 800/682-4637. Bring your own booze.

MOUNT SNOW RESORT
(approximately 3 miles from airport)
Route 100, Mount Snow, VT 05356; Tel: 800/245-SNOW; Internet:
www.mountsnow.com

You probably have already noticed Mt. Snow's 3,600-foot summit during your approach to the airport. Two lifts, including the new high-speed quad, take you to 133 trails covering 51 miles on five mountains. Sixty percent of trails are for intermediate level skiers, and the vertical drop is 1,700 feet. If you are renting skis or taking lessons, avoid waiting in line at the ticket counter by buying your ticket at the rental or ski school shop. Try snowboarding at Un Blanco Gulch, Vermont's biggest snowboarding park. Like most

VT

places, it gets pretty busy on weekends, so try and arrange to have your lunch at Haystack or Carinthia, which are part of the five-mountain ski area.

WHILE YOU'RE THERE: As typical for New England, the Mount Snow area is also a beautiful place during summertime for mountain biking and hiking. Rent bikes at **Mt. Snow Mountain Bike Center** 802/464-3333.

NOTES:

Basye
Sky Bryce Airport

NOTE: PRIVATE AIRPORT
CONTACT 800/821-1444 FOR DETAILS

BRYCE RESORT
(year-round resort adjacent to private airport)
P.O. Box 3, Basye, VA 22810; Tel: 800/821-1444 or 540/856-2121;
Internet: www.bryceresort.com

Virginia's scenic Shenandoah Valley is the backdrop for this private airport. Conveniently located next to the runway are an 18-hole championship golf course, ski facilities, and tennis courts. A private lake with grassy beach area invites for swimming, boating, fishing or a 3-mile hike around the lake.

☞ *Lodging:*
Basye: Bryce Resort 800/821-1444 or 540/856-2121

Luray Caverns Airport

(W45)
Airport is located 2 miles west of town.

☞ *Airport Information:*
Location: Cincinnati sectional N38.40.02 W78.30.04
Attended: Apr-Oct 1400-2200Z; Nov-Mar 1400-2100Z
Elevation: 902 feet
Fuel: 100LL
TPA: 1700 feet msl
Runway: 04-22: 3125 x 75 asph
FBO: Luray Caverns 540/743-6070

VA

☞ *Communication:*
CTAF:　　122.8
Unicom:　　122.8
App/Dep:　　Washington Center 133.2

☞ *Transportation:*
Taxi:　　　540/743-5735
Car Rental: Luray Motor Co.
　　　　　　540/743-5128

☞ *Lodging:*
Luray: The **Ramada Inn** 540/743-4521
has an outdoor pool and mini golf facility.
The **Mayne View** 540/743-7921 is a
Victorian home turned bed & breakfast
with good views.

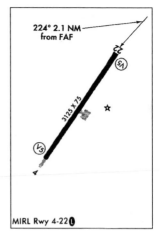

LURAY CAVERNS
(approximately 1 mile from airport)
Route 211, Luray, VA 22835; Tel: 540/743-6551; Internet: www.
luraycaverns.com
Open year round.
Admission is $14 for adults and $6 for children 7 to 13 years old.

The Luray Caverns are the largest and most popular caverns on the
East Coast. Formed into limestone by water seepage over millions of
years, gigantic formations called stalactites and stalagmites dazzle
the eye. Entrance fee also covers admission to the adjacent Historic
Car and Carriage Exhibit, which displays a 1892 Benz.

WHILE YOU'RE THERE: The **Luray Caverns Country Club**
540/743-7111 is a fine, if hilly, golf course with attractive Blue Ridge
scenery. It's adjacent to the airport.

Newport News
Williamsburg Int'l
Airport (PHF)

Airport is located 9 miles northwest of town.

☞ *Airport Information:*

Location: Washington sectional N37.07.91 W76.29.58
Airspace: Class D service 1100-0400Z*
Attended: Continuously
Elevation: 43 feet
Fuel: 100LL, Jet A
TPA: 900 feet msl
Runway: 07-25: 8003 x 150 concrete
         02-20: 6526 x 150 concrete
FBO: Rick Aviation 757/874-6415
         Flight Int'l. 757/877-6401

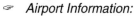

☞ *Communication:*

CTAF: 118.7
Unicom: 122.95
App: Norfolk 125.7
Dep: Norfolk 124.9
Tower: 118.7 (1100-0400Z*)
Ground: 121.9
Clnc Del: 124.9 (when tower closed)
         121.65 (also pre-taxi clnc frequency)
ATIS: 128.65 (1100-0400Z*)

☞ *Transportation:*
Taxi: 757/877-0279

☞ *Lodging:*
Yorktown: The **Duke of York Motor Hotel** 757/898-3232 is located in the center of town, overlooking the York River.
Newport News: The **Comfort Inn** 800/368-2477 is centrally located.
Hampton Inn-Newport News Airport Hotel 757/249-0001.
Hampton: Located on the waterfront and next to the Virginia Air and Space Center is the **Radisson Hotel Hampton** 800/333-3333.

☞ *Restaurants:*
Yorktown: **Nick's Seafood Pavillion** 757/887-5269 has been under

the same ownership since 1944. Steak lovers may drop in at
Sammy and Nick's Restaurant 757/898-3070, where seafood is on
the menu as well.

VIRGINIA AIR AND SPACE CENTER
(museum approximately 10 miles from airport)
600 Settlers Landing Rd, Hampton, VA 23669; Tel: 800/296-0800 or
757/727-0900; Internet: www.vasc.org
Open daily.
Admission is $9 for adults, $7 for children 3 to 11 years old.

An interesting place for all aviators and non-aviators alike. As the
official visitor center for NASA's Langley Research Center, the
Virginia Air and Space Center features historic aircraft and spacecraft. Exhibits include an Apollo 12 command module, a lunar rock, a
Mars meteorite, and the very latest in transportation devices. One of
the aircraft on display, a Convair F-106, was used to conduct
lightning research. Purposely flown into thunderstorms, it was struck
by lightning 700 times. A detailed 1/144th scale model of the new
International Space Station is one of the newer exhibits. A large, 5-
story-screen IMAX theater features documentaries and films in
oversized format. The price of admission includes one film.

YORKTOWN BATTLEFIELD
(approximately 8 miles from airport)
Box 210, Yorktown, VA 23690; Tel: 757/898-3400
Visitor Center is open daily.
Admission is $4 for adults. Children under 16 are free.

It is here that the final battle of the Revolutionary War was fought in
1781. The American and French forces surrounded British troops,
which surrendered. Visit the observation deck to get a good view of
strategic points in the battle. George Washington's original field tent
is displayed in the museum.

YORKTOWN VICTORY CENTER
(museum approximately 7 miles from airport)
P.O. Box 1607, Williamsburg, VA 23187; Tel: 757/253-4138 or
888/593-4682
Open daily except Christmas and New Year.
Admission is $10.25 for adults and $5 for ages 6 to 12.

The American Revolution unfolds here through dramatic galleries,
powerful film, and living history. A Continental Army encampment

VA

284

and 18th-century tobacco farm with costumed interpreters demonstrate medicine, military technique, and cooking.

WHILE YOU'RE THERE: The **Mariners' Museum** 757/596-2222 features vintage boats, ship models, figureheads, a working steam engine, and other nautical artifacts, including a special exhibit on the *Titanic*. See Hampton Roads Harbor, historic Fort Wool and the world's largest naval base by cruising with **Miss Hampton II Harbor Cruises** 757/722-9102.

Norfolk Int'l Airport
(ORF)

Airport is located 3 miles northeast of town.

☞ *Airport Information:*

Location: Washington N36.53.68 W76.12.08
Airspace: Class C
Attended: Continuously
Elevation: 27 feet
Fuel: 100LL, Jet A
TPA: 1000 feet msl non-turbine acft
2500 feet msl turbine acft
Runway: 05-23: 9001 x 150 asph, concrete
14-32: 4876 x 150 asph
FBO: Piedmont Aviation
757/857-3463

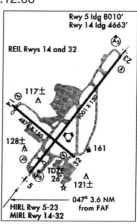

☞ *Communication:*

Unicom: 122.95
App: 118.9 (010-080º), (180-310º)
125.7 (311-009º), 118.9 (010-080º), (180-310º)
Dep: 125.2
Tower: 120.8
Ground: 121.9
Clnc Del: 118.5
ATIS: 127.15

VA

☞ *Transportation:*
Taxi:　　757/583-4079; 757/467-3181
Car Rental: Dollar 757/855-1988; National 757/857-5384

☞ *Lodging:*
Norfolk: A convenient downtown and waterfront location can be found at the **Norfolk Waterside Marriott Hotel** 757/627-4200.

☞ *Restaurants:*
Hampton: The Great Steak's 757/827-1886 menu includes chicken and seafood as well as steaks that you can grill yourself!
Norfolk: Pub-lovers should visit the authentic **Reggie's British Pub** 757/627-3575 for pub fare and ales. **La Galleria** 757/623-3939 has gained renown among the locals. Try their delicious pastas.

CHRYSLER MUSEUM
(fine art museum approximately 7 miles from airport)
245 W. Olney Road, Norfolk, VA 23510; Tel: 757/664-6200
Closed Mondays.
Admission is $5 for adults.

Housing the collection of car magnate Walter Chrysler Jr., the Chrysler Museum is ranked as one of the nation's top fine art museums. Exhibits display treasures from various parts of the world, including Lalique and Tiffany glassware.

NAUTICUS: THE NATIONAL MARITIME CENTER
(approximately 8 miles from airport)
One Waterside Drive, Norfolk, VA 23518; Tel: 757/664-1000
Open daily mid-May to mid-September. Rest of the year closed on Mondays.
Admission is $7.50 for adults and $5 for ages 4 to 17.

The museum, in the shape of a battleship, has an interesting mix of interactive oceanography exhibits, oversized-screen films, and virtual reality experiences.

NORFOLK NAVAL BASE
(approximately 7 miles from airport)
9079 Hampton Boulevard, Norfolk VA 23505; Tel: 757/444-7955;

A year-round operating naval base and the largest in the world. Take a narrated tour to see some of the ships of the Atlantic and Mediterranean fleet.

VA

WHILE YOU'RE THERE: The annual **Virginia Waterfront International Arts Festival** 757/664-6492 is an 18-day affair around the beginning of May. Watch music, dance, theater performances from around the globe. If you enjoy touring large U.S. and foreign ships, inquire at the **International Pier** 757/664-1000 to check if any are in town and available for touring. **Tidewater Adventures Kayak Ecotours** 757/480-1999 has tours along the Atlantic beach, wildlife refuges, or lakes.

Orange Co. Airport (W93)

Airport is located 3 miles east of town.

☞ *Airport Information:*

Location:	Washington sectional N38.14.84 W78.02.74
Attended:	Oct-Mar 1300-2300Z*
	Apr-Sep 1300-0100Z*
Elevation:	465 feet
Fuel:	100LL
TPA:	1500 feet msl
Runway:	07-25: 3200 x 75 asph
FBO:	Glick Fields 540/672-2158

☞ *Communication:*

CTAF:	122.8
Unicom:	122.8
App/Dep:	Richmond 132.85

☞ *Transportation:*

Taxi:	540/672-1532
Car Rental:	Reynolds 540/672-3701

MURRAY'S FLY FISHING SCHOOL

(fly fishing school approximately 7 miles from airport)
P.O. Box 156, Edinburg, VA 22824; Tel: 540/984-4212; Internet: www.murraysflyshop.com

Harry Murray is an author of numerous magazine articles and books on fly fishing. Sharpen your skills by attending one of his schools. Although the school and the shop are located in Edinburg, the meeting point for the trout school is in Madison for fishing on the Rapidan River. Orange County Airport is approximately seven miles

VA

287

from the meeting point. Almost the entire time is spent on the stream fishing, so even beginners come away with a thorough understanding of the art of fly angling. Covered are reading the water, proper fly selection, casting and how to fish drys, nymphs, and streamers for trout in freestone streams. Because Murray also has the shop you can choose from a wide variety of gear free of charge. There are only a few schools a year during the spring, so it is advised to make your reservation early. Guided fly-fishing trips are available as well.

Richmond Int'l Airport

(RIC)
Airport is located 6 miles east of town.

☞ *Airport Information:*

Location:	Washington sectional N37.30.31 W77.19.18
Airspace:	Class C
Attended:	Continuously
Elevation:	168 feet
Fuel:	100LL, Jet A
TPA:	1200 feet msl lgt acft
	1700 feet msl hvy acft
Runway:	16-34: 9003 x 150 asph
	02-20: 6607 x 150 asph
	07-25: 5316 x 100 asph
FBO:	Million Air 804/222-3700
	Richmond Jet Center
	804/226-7200

☞ *Communication:*

Unicom:	122.95
App:	126.8 (171-263º), 126.4 (360-170º),134.7 (264-359º), 118.2
Dep:	126.8 (171-163º), 126.4 (360-170º),134.7 (264-359º)
Tower:	121.1
Ground:	121.9
Clnc Del:	127.55
ATIS:	119.15 (1100-0400Z*)

☞ *Transportation:*

Taxi:	804/222-7222

Car Rental: Thrifty 804/222-3200; Hertz 804/222-7228

☞ *Lodging:*
__Richmond:__ Stay in grand style at the **Jefferson Hotel** 804/788-8000 or 800/424-8014, a National Historic Landmark downtown. The **Midtown Inn & Conference Center** 804/359-4061 is located near the Fine Art Museum. The **Linden Row Inn** 800/348-7424 is a historic property of red-brick Georgian terrace houses. **Holiday Inn Airport** 804/222-6450

☞ *Restaurants:*
__Richmond:__ Try Richmond's specialty, barbecue, at **Bill's Barbecue** 804/270-9722. They have several locations around town.

EDGAR ALLAN POE MUSEUM
(approximately 7 miles from airport)
1914-16 E. Main Street, Richmond, VA 23223; Tel: 804/648-5523
Open daily.
Admission is $6 per person.

Edgar Allan Poe spent much of his time in Richmond and considered it his hometown. The museum commemorating his life is housed in the oldest building in Richmond. View Poe memorabilia and a model of Richmond as it was during his time.

MUSEUM AND WHITE HOUSE OF THE CONFEDERACY
(approximately 7 miles from airport)
1201 E. Clay Street, Richmond, VA 23219; Tel: 804/649-1861
Open daily.
Admission is $8 for a combination ticket.

Confederate artifacts and the history of the Civil War are the highlights of the museum. The White House has been restored to its Victorian elegance. It was the official residence of president Jefferson Davis.

SCIENCE MUSEUM OF VIRGINIA
(approximately 9 miles from airport)
2500 W. Broad Street, Richmond, VA 23220; Tel: 804/367-6552 or 800/659-1727; Internet: www.smv.mus.va.us
Open daily, except Christmas.
Admission is $5.

VA

Known for its more than 250 hands-on exhibits, it also features multimedia planetarium shows. A five-story OMNIMAX theater screens films. The museum is housed in what used to be a huge, domed train station.

VIRGINIA AVIATION MUSEUM
(located on field)
Tel: 804/236-3622; Internet: www.smv.mus.va.us/wvamhome.html
Open daily except Thanksgiving and Christmas.
Admission is $5 for adults and $3 for children.

Find more than 20 vintage aircraft from circa 1914 to the 1930s, including the first American research plane to fly over Antarctica with famous Virginian Admiral Richard E. Byrd. Aviation films and the Virginia Aviation Hall of Fame are part of the museum as well. You will receive a small handout with explanations upon entering the premises. A self-guided tour through the facility takes approximately one hour.

VIRGINIA MUSEUM OF FINE ARTS
(approximately 9 miles from airport)
2800 Grove Ave, Richmond, VA 23221; Tel: 804/367-0844; Internet: www.vmfa.state.va.us
Open daily, except Mondays. Free admission (donation suggested).

Art from ancient Egypt, Greece and India. Paintings by Picasso, Degas, Renoir, Goya, van Gogh and Monet. Frank Lloyd Wright furniture. Hindu and Buddhist sculpture from the Himalayas. Works of Carl Fabergé.

VIRGINIA STATE CAPITOL
(approximately 7 miles from airport)
9th and Grace Streets, Richmond, VA 23219; Tel: 804/786-2441
Open Monday to Saturday. Admission is free.

Designed by Thomas Jefferson and in use since 1788, it offers a scenic view over Richmond from its columned portico. Inside the domed central rotunda is a Houdon statue of George Washington. Sculptures of the other eight Virginia-born U.S. presidents line the perimeter.

WHILE YOU'RE THERE: Cruise on the **Annabelle Lee Riverboat** 804/644-5700, a 400-passenger paddlewheel boat during the months of April through December.

VA

290

Saluda
Hummel Field (W75)

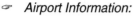

Airport is located 6 miles east of town.

☞ *Airport Information:*
Location: Washington sectional N37.36.15 W76.26.80
Attended: 1400-2200Z*
Elevation: 30 feet
Fuel: 100LL
TPA: 800 feet msl
Runway: 18-36: 2270 x 45 asph
FBO: Airwrench 804/758-3558

☞ *Communication:*
CTAF: 123.0
Unicom: 123.0
App/Dep: Norfolk 126.05

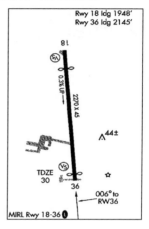

☞ *Transportation:*
Car Rental: Saluda Auto Sales
804/758-4824

☞ *Lodging:*
Saluda: See entry for **The Tides Inn** 800/843-3746 or 804/438-5000 following. The **Pilot House Inn** 804/758-2262 is adjacent to the airport.

☞ *Restaurants:*
Saluda: **Oasis** 804/758-4227

THE TIDES INN
(golf courses and resort approximately 5 miles from airport)
480 King Carter Drive, Irvington, VA 22480; Tel: 800/843-3746 or 804/438-5000
Closed during the winter.

A charming resort nestled on the Rappahannock River. It was awarded four diamonds by AAA and offers an atmosphere of leisure and quiet luxury in an idyllic setting. Complete resort facilities include yacht cruises, boat rental, canoeing, tennis, swimming in the salt water pool, biking, music and dancing. One of the two 18-hole golf courses, the Golden Eagle, is consistently ranked as one of the top

VA

courses in Virginia. Designed by George Cobb, it rewards good shots and penalizes poor ones. It is built on gentle wooded hills with plenty of water hazards. The Tartan course has tree-lined fairways with Carter Creek meandering through it. The original nine holes were designed by Sir Guy Campbell, with the second set of nine holes done by George Cobb.

Tangier Island (TGI)
Airport is located 4 miles west of town.

☞ *Airport Information:*

Location: Washington sectional N37.49.51 W75.59.87
Attended: Apr-Dec, Thu-Tue 1300-2200Z*
Airport closed sunset to sunrise daily.
Elevation: 7 feet
Fuel: Not available
TPA: 607 feet msl lgt acft
1507 feet msl hvy acft
Runway: 02-20: 2950 x 75 asph
FBO: 757/891-2496

☞ *Communication:*

CTAF: 122.8
Unicom: 122.8
App/Dep: Patuxent 120.05
(1200-0400Z*)
Washington Center 132.55
(0400-1200Z*)

☞ *Transportation:*
Taxi: 757/891-2215

☞ *Lodging:*
Tangier: **Chesapeake House Hotel** 757/891-2331 is adjacent to the airport.

☞ *Restaurants:*
Tangier: **Chesapeake House** 757/891-2331

CHESAPEAKE HOUSE HOTEL
(located adjacent to airport)
Box 194, Tangier, VA 23440; Tel: 757/891-2331

This place is open from mid-April to mid-October and well worth a
visit. It's fun to wander around the island or listen to the locals speak
an old dialect of English from the colonial period. You won't be able
to recognize a word but they will switch to a more understandable
version for visitors. Spend the night at the Chesapeake House Hotel
or eat family style at long tables in their restaurant.

Williamsburg-Jamestown Airport

(JGG)
Airport is located 3 miles southwest of town.

☞ *Airport Information:*

Location: Washington sectional N37.14.35 W76.42.97
Attended: 1200Z* till dark
Elevation: 49 feet
Fuel: 100LL, Jet A
TPA: 849 feet msl single acft
1049 feet msl twin, turbine
acft
Runway: 13-31: 3204 x 60 asph
FBO: 757/229-9256

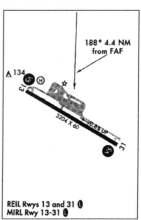

☞ *Communication:*
CTAF: 122.8
Unicom: 122.8
App/Dep: Norfolk 119.45

☞ *Transportation:*
Taxi: 757/229-9256
Car Rental: Enterprise 757/229-9256
Colonial Rent-A-Car 757/220-3399

☞ *Lodging:*
__Williamsburg:__ For colonial atmosphere contact **Colonial
Williamsburg** 757/229-1000 or 800/447-8679 which runs the

VA

Williamsburg Inn, Williamsburg Lodge, and the Governor's Inn. Just two blocks from Colonial Williamsburg is **The Williamsburg Hospitality House** 800/932-9192. The **Legacy of Williamsburg B & B** 757/220-0524 or 800/962-4722 is an elegant 18th-century award-winning place. **Embassy Suites** 757/229-6800; **Best Western Colonial Capitol Inn** 757/253-1222; **Days Inn** 757/253-1166; **Comfort Inn** 800/544-7774

☞ *Restaurants:*
Williamsburg: For a very upscale dinner visit the **Regency Room** 757/229-1000 in the Williamsburg Inn. The **Polo Club** 757/220-1122 has excellent food and is near the airport.

BUSCH GARDENS
(theme park approximately 4 miles from airport)
One Busch Garden Boulevard, Williamsburg, VA 23187; Tel: 757/253-3350; Internet: www.buschgardens.com
Open March to November.
Admission is $35 for adults, $28 for children 3 to 6 years old.
Combination tickets with Water Country are available.

A perennial favorite with kids, this theme park on 100 acres of rolling, wooded hills features nine mock hamlets recreating the villages and lifestyles of 17th-century Europe, which also please adults. More than 35 thrilling rides, dazzling shows, quaint shops, and European cuisine entertain the whole family. Their newest addition, Apollo's Chariot, rises on a purple track to plunge 210 feet into a ravine only to skim the top of Rhine River to rise back towards the sky again. Top speeds of over 80 miles per hour are reached with a pull of 4.5 G's!

COLONIAL WILLIAMSBURG
(restored area approximately 3 miles from airport)
P.O. Box 1776, Williamsburg, VA 23185; Tel: 757/220-7645 or 800/HISTORY
Visitor center is open daily.
Tickets are $27 for adults and $16 for children 6 to 12 years old for a day pass (does not include Carter's Grove Plantation, Governor's Palace, Bassett Hall Museum). Check into combination tickets. Free shuttle buses are included in the ticket price; no cars are allowed.

Colonial Williamsburg is an 18th-century town restored to the time when it was the political and cultural center of Britain's largest colony in the New World. The restoration began in 1926 and still continues.

VA

Many original 18th- and 19th-century structures have been restored and more than 220 period rooms are furnished to authenticity. Tradesman in period clothing practice 30 historic trades and domestic crafts. Even gardens and greens reflect the times. Stroll through cobblestone streets and feel yourself transported back to the "olden days." Visit the taverns to taste the food approximating that of 200 years ago. Don't miss the highlights such as the courthouse, capitol, governor's palace, and William and Mary, the second oldest college in the USA.

Colonial Williamsburg is worth a visit, especially during Christmas time, although it can get rather crowded.

FORD'S COLONY COUNTRY CLUB
(golf approximately 3 miles from airport)
240 Fords Colony Drive, Williamsburg, VA 2318; Tel: 757/258-4130

Ford's Colony has a total of 36 holes that were designed by Dan Maples. Framed by oak, dogwood and hickory, the fairways allow a challenge for all golfers. Rolling hills are a welcome respite from the plentiful sightseeing Ford's Colony is surrounded with.

JAMESTOWN SETTLEMENT
(living history museum approximately 3 miles from airport)
Jamestown Yorktown Foundation, P.O. Box 1607, Williamsburg, VA 23187; Tel: 757/253-4838
Open daily, except Christmas and New Year's.
Admission is $10.25 for adults, $5 for children 6 to 12 years old.

Jamestown Island was the first permanent English settlement in North America where in 1607 the colonists built a fort and planted the flag of England. Nearby, at Jamestown Settlement you get close to the sights and sounds that Captain John Smith, Pocahontas and the Jamestown colonists knew in the early years of the 17th century. Full-sized replicas of three tall-masted ships, that carried the first settlers here, lie at anchor in the James River. In the woods, a recreated colonial fort encircles the wattle-and-daub buildings within. Costumed interpreters will recount the difficult life colonists faced as they struggled to sustain themselves through hard work, prayer, and military skill. Reed-covered dwellings of a Powhatan Indian Village are just beyond. Watch or participate in scraping hides, making pottery and ropes, or building a canoe. Indoor galleries display original artifacts and exhibits.

VA

KINGSMILL RESORT

(golf resort approximately 3 miles from airport)
1010 Kingsmill Road, Williamsburg, VA 23185; Tel:757/253-1703 or
800/832-5665; Internet:www.kingsmill.com

Play a round of golf on the course of the famous PGA Anheuser-
Busch Classic here at Kingsmill. The River Course was designed by
Pete Dye and has a 135 championship slope rating. Expansive
views of the historic James River are interspersed with woods and
ponds. Arnold Palmer's Plantation Course challenges with water
hazards. But you surely will not get bored here with a total of 63
holes of championship golf to choose from. After a hard day of golf,
visit the spa for invigoration or go for a swim at the pool. Try a game
of tennis at one of the 12 all-weather courts. The marina supplies all
your fishing needs. Luxurious villas provide the accommodation at
this Mobil 4-star resort.

WATER COUNTRY USA

(approximately 4 miles from airport)
P.O. Box 3088, Williamsburg, VA 23187; Tel: 757/229-9300;
Internet: www.watercountryusa.com
Open Memorial through Labor Day daily and weekends May and
early September.
Admission is $27 for adults, $19.50 for children 3 to 6 years old.

The Mid-Atlantic's largest water play park features water rides, a
huge wave pool, slides and entertainment, all set in a beach theme
from the 1950s and '60s. A new drag-racing water adventure is sure
to quench almost everyone's need for speed. Get wet and have
some fun!

WILLIAMSBURG INN

(golf resort approximately 3 miles from airport)
P.O. Box B, Francis Street, Williamsburg, VA 23187; Tel: 757/229-
2141

One of the most distinguished hotels, this award-winning gem also is
home to the Golden Horseshoe, which consists of 45 holes of
excellent golf. Robert Trent Jones's design of the Gold Course is
regarded as one of his best works. Virginia's picturesque Tidewater
Area makes a fitting background with rolling terrain. The Green is a
Rees Jones–built course, opened in 1991. The Williamsburg Inn
itself is a landmark of gracious style and impeccable hospitality that
has seen visitors such as Queen Elizabeth II, the Emperor of Japan,

VA

Sir Winston Churchill and quite a few movie personalities. Individually designed rooms are furnished in Regency style antiques and reproductions. Located adjacent to Colonial Williamsburg historic area, it was built in 1937. Facilities include in- and outdoor pools, tennis, and health spa.

WHILE YOU'RE THERE: Guided tours and tastings can be had a the **Williamsburg Winery** 757/229-0999. Bicycles can be rented at the **Williamsburg Lodge** 757/229-1000 to explore Colonial Williamsburg, which bans motor vehicles. Horse-drawn carriage rides can be booked through **Greenhow Lumber House** 757/229-1000. Search for bargains of all kinds and varieties at the well known **Williamsburg Pottery Factory** 757/564-3326.

Beckley (BKW)
Raleigh Co. Mem. Airport
Airport is located 3 miles east of town.

☞ *Airport Information:*
Location: Cincinnati sectional N37.47.24 W81.07.45
Attended: 1100-0300Z*
Elevation: 2504 feet
Fuel: 100LL, Jet A
TPA: 3300 feet msl lgt acft
3650 feet msl hvy acft
Runway: 01-19: 6750 x 150 asph
10-28: 5000 x 100 asph
FBO: 304/255-0476

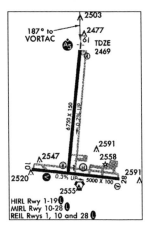

☞ *Communication:*
CTAF: 123.0
Unicom: 123.0
App/Dep: Charleston 118.95

☞ *Transportation:*
Taxi: 304/253-2254
Car Rental: Enterprise 304/252-1227

☞ *Lodging:*
Beckley: **Best Western** 304/252-0671; **Days Inn** 304/255-5291; **Bavarian Gasthaus** 304/253-1140

☞ *Restaurants:*
Beckley: **Captain D's Seafood Restaurant** 304/255-4636 serves seafood at reasonable prices.

THEATRE WEST VIRGINIA
(outdoor dramas approximately 9 miles from airport)
P.O. Box 1205, Beckley, WV 25802; Tel: 800/666-9142; Internet: www.wvweb.com/www/TWV

Tickets are $12 for adults and $6 for children under 12.
Season is June through August.

Cliffside Amphitheatre in Grandview is the stage for outdoor drama
productions such as *Hatfields and McCoys*, depicting the famous
feud, and *Honey in the Rock*, a Civil War story, as well as a different
musical each season. Spend the day exploring scenic New River
Gorge National River with picnic area, secluded trails, rock
formations, and stunning overlooks of the gorge and top it off with a
drama or musical under the stars.

WHILE YOU'RE THERE: **Pedals & Spokes** 304/255-6005 or
888/548-6005 rents mountain and road bikes and can provide
guided trips on request.

Fayetteville Airport (I89)
Airport is located 2 miles southwest of town.

☞ *Airport Information:*
Location: Cincinnati sectional N38.01.61 W81.07.19
Attended: Daylight hours
Elevation: 1960 feet
Fuel: 80
TPA: 2800 feet msl
Runway: 03-21: 2010 x 20 asph
FBO: Thomas Flying Service 304/574-1035

☞ *Communication:*
CTAF: 122.8
Unicom: 122.8

☞ *Transportation:*
Taxi: 304/574-3475
Car Rental: Enterprise 304/465-5830

☞ *Lodging:*
Fayetteville: The **Comfort Inn** 304/574-3443 is one mile from the
New River Gorge Bridge. It is a five-minute drive from **The County
Seat B & B** 304/574-0823 to the New River Gorge. The **Woodcrest
B & B** 304/574-3870 has 15 rooms on 100 acres with pool.

WV

☞ *Restaurants:*
Ansted: For a dining experience with a view, visit the **Hawks Nest Restaurant** 304/658-5212 perched atop spectacular New River Canyon.
Fayetteville: Seafood and southwestern favorites are served at the **Sedona Grille** 304/574-3411 downtown. Late night cravings can be taken care of at the 24-hour **Western Pancake House** 304/574-1240.

CLASS VI RIVER RUNNERS
(raft trips approximately 4 miles from airport)
Ames Heights Road, P.O. Box 78, Lansing, WV 25862; Tel: 800/ CLASS VI or 304/574-0704; Internet: www.raftwv.com

The New and Gauley River are two of North America's premier whitewater rivers. They offer a variety of experiences, from family adventure trips on the upper sections of the New River to the exhilarating challenges of the Gauley. Tucked deep within the remote mountain folds of West Virginia's Monongahelas, the Upper Gauley River plunges in drops of up to ten feet and you face five monster rapids in a row. It is not the place to find out if you are afraid of big rapids! But over 80% of the National River section of the New River is perfect for families, those new to whitewater, or multi-generational groups. Qualified staff is available to help you choose just the right amount of whitewater to get your adrenaline going. Each morning a Class VI staff person logs onto the U.S. Army Corps of Engineers computer for access to the latest and most accurate water levels. The levels dictate which section is being rafted and which type of raft is being used. Choose from day, multi-day, combination river trips, kayaking clinics, raft/mountain biking packages, raft/rock climbing packages, and even fishing trips in rafts with rigid, inflatable floors and pedestal seats. Fish for great smallmouth bass and muskies in these beautiful, remote, and wild rivers.

WHILE YOU'RE THERE: Contact the **Canyon Rim Visitor Center** 304/574-2115 at the northern end of the **River Gorge National Park** (next to the New River Gorge Bridge, whose span rises 900 feet above the river) for detailed hiking guides and a slide presentation. **ACE Adventure Center** 800/787-3982 has rafting, rock climbing, mountain biking, horseback riding trips, and kayak instruction. **Cast-Away** 304/465-5128 or 800/426-0511 offers guided float and wade trips for spin or fly fishermen. Fish for small mouth bass, muskie, walleye, and trout on the New, Gauley, and Greenbrier

Rivers. Contact the **Canyon Ranch** 304/574-3111 for horseback riding in the Gorge. Hunters can contact the **Plateau Pheasant Reserve** 304/465-8882 to hunt pheasant and quail on 500 acres of open field and strip mine flats. Dogs are provided.

Morgantown Munic. Airport - Hart Field (MGW)

Airport is located 3 miles east of town.

☞ *Airport Information:*

Location: Cincinnati sectional N39.38.58 W79.54.98
Airspace: Class D service 1200-0400Z*
               Other times Class E
Attended: 1100-0400Z*
Elevation: 1248 feet
Fuel: 100LL, Jet A
TPA: 2048 feet msl lgt acft
               2248 feet msl hvy acft
Runway: 18-36: 5199 x 150 asph
               05-23: 2769 x 75 asph
FBO: Aero Services 304/296-2359

☞ *Communication:*

CTAF: 120.0
Unicom: 122.95
App/Dep: Clarksburg 121.15 (1200-0400Z*)
               Cleveland Center 126.95 (0400-1200Z*)
Tower: 120.0 (1200-0400Z*)
Ground: 121.7

☞ *Transportation:*

Taxi: 304/292-7441
Car Rental: Avis 304/291-5867; Budget 304/296-3335
               Hertz 304/296-2331

☞ *Lodging:*

Morgantown: **Comfort Inn** 304/296-9364; **Lakeview Resort** 304/594-1111; **Holiday Inn** 304/599-1680

WV

LAKEVIEW RESORT

(golf approximately 5 miles from airport)
1 Lake Vie Drive, Morgantown, WV 26508; Tel: 304/594-1111

Lakeview golf course has been ranked 4th in West Virginia by *Golf Digest*. Eighteen holes of challenging but enjoyable golf amidst scenery that one keeps remembering. Lakeview Resort is home to both the Lakeview and Mountainview courses (the latter rather hilly and tight).

Wheeling
Ohio Co. Airport (HLG)

Airport is located 8 miles northeast of town.

☞ *Airport Information:*

Location: Cincinnati sectional N40.10.50 W80.38.78
Airspace: Class D service Mon-Fri 1200-0300Z*
Sat-Sun 1500-0100Z*
Other times Class E
Attended: Mon-Fri 1200-0300Z*
Sat-Sun 1300-0100Z*
Elevation: 1195 feet
Fuel: 100LL, Jet A
TPA: 2000 feet msl
Runway: 03-21: 5000 x 150 asph
16-34: 4497 x 150 asph
FBO: Ohio Valley Aviation
304/277-2121

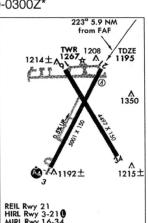

☞ *Communication:*
CTAF: 118.1
Unicom: 122.95
App/Dep: Pittsburg 127.95
Tower: Wheeling 118.1 (Mon-Fri 1200-0300Z*)
(Sat-Sun 1500-0100Z*)
Ground: 121.75
ASOS: 127.375

☞ *Transportation:*
Taxi: 304/737-8902; 304/232-5151

Car Rental: Enterprise 304/233-9582

☞ *Lodging:*
Wheeling: Oglebay Resort 304/243-4000 or 800/624-6988 see below. The **Stratford Springs** 304/233-5100 or 800/521-8435 is a historic inn on 30 secluded acres.

OGLEBAY RESORT
(golf approximately 8 miles from airport)
Wheeling, WV 26003; Tel: 304/243-4000 or 800/624-6988; Internet: www.oglebay-resort.com

Oglebay's newest course was designed by legendary Arnold Palmer with a championship layout designed to accommodate golfers on all skill levels. If you are in search of a challenge play the 7,000-yard, 18-hole, Robert Trent Jones–designed Speidel Course. It was home to the West Virginia LPGA Classic for 11 years and offers rolling, bentgrass fairways with four lakes coming into play on four holes. The Crispin Course is less expensive as well as less difficult and will boost your ego after playing the Speidel. It's not just all golf at Oglebay, though. Tennis enthusiasts will find 11 courts to play on. Winding brick walks surrounded by flowers, fountains, and majestic trees invite a stroll. Kids will enjoy the zoo, a mile-long train ride, and the paddle boats on Schenk Lake. Indoor and outdoor pools.

WV

INDEX BY ACTIVITY

Page numbers shown in bold are activities described in detail.
An "r" indicates activity at resort generally requiring overnight stay.

AMUSEMENT PARK
> **FL 29, FL 30,** FL 31, **FL 39, GA 45, IN 67, KY 77, MD 104,
> NC 187, OH 205, OH 220, PA 232, TN 261,** TN 272, **VA 294**

ANIMAL PARK/ZOO
> **FL 25, FL 27,** FL 32, FL 35, **GA 57, GA 60,** IN 66, KY 78,
> **SC 249**

AQUARIUM
> **CT 3,** FL 36, **FL 39, MD 96, NY 175, TN 262**

BEACH
> **FL 12r, FL 27r, FL 31r, MD 107, MA 111r, MA 113, MA 118,
> MI 129r, MI 139r, NC 189, SC 252r, SC 258**

BIKING
> **FL 18r,** FL 22, **FL 24, GA 48r,** GA 48, GA 50, **GA 57r, KY
> 70, KY 71, ME 82, ME 83, ME 85,** ME 88r, **ME 90, ME 91r,
> MD 105,** MA 115, MA 119, MA 122, **MI 124, MI 125r, MI
> 129r,** MI 138, **NJ 151,** NJ 156, **NY 165, NY 166, NY 167,** NY
> 173, **NC 192,** NC 193, **NC 197r, OH 217, PA 222r,** PA 228,
> **PA 228r, PA 229, PA 231,** PA 235, **RI 241,** RI 242, **SC 246,
> SC 252r, TN 264r, TN 272, VT 277, VT 278r, VT 278,** VT
> 280, VA 297, WV 299, **WV 300**

BIRD-WATCHING
> **CT 2, FL 17, FL 42, KY 73, ME 83, MD 107, NJ 149, NJ
> 156, NC 189, NC 196r, OH 222r, PA 238, RI 241,** RI 244,
> **SC 246, TN 271, VT 277**

BOAT CRUISES/TOURS
> ANIMAL WATCHING FL 12, **FL 17,** FL 22, **FL 34,** GA 48, **GA 51,**
> GA 53, **ME 83, MA 113, MA 116, MA 119,** NH 146, NJ 150,
> NJ 156, NY 170, NC 194, **SC 259,** VA 287
> DINNER/DANCE FL 32, GA 32, GA 53, NC 194

305

FISHING **CT 4,** CT 5, **FL 13,** FL 15, **FL 31r,** FL 32, FL 35, GA 48,
GA 53, ME 84, MD 94, **MD 109,** MA 119, NH 146, NJ 150,
NJ 153, NY 167, NY 170, **NC 189,** NC 193, NC 194, **NC
196r, OH 217, RI 241, SC 254,** SC 255, **SC 257**
OTHER ME 84, **ME 91,** MA 122, MD 93, NJ 153, NJ 156, NY 170,
NY 175, NY 176, SC 246, SC 256, TN 270, VA 290
SIGHTSEEING **CT 4,** CT 5, **FL 31r,** FL 32, GA 53, MD 97, NH
146, NY 164, **NY 176,** RI 244, SC 248, TN 263, TN 270, VA
285

BOAT RENTAL
FL 13, FL 17, FL 28, **FL 34,** GA 47, **GA 51,** IN 67, **KY 71,**
ME 84, **ME 87, ME 90,** MD 93, MD 107, **MD 109, MA 111r,**
MA 113, MA 122, **MI 29r, MI 124, MI 124r, MI 130,** NH 146,
NJ 156, **NY 165, NC 189,** OH 220, **RI 241, RI 243,** SC 246,
SC 255, **SC 257,** VT 274

BOTANICAL GARDEN
DE 10, GA 57, NY 162, NY 172, NC 185, NC 186, NC 194,
NC 197, PA 232, **PA 238, RI 244, SC 246, SC 250**

CANOEING/KAYAKING
FL 17, FL 22, **FL 24, FL 27r, FL 34, FL 42, GA 49, GA 51,
KY 70, KY 71, ME 82, ME 87, ME 88, ME 90, MD 105, MD
109,** MA 113, MA 117, **MI 124, MI 139r, NY 165, NC 192,
NC 196r, PA 227, PA 228r,** PA 228, **RI 241, RI 243,** SC 246,
SC 250, **SC 252r,** SC 256, **SC 259,** VT 274, **VT 277,** VT 287,
WV 300

CAVES
KY 70, KY 72, PA 223, TN 263, **VA 282,**

DOG RACING
FL 39

DRIVING/RACING SCHOOL
FL 37, GA 52, OH 210, PA 225

FARM
VT 274

FARMERS MARKET
CT 6, PA 235

306

FESTIVAL/EVENT

CT 4, FL 24, KY 77, ME 91, MD 93, MA 113, MI 136, MI
141, **NJ 156, NY 158,** NY 179, **NC 184,** NC 186, NC 193,
OH 213, PA 228, PA 232, RI 243, TN 263, VA 287

FISHING

CT 4, CT 5, **FL 11r, FL 13, FL 15, FL 31r,** FL 32, FL 35, **FL
40r, FL 42,** FL 42, **GA 48r, GA 49, GA 51,** GA 53, **GA 57r,
KY 70, KY 71,   KY 73,** ME 84, **ME 85,** ME 88r, MD 94, **MD
109, MA 111r,** MA 113, MA 119, **MI 125r, MI 129r, MI 130,
MI 134r, MI 139r, MI 140r,** NH 146, NJ 150, NJ 153, **NY
161r, NY 165,** NY 167, **NY 168,** NY 170, **NY 171r, NY 173r,
NC 189,** NC 193, NC 194, **NC 196r, OH 217, PA 222r,** PA
228, **RI 241, SC 252r, SC 254,** SC 255, **SC 257, TN 271, TN
272r, VT 277, VT 278, VA 281r, VA 287, VA 296r, WV 300**

GAMBLING

CT 3, NJ 151

GOLF

CT 6, FL 11, FL 18, FL 19, FL 20, FL 27, FL 29, FL 30, FL
31r, FL 40, GA 47, GA 48, GA 53, GA 57, IN 63, IN 65, KY
74, KY 75, ME 85, ME 90, MD 103, MD 105, MD 107, MA
110, MA 111, MA 122, MI 125, MI 129, MI 131, MI 134, MI
137, MI 139, MI 140, NH 144, NH 146, NH 147, NJ 149, NJ
152, NJ 153, NY 161r, NY 162, NY 170, NY 171, NY 173r,
NY 176, NC 192, NC 195, NC 197, OH 202, OH 205, OH
214, OH 220, OH 221, PA 222r, PA 227, PA 232, PA 236,
SC 247, SC 252, SC 258, SC 259, TN 264, TN 265, VA
281r, VA 282, VA 295, VA 296, WV 302, WV 303

HIKING

CT 2, FL 24, FL 42, GA 51, KY 70, KY 71, KY 73, KY 80,
ME 83, ME 85, ME 87, ME 88r, ME 91, MD 107, MI 129r,
MI 130, MI 134r, MI 137r, NH 147r, NJ 149, NY 165, NY
167, NY 173r, NY 173, NY 175, NC 193, PA 222r, PA 227,
PA 228r, SC 246, TN 271, VT 277r, VT 280, VA 281r, WV
300

HORSE BUGGY RIDE

ME 84, **MI 137r, MI 138, NH 147r,** NC 199, **OH 215, PA
235, PA 239, SC 248, VT 277r, VA 278r,** VA 297

HORSE RACING
IN 62, KY 75, **NY 171,** NY 180

HORSEBACK RIDING
GA 48r, GA 53, **IN 63r, KY 70, KY 72, KY 79,** MA 119, MA 122, MI 138, **NH 147r,** NY 164, **NY 165,** NY 170, **NY 171r, Y 173r,** NY 173, **NY 179r,** NC 189, **NC 196r, NC 197r, PA 228r,** PA 228, **PA 229, PA 239,** RI 242, **SC 252r, TN 264r, TN 272,** VT 278, WV 300, WV 301

HOT-AIR BALLOONING
CT 7, PA 235

HUNTING
FL 42, ME 88r, **MD 109, MI 129r, MI 130,** NY 167, SC 255, WV 301

KAYAKING/CANOEING
FL 17, FL 22, **FL 24, FL 27r, FL 34, FL 42, GA 49, GA 51, KY 70, KY 71, ME 82, ME 87, ME 88, ME 90, MD 105, MD 109,** MA 113, MA 117, **MI 124, MI 139r, NY 165, NC 192, NC 196r, PA 227, PA 228r,** PA 228, **RI 241, RI 243,** SC 246, SC 250, **SC 252r,** SC 256, **SC 259,** VT 274, **VT 277,** VT 287, **WV 300**

MILITARY BATTLEFIELD
PA 229, TN 261, VA 284

MOUNTAIN CLIMBING
ME 84, **ME 86, NY 165,** NY 167, NY 173, **NC 192, PA 227,** WV 300

MUSEUMS
AVIATION **CT 8, FL 23, FL 26, FL 29, FL 32, FL 43, GA 54, GA 59, KY 74, ME 90, MD 97, MD 99, MD 100, MI 128, MI 136, NJ 154, NY 159, NY 177, NY 181, NC 183, NC 187, NC 190, NC 192, OH 208, OH 209, PA 233, SC 251, VA 284, VA 290**
LIVING HISTORY **FL 34, KY 71, MA 115, MA 117, MA 120, NY 58, VA 295**
MARITIME **CT 3, CT 4, FL 22,** ME 84, MD 93, **MD 95, MA 113,** MA 117, **MI 124,** NC 189, NC 199, RI 244, **SC 256,** VA 285, **VA 286**

308

OTHER **DE 10, FL 21,** FL 28, **FL 36,** FL 42, **GA 50, IN 65,** IN 66, **KY 75, KY 77,** KY 78, **MD 95, MD 96,** MD 97, **MD 101,** MA 117, **MI 126, MI 133, MI 137,** MI 138, **NH 145, NY 157,** NY 158, **NY 162,** NY 167, **NC 185, NC 186,** NC 190, NC 196, NC 199, **OH 201,** OH 205, **OH 206,** OH 208, **OH 218, RI 243, RI 244, SC 246,** TN 262, **TN 266,** TN 267, **TN 269,** TN 270, **VT 274, VA 284, VA 286, VA 289, VA 290**

SCIENCE **FL 39, GA 46, MD 96,** NC 188, OH 207, TN 262, **VA 289**

MUSICAL PERFORMANCE
KY 68, MA 115, NY 175, NY 180, OH 212, RI 243, SC 253, **TN 269, VT 278r**

PARA-SAILING/HANG GLIDING
NH 142, NY 161, **NC 192,** OH 218, **RI 241, SC 257**

PLANETARIUM
KY 71, MD 100

RANCH
NY 161, NY 173, NY 179

RESORT/SPA
FL 11, FL 18, FL 27, FL 31, FL 40, GA 48, IN 62, ME 90, MA 111, MA 114, MI 125, MI 129, MI 131, MI 134, MI 137, MI 139, MI 140, NH 147, NJ 149, NY 169, NY 171, NY 172, NY 173, NC 195, NC 197, PA 222, PA 227, PA 236, SC 247, SC 252, TN 264, VT 277, VT 278, VA 281, VA 291, VA 296, WV 303

SAILING
CT 2, CT 5, **FL 20, FL 31r, GA 48r,** ME 84, ME 91, **MD 93,** MD 107, **MD 109,** MA 122, **MI 124, MI 125r,** NJ 156, **NC 192, NC 196r, NC 197r, NC 199,** OH 220, **RI 243, SC 252r, SC 258**

SAILPLANE SOARING
MA 111, NY 160

SCUBA DIVING
FL 31r, FL 32, NY 173, NC 199

INDEX

SIGHTSEEING (no tour — self guided)
FL 18, FL 22, **MD 93,** MD 96, MD 102, MD 103, **MI 124, MI 137,** NJ 150, **NJ 156,** NY 170, NC 189, NC 194, NC 199, OH 208, OH 210, **OH 215, OH 218,** PA 235, SC 248, TN 263, **VA 290, VA 293, VA 294**

SIGHTSEEING (guided tours)
FL 21, FL 34, FL 41, KY 73, KY 75, KY 77, ME 84, **MD 93, MD 101,** MD 103, **MA 118,** MI 141, **NJ 156,** NY 167, NY 158, **NY 175,** NC 199, OH 208, **OH 215, PA 229, PA 232, PA 235, SC 246, SC 248, TN 261,** TN 263, **VA 286**

SKYDIVING
FL 13, FL 16, GA 55, PA 224

SNORKELING
FL 12r, FL 22

SURFING/WINDSURFING
FL 11r, FL 15, FL 22, **FL 31r, GA 48r, MD 109,** MA 122, **MI 124,** NY 167, **NC 189,** NC 193, **SC 252r, SC 258,** VT 274

TENNIS
FL 11r, FL 18r, FL 31r, FL 36, FL 40r, GA 48r, GA 57r, IN 63r, KY 79, ME 91r, MA 111r, MI 125r, MI 229r, MI 137r, MI 141r, NH 147r, NJ 149r, NY 171r, NY 173r, NC 197r, PA 222r, PA 228r, PA 237r, SC 248r, SC 252r, SC 253r, TN 264r, VT 278r, VA 281r, VA 296r, VA 297r, WV 303r

THEATER/OUTDOOR DRAMA
KY 68, NC 194, OH 203, OH 216, WV 298

VARIOUS OTHER ACTIVITIES/ATTRACTIONS
FL 29, FL 41, GA 45, GA 50, MD 99, MD 100, MD 101, NJ 151, NY 166, NY 168, OH 202, **TN 267, TN 270**

WATER PARK
FL 30, FL 31, FL 39, GA 53, **IN 64, IN 67, KY 77, MD 104, NH 145, NY 163, NC 187, OH 205,** OH 220, PA 228, SC 258, **VA 296**

INDEX

WATER SPORTS

CANOEING, KAYAKING, SCUBA DIVING, SAILING, SNORKELING, SURFING, WHITE-WATER RAFTING, AND WINDSURFING are indexed individually under the appropriate alphabetical order.

FL 12r, FL 22, **FL 27r,** FL 28, **FL 31r, GA 49,** IN 67, **MD 105, MI 124, MI 139r,** NJ 156, NY 164, **NY 173r, NC 189, PA 227,** PA 228, **RI 243, SC 257, SC 258**

WHITE-WATER RAFTING

ME 88, MD 105, NY 167, **NY 182, PA 227, PA 230, WV 300**

WINDSURFING/SURFING

FL 11r, FL 15, FL 22, **FL 31r, GA 48r, MD 109,** MA 122, **MI 124,** NY 167, **NC 189,** NC 193, **SC 252r, SC 258,** VT 274

WINERY

NY 159, NY 173, VA 297

WINTER SPORTS

ME 83, ME 85, ME 88r, **ME 91r, MD 105, MI 125, MI 129r, MI 130, MI 132, MI 134, MI 141r,** NH 147, NJ 154, **NY 161r, NY 165, NY 166,** NY 167, **NY 171r, NY 173r, NY 179r, OH 213, PA` 222r, PA 227, PA 228r,** PA 231, TN 272, **VT 275, VT 277, VT 277r, VT 278r,** VT 278, **VT 279, VA 281r**

ZOO/ANIMAL PARK

FL 25, FL 27, FL 32, FL 35, **GA 57, GA 60,** IN 66, KY 78, **SC 249**

INDEX

INDEX BY ATTRACTION

INDEX

E

F

G

H

I

J

K

INDEX

INDEX

T

INDEX

INDEX

Y

INDEX

WRITE TO US

No matter how carefully facts are checked, businesses close, addresses change, places open or have been overlooked, and others don't meet your expectations. We'd like to hear from you!

Your feedback is greatly welcome at:
Beyond the Clouds, P.O. Box 257, Chester, MD 21619
e-mail: Poldimi@aol.com

HAVE A SAFE FLIGHT AND ENJOYABLE TRIP!

NOTES:

NOTES:

ABOUT THE AUTHOR

Poldi Mikula is a private pilot, expedition leader for the Mt. Everest region, and tour director in Canada. She was born and raised in Vienna, Austria. When Poldi is not above the clouds doing what she loves best, she resides in Chester, Maryland. Enjoying the destination as much as the journey has prompted her to write this recreational flying guide. This book reflects her experience as a pilot who also loves to have fun on the ground. She previously co-authored and published a well-received Hong Kong guidebook and tourist map.